Sara Moulton **cooks at home**

Sara Moulton

cooks at home

Recipes developed with Charles Pierce

Photography by Elizabeth Watt

Wine advice by Michael Green

BROADWAY BOOKS

New York

Broadway Books titles may be purchased for business or promotional use or for special sales. For information, please write to: Special Markets Department, Random House, Inc., 1540 Broadway, New York, NY 10036.

PRINTED IN THE UNITED STATES OF AMERICA

Broadway Books and its logo, a letter B bisected on the diagonal, are trademarks of Broadway Books, a division of Random House, Inc.

Visit our website at www.broadwaybooks.com

Library of Congress Cataloging-in-Publication Data
Moulton, Sara, 1952–
    Sara Moulton cooks at home / Sara Moulton; recipes developed with Charles Pierce.—1st. ed.
        p.   cm.
    Includes index.
        1. Cookery.   I. Pierce, Charles.   II. Title.

TX714 .M717 2002
641.5—dc21

2001056615

FIRST EDITION

Book design by Marysarah Quinn
Food styling by William Smith
Prop styling by Lisa Sacco

ISBN 0-7679-0770-1

10   9   8   7   6   5   4   3   2   1

To Wayne Cummings

a dear friend and collaborator, I miss you

contents

acknowledgments

In addition to the greater Moulton and Adler families, who contributed so many ideas and recipes to this book, I have many people to thank:

Judith Weber, my agent, who took me on many years ago

Jennifer Josephy, my editor, who really understood what I was trying to do with this book and helped me to make it better

Charles Pierce, my ace recipe tester, for keeping me on track and staying calm

Andrea Hagan, my tireless assistant recipe tester, for making all those recipes over and over again

Michael Green, for writing about wine the way I strive to write about cooking: accessibly

Magda Alcayaga, my longtime housekeeper, for being so patient during all those months of chaos in the kitchen

Jane Grenier, my boss at *Gourmet,* for being so flexible about my day-to-day schedule while I was writing this book

Jackie Bobrow, my ex-second-in-command at *Gourmet,* for holding down the fort

Jennifer Baum, my tireless publicist and friend

Georgia Downard, my producer, and the team at "Cooking Live"

All my friends at *Good Morning America,* for putting me on television for the first time, and especially **Margo Baumgart,** for continuing to support me

All my old friends and colleagues who contributed to this book

Julia Child, Jean Anderson, and **Jacques Pépin,** for being such inspirations

My parents, **Henry** and **Elizabeth Moulton,** for instilling such a love of food and cooking in me and for encouraging me at every step

My children, **Ruth** and **Sam,** for putting up with a year's worth of weird dinners: all soups one night, all appetizers the next, all starches the third, etc.

My husband, **Bill,** for being my biggest supporter and best friend

introduction

When I started putting together this cookbook, I really had very little notion of what its final shape was going to be. My only idea was to compile all the recipes I've ever loved and from those to choose the ones that would be most useful to home cooks. But after I'd dug up and dusted off several heirloom recipes—recipes that recalled my grandmother Ruth or my husband's great-aunt Rifka—I began to see that I was writing a kind of piecemeal autobiography based on a lifetime of cooking and eating. When it came time to write the headnote to each recipe, my mind seemed naturally to flash back to the first time I'd ever tried the dish in question. How old was I then? Where was I living? Who was the cook? And, then, why have I continued to love it?

Of course, there is no separating cooking and dining from friends and family, time and place, and life as we live it. In my own case I think of all the wonderful meals I've eaten and understand as I never did before just how charmed my life has been. How lucky I was to be born in New York City to parents with taste and means, a farm in the country, and strong New England roots. How lucky I was as a kid to be able to wander the most cosmopolitan city in the world, sampling dozens of foreign cuisines. How lucky to get away from New York and go to college in the Midwest, where I met the Nice Jewish Boy who would become my husband. How lucky to be able to attend the Culinary Institute of America—and to extend my formal culinary education with an apprenticeship in France. How incredibly lucky to meet and work with Julia Child. How lucky to get a job with Chef Sally Darr at La Tulipe when I came back to New York and to work alongside Jacques Pépin in her kitchen when he was a guest chef there. How lucky to land at *Gourmet* magazine when I decided to retire from restaurant work and start raising a family of my own. How great to work in the test kitchen there and get paid to expand my knowledge of international cuisines and how exciting afterward to work as the chef in *Gourmet*'s dining room. How lucky to have been able to round out my own culinary education as a teacher at Peter Kump's New York Cooking School, where I discovered that, indeed, teaching might be the thing I do best. How lucky to have met Jean Anderson and traveled with her on food-and-wine assignments to Holland, Portugal, and Brazil. How lucky to have spent years backstage at "Good Morning America," where I had the chance to meet and work closely with such great contemporary chefs as Wolfgang Puck, Marcella Hazan, Martin Yan, and Emeril Lagasse. How lucky to be able to work at the Food Network on a live call-in show with an audience that never ceases to challenge and educate me. How blessed, finally, to have had children and to watch them grow, great kids who keep me young and curious and on my toes.

Looking back, however, it seems as though my professional life came together in much the same fashion as this cookbook. There was very little planning. Like everyone else, I just made it up as I went along, the only constants being my appetite and the quest for culinary knowledge. But here I am, twenty-five years after graduating from cooking school, a chef, a teacher, and, now, an author. I'd say a pattern has emerged.

This is a great time to be cooking in America. The culinary advances of the last forty years have been amazing. When I was a kid, TV dinners and Hamburger Helper were big. The cardboard tomato was king. Lettuce was Iceberg. Mushrooms were button. A leek was exotic. Parsley was the only fresh herb (unless you were one of the few pioneering souls who grew a variety of herbs in your own backyard).

But then Julia Child started appearing on television with a message of pure empowerment: You—yes, *you*—can cook well at home, and if you can't find leeks at your local market, then let your local purveyor know he ought to think about stocking them. James Beard began singing the praises of American cooking, freeing us from our slavish devotion to Europe. Alice Waters encouraged us always to reach for the freshest local produce—or grow our own. And all the while the opportunity to acquire a formal culinary education in America was exploding, led by the Culinary Institute of America and Johnson & Wales, followed by the introduction of cooking courses at community colleges from coast to coast.

Today local organic produce is widely available in a way it never was before. So are organic and "natural" meats and artisanal breads, cheeses, and oils. Regional American cuisines are flourishing, and once-exotic ingredients from around the world are often as close as the neighborhood supermarket. Superstar chefs advise us about the politics of food: the necessity of supporting sustainable agriculture and protecting heirloom crops and endangered fish, the importance of the emerging "slow food movement" to counter the fast-fooding of America. I think it's vital for us to support these trends, if only to forestall the day when we're all eating astronaut food.

I also think it's important to cook and eat at home. Indeed this is a home cookbook. Very broadly, it includes two kinds of recipes: recipes you can cook up and get onto the table in the midst of a busy week, and slightly more lavish recipes for weekend entertaining. I have tried to make this an accessible cookbook. If an ingredient is exotic, we give you sources for it. If you still can't get your hands on it, you can use the more commonly available substitutes we list. I've also tried to provide you with as many shortcuts and tips as I know. Cooking well is cooking with intelligence, identifying the best tools and techniques and produce so as to make the most out of your labor with the least wasted motion. (Many of these tips came to me from our viewers and from the guests on the show. Indeed, I necessarily learn a ton of new stuff simply prepping for four new shows every week.) And, as mentioned, this is an heirloom cookbook. I feel strongly that my grandmother lives on through her recipes. A similar belief has inspired many of my viewers to put together their own family cookbooks—which is why we've listed several sources at the back of this book (page 370) that will tell you how to make one of your own.

I have always loved to eat. If I'd had a bad day as a kid but my mom made Meatball Stroganoff for dinner, the world suddenly looked brighter to me. I think most people feel that way about food. It comforts us and brings us together. Birthdays and special occasions are always built around a special meal. My son Sam is sure to request spaetzle and matzo ball soup for his birthday. My daughter Ruthie asks for lamb and, for dessert, something real chocolaty. On those rare occasions when three generations of Moultons get together at the family farm, we all tend to run around like hamsters during the day so that we can guiltlessly dig into the extravagant dinner we prepare for that evening.

A home-cooked meal is always a great gift, as is sitting down to dine. It's probably the one chance everyone in the family has every day to slow down and catch up with one another. Even if you live alone—as over 28 percent of Americans do—you shouldn't be shy about giving these gifts to yourself. It's important to take care of yourself and cook for yourself, to set the table and sit down and eat and taste what you're eating. It's much healthier in all ways than driving to the nearest fast-food franchise or reaching for the phone and ordering some takeout to eat in front of the TV.

The great French gastronome Jean Anthelme Brillat-Savarin published *The Physiology of Taste* in 1825 after some thirty years of research. The book leads off with twenty Aphorisms from the Professor. Here's my favorite: "The pleasures of the table are for every man, of every land, and no matter of what place in history or society; they can be part of all his other pleasures, and they last the longest, to console him when he has outlived the rest." To the extent that I can be sure that the professor was writing of women as well as men, I agree with him utterly.

Sara Moulton
New York City
August 2002

notes on how to use this book

Please read each recipe in its entirety before you start and then follow it *exactly*, at least the first time you make it. After you've made it once or twice, of course, you're welcome to improve it however you see fit.

Most of the chapters in this book fall into the usual categories: hors d'oeuvres, soups, and so on. Then there is the chapter devoted to light lunches. Those recipes really are appropriate for a light lunch, but they could also serve as appetizers if you pared them down. Alternatively, with the addition of the right side dishes, most of them could work as the main course for a weekend supper.

There's a very friendly wine chapter at the end of the book because I believe that good wine immeasurably enhances good food. The chapter was written by my friend and *Gourmet* colleague Michael Green, who sets out a wonderful commonsense system for understanding the art of wine-and-food pairing and then illustrates it by pairing up a couple of my recipes with appropriate wines. Elsewhere in the book you'll come across a recipe every once in a while for which we provide specific wine recommendations, but that's only for those extra-special recipes you make when guests are coming.

I have suggested side dishes to go along with the entrees.

Unless otherwise indicated:

Salt is kosher.

Black pepper is freshly ground.

Butter is unsalted.

Flour is all-purpose.

Vanilla extract is pure.

Vegetable oil is whichever brand you prefer.

Brown sugar is firmly packed when measured.

Bay leaves are from Turkey.

Dried apricots are from California.

Avocados are from California (also known as Hass avocados).

Maple syrup is grade B (see Mail Order Sources at the back of the book).

Bread crumbs are fresh and homemade (see page 347).

Milk, yogurt, and similar dairy products are whole. (If you want to slim down the recipe, you can use lower-fat alternatives. However, you should stay away from no-fat products. I think they have no flavor.)

Heavy cream is pasteurized, not ultrapasteurized. (The latter tastes cooked to me and tends to break faster than the pasteurized when whipped.)

Lemon, lime, and **orange juices** are freshly squeezed.

Lemon, lime, and **orange zests** are freshly grated. (Note: The best tool for this job is called a *microplane*. It is sold in many kitchenware stores. See Mail Order Sources.)

Parmigiano-Reggiano is freshly grated. (Again, reach for the microplane.)

Eggs are large.

A few recipes in this book call for fresh **raw egg whites**. Although the risk of salmonella is real, it is minuscule. However, if you are cooking for one of the high-risk groups—the immune-impaired, the elderly, or the very young (under five years old)—you should reach for alternatives. Substitute pasteurized egg whites or powdered egg whites (I've used a brand called Just Whites with great success), available at many supermarkets.

One tablespoon **fresh herbs** equals 1 teaspoon dried herbs.

Poultry is organic, "natural" (minimally processed), or kosher, if possible.

Meat is "natural" (minimally processed) or organic, if possible.

Fish is not endangered. Overfishing, wasteful practices, and habitat destruction have endangered many species of fish. The fish I chose to use were not in the high-risk category at the time I was writing this book. But the situation keeps changing. It's not always easy, anyway, to know whether a fish is endangered. For up-to-date information on the status of any fish, please go to the Seafood Choices Alliance website at www.seafoodchoices.com or call (866) 732-6673. If the fish of your desire is indeed endangered, the Seafood Choices Alliance will provide you with alternative choices.

Wine is drinkable. Never use "cooking wine."

Hors d'oeuvres

Roasted Asparagus Bruschetta

1 pound medium asparagus spears

2 tablespoons extra virgin olive oil

Kosher salt and freshly ground black pepper to taste

Six ⅓-inch-thick slices rustic country bread, cut from a 6-inch-high loaf

1 garlic clove, halved

¼ pound Parmigiano-Reggiano

2 tablespoons balsamic vinegar

2 tablespoons white truffle oil*

*Available at specialty food shops or see Mail Order Sources.

SERVES 6

My favorite way to cook asparagus is to roast it at high heat, which caramelizes and concentrates its flavor. After it's been roasted, asparagus dresses up very easily. Here I have put it on grilled bread, tossed it with a little balsamic vinegar and white truffle oil, and finished it with some shaved Parmigiano-Reggiano. Simple as it is, people go crazy for this hors d'oeuvre. You can grill the bread and roast the asparagus a day ahead. Just don't toss it with the vinegar and truffle oil until the last minute.

Preheat the oven to 450°F. Break off the tough ends of the asparagus and discard. Peel the stalks of the asparagus halfway up the length and arrange in one flat layer over the bottom of a roasting pan or baking sheet. Drizzle on the olive oil and season with salt and pepper. Roast on the middle rack of the oven until just tender, about 10 minutes. Cool and cut in half crosswise.

Prepare a charcoal fire. When the flames have died down and the coals are glowing, place the grill 3 to 4 inches from the source of heat. Alternatively, preheat a grill pan over medium-high heat until very hot. Grill the bread until lightly toasted, turning often. Rub one side of each slice with the cut garlic clove while hot.

Using a swivel-bladed peeler, shave large paper-thin slices of cheese off the wedge, making enough cheese slices to cover the 6 slices of bread. (Reserve any remaining cheese for another use.) Cover the bread with the cheese. Toss the asparagus with the vinegar and half the truffle oil. Season with salt and pepper. Top each slice of bread with asparagus, mounding it in the center. Drizzle with the remaining truffle oil and serve at room temperature.

roasting vegetables

My preferred way to cook almost any vegetable is to roast it at high heat. You just have to cut it down to size before you put it in the oven so it will cook properly. Other vegetables that work well besides asparagus are broccoli and cauliflower (cut into 1-inch florets), carrot sticks or baby carrots, and green beans. The drill is the same for all of them: preheat the oven to 450°F, arrange the vegetables in one layer, lightly drizzle with oil, add salt and pepper to taste, and roast for 10 minutes or until just cooked through and caramelized. If you want to cut way back on fat, just spray them with one of those vegetable oil sprays. This is a very satisfying recipe for dieters.

truffle flavor

There are many truffle products out there besides the very expensive whole fresh item. You can find truffles canned, frozen, in peelings, powdered, in butter, and in oil. It is fun to play around with all of these more affordable versions of the whole truffle, but my favorite is truffle oil. The best stuff is made by soaking truffles in olive oil. It keeps well on the door of the fridge for quite a while. A little goes a long way.

Tonnato-Stuffed Eggs

6 large eggs

¼ cup mayonnaise

One 3.5-ounce can tuna (Italian tuna packed in oil for more flavor, American tuna packed in water for fewer calories), drained

5 anchovy fillets, coarsely chopped

1 tablespoon drained bottled capers

1 tablespoon fresh lemon juice

1 tablespoon extra virgin olive oil

Kosher salt and freshly ground black pepper to taste

Celery leaves and Niçoise olives for garnish

MAKES 12 STUFFED EGGS

One of my husband Bill's favorite dishes is Vitello Tonnato. Cold sliced veal with a tuna sauce, it is an Italian version of surf and turf. Trying to imagine another recipe on which to use this tasty sauce, I thought of eggs. I love stuffed eggs. My mom has never stopped making them, even though the food police decreed them taboo for the longest time. In fact, as of October 2000, the position of the American Heart Association is that an egg a day is OK.

Eggs and tuna, like veal and tuna, are a happy marriage, and a couple of these stuffed eggs are substantial enough to make up a light lunch.

The most important thing to learn from this recipe is how to boil eggs. In fact, as Julia Child taught me, the paradoxically correct method is *not* to boil them. You start the eggs in cold water, bring them just up to the boil, pull them off the heat and let them sit. "Boiling" the eggs this way eliminates tough, chewy whites *and* the nasty green line that otherwise runs between the yolks and the whites. Try it. You'll be amazed.

Place the eggs in a large saucepan and pour in enough cold water to cover by 1 inch. Bring to a boil over high heat. Remove from the heat, cover, and set aside for 15 minutes. Transfer the eggs to a bowl of half ice and half water. Cool completely, then peel under cold running water.

Cut the eggs in half lengthwise and remove the yolks. Keep the halves of the whites intact. Place the yolks in a strainer set over a large bowl and force through with the back of a large spoon. Add the mayonnaise and stir until smooth.

Combine the tuna, anchovies, capers, lemon juice, and olive oil in a food processor. Process until smooth and creamy. Stir into the yolks and season with salt and pepper. Mound a heaping spoonful of the yolk mixture into the cavity of the whites. Garnish with a celery leaf and an olive. Keep chilled until ready to serve.

eggs

Have you ever had a hard time peeling your hard-boiled eggs? They were too fresh. This is the one time when an older egg is a good thing. For just about everything else, very fresh is best because fresh eggs will have greater volume when beaten. When eggs are "harvested" from the hen, they are rinsed off, which removes not only henhouse detritus (chicken poop among other things) but also nature's protective oily coating. As soon as this coating is removed, the shell is much more permeable and the egg starts to develop an air pocket between the shell and the egg itself. The older the egg, the larger the air pocket. The larger the air pocket, the easier the egg is to peel. How do you know the age of the egg besides the date on the carton? Try this experiment: Put a raw egg in the shell in a bowl of water. If it lies flat on its side, it is very fresh. If it stands up, it is getting older and is probably a good candidate for boiling. Most eggs you get at the supermarket are somewhere between the two. An egg that floats is an old egg. Toss it.

Baby Egg Rolls with Soy Sesame Dipping Sauce

For the egg rolls:

1/4 cup olive oil

One 2-inch piece fresh ginger, peeled and minced

1 garlic clove, minced

One 1/2-pound boneless pork chop, cut into thin strips

2 scallions, white and 1 inch of the green parts, thinly sliced

1 carrot, julienned

1 large red bell pepper, julienned

1 cup thinly sliced napa cabbage

1/4 cup chicken stock, preferably homemade (page 338)

2 tablespoons soy sauce

30 square wonton wrappers*

For the dipping sauce:

6 tablespoons soy sauce

1/4 cup rice vinegar

2 teaspoons Asian (toasted) sesame oil**

2 teaspoons sugar

*Available in the frozen food section of many supermarkets or at Asian markets.

**Available at most supermarkets or see Mail Order Sources.

MAKES 30 EGG ROLLS

It's always a pretty scary proposition when my kids come onto the show to cook with me. Unlike almost all of my other guests, they're not chefs or grown-ups or practiced television performers. They're sweet and funny, of course, but they are children, and they're unpredictable, which is to say unscriptable, and that can be pretty nerve-racking.

We developed this recipe in anticipation of a show with my kids. I was trying to think of all their favorite foods and what they might enjoy preparing as well as eating. Chinese egg rolls seemed like a good idea at first, but egg rolls are deep-fried, and we were not about to fire up a pot of hot oil with the kids around. Our solution was to develop a lighter version, in which the egg rolls are sautéed with just a little oil in a nonstick pan. We put in all the ingredients from the original recipe, including tofu, and the kids just loved them—and loved making them, too.

This was a very pleasant surprise. I'd made healthy homemade versions of some of the kids' fast-food faves when they were younger, but somehow my lovingly prepared macaroni and cheese, pizza, and baked coated chicken tenders just couldn't compete with mac and cheese from the box, pizza from the dollar-a-slice spot on the corner, and those insidious little brand-name chicken nuggets.

I have since perfected this recipe and made it many times with my kids and their cousins, Katie and Peter. These egg rolls make great hors d'oeuvres for kids and grown-ups alike. If you make a double batch, you can freeze half for the next time. But when the time comes, don't bother to defrost them first. Cook them straight out of the freezer, giving them just a little extra time in the pan.

To make the eggrolls, heat 2 tablespoons of the olive oil in a large skillet or wok over medium heat. Add the ginger and garlic and cook, stirring, until slightly softened, about 2 minutes. Add the pork and stir until it turns white, about 2 minutes. Transfer the pork to a plate and set aside. Add the scallions, carrot, and red pepper to the skillet. Cook, stirring, until slightly softened, about 2 minutes. Add the cabbage, stock, and soy sauce. Reduce the heat to medium-low and simmer until the liquid has evaporated and the vegetables are tender, about 5 minutes. Return the pork to the skillet and let the contents of the skillet cool to room temperature. You should have about 2 cups.

Lay the wrappers flat on a work surface. Brush the edges lightly with water. Top with about 1 tablespoon of the filling and roll into a cylinder, tucking in the sides and pressing the edges to seal. (The egg rolls can be frozen at this point.) Heat the remaining olive oil in a large nonstick skillet over medium-high heat until almost smoking. Working in batches, add the rolls and cook, turning often with tongs, until golden brown on all sides, 5 to 7 minutes. Cool slightly before serving.

To make the dipping sauce, combine the soy sauce, vinegar, sesame oil, and sugar in a small bowl. Stir well and serve on the side with the rolls.

Tahini Crab and Sliced Radishes on Cayenne Toasts

For the toasts:

2 tablespoons vegetable oil

2 teaspoons Asian (toasted) sesame oil*

1/4 teaspoon cayenne pepper

Two 6-inch pita breads with pockets

Kosher salt to taste

For the crab:

1/4 cup tahini (sesame paste)*

1 garlic clove, minced

2 tablespoons fresh lemon juice

1 tablespoon olive oil

Kosher salt and freshly ground black pepper to taste

1/4 pound jumbo lump crabmeat, about 1 cup, picked over

4 large radishes, thinly sliced

*Available at most supermarkets or see Mail Order Sources.

MAKES 24 HORS D'OEUVRES

Back in the late seventies I worked at the Harvest Restaurant in Cambridge under Chef Laura Boehmer, who had Crab Rangoon on the menu. (How long ago was that? Now there is no more Burma, and Rangoon turns out to be the capital of a country called Myanmar.) Crab Rangoon was crab tossed with a tahini sauce, folded into a wonton wrapper, and deep-fried. We served it with an apricot dipping sauce, and it was delicious.

I wanted a version of Crab Rangoon for this book, but without the deep frying. So I took the sesame crab mixture and put it on pita crisps and threw in a few radishes for color and crunch. This is an elegant little hors d'oeuvre that is really easy to make, but please use real crabmeat. The imitation stuff is highly processed, and I don't recommend it.

To make the toasts, preheat the oven to 400°F. Whisk the vegetable oil, sesame oil, and cayenne in a small bowl. Split each pita into 2 rounds and brush the rough sides with equal amounts of the cayenne mixture. Cut each round into 6 triangles and arrange in one flat layer on a large baking sheet. Bake until golden and crisp, about 5 minutes. Sprinkle with salt while hot.

Whisk the tahini, garlic, lemon juice, and olive oil with salt and pepper in a small bowl. Gently fold in the crab. Add water if the mixture appears too dry. Arrange a few radish slices on top of each pita triangle and top with a teaspoonful of the crab.

Herbed Yogurt Cheese

I was still in high school when my mom introduced me to delicious garlic-and-herb-flavored French Boursin, a soft, spreadable cow's milk cheese. Years later, working in the test kitchen at *Gourmet,* I set myself the task of developing a homemade alternative to Boursin that somehow retained all the rich flavors of the original with far fewer calories. Eventually it dawned on me that yogurt was the way to go. If you drain yogurt overnight you'll discover the next day that it's acquired a decidedly cheeselike solidity. At that point you can flavor it with anything. (You are not required to go the Boursin wanna-be route.)

You're welcome to make this recipe with low-fat or nonfat yogurt, but you'll naturally end up with low-flavor or no-flavor cheese. Serve in a crock with Bette's Melba Toast (page 29), Oven-Baked Rosemary Potato Chips (page 14), or Pita Croutons (page 56), and it is even better a few days later.

2 cups whole-milk yogurt

1 tablespoon snipped fresh chives

1 tablespoon finely chopped fresh parsley

1 teaspoon chopped fresh tarragon leaves

1 teaspoon finely chopped fresh thyme, preferably lemon thyme

1 small shallot, minced

1 garlic clove, minced

1 tablespoon extra virgin olive oil

Kosher salt and freshly ground black pepper to taste

MAKES ABOUT 1 3/4 CUPS

Line a large strainer with a double layer of rinsed and squeezed cheesecloth or a layer of rinsed and squeezed paper towels. Spoon the yogurt into the strainer and set over a bowl to drain. Cover with plastic wrap, put in the refrigerator, and drain for at least 4 hours, preferably overnight. Remove the yogurt cheese from the cheesecloth and place in a small bowl. Stir in the remaining ingredients. Spoon into a decorative crock and refrigerate for up to 3 days.

Finnan Haddie Brandade

1 small onion, thinly sliced

1 small celery rib, sliced

4 fresh parsley sprigs

1/2 teaspoon black peppercorns

3/4 pound finnan haddie (smoked haddock),* cut into 6 pieces

1 small Yukon Gold potato, peeled and halved

Kosher salt to taste

1/4 cup extra virgin olive oil

2 garlic cloves, minced

2 tablespoons half-and-half

2 teaspoons fresh lemon juice

Freshly ground black pepper to taste

Chopped fresh parsley, Niçoise olives, roasted red pepper strips, and toasted slices of French bread or Bette's Melba Toast (page 29) for garnish

*See Mail Order Sources.

SERVES 4 TO 6

I once asked my dad to come onto the show for Father's Day, but I never really thought he'd go for it. Not Hump. Too doggone shy.

I was wrong. He jumped at the chance. As a younger man, yes, he was shy. But my father in his golden age has become quite the dinner table raconteur, a development I'd conveniently forgotten. These days he loves to regale us—at length—with tales of his foreign travels with my mother. Indeed, it's gotten so that the rest of us think twice before saying, "Hey, Hump, how was Italy?" And now television was beckoning? He was ready.

My dad has exactly two recipes in his repertoire: scrambled eggs (cooked slow and low) and fish chowder. As Father's Day on "Cooking Live" approached, we both wondered, separately, what he was going to do for an hour while I cooked furiously around him. But on the appointed day the man was prepared. He'd done his homework on the two culinary subjects that interested him: finnan haddie (Scottish smoked haddock) and johnnycakes. Neither of them was on the menu for the evening, but a detail like that wasn't going to slow down Hump. In fact, as soon as he started talking about finnan haddie, the floodgates opened. A bunch of viewers called to express their gratitude for Hump's learned celebration of this esoteric product and their solidarity with the man himself. One viewer even took the trouble to write to me with information about where my dad and his fellow finnan haddie fanatics could find the coveted item (see Mail Order Sources).

Impressed by these declarations of passion, I wondered if a recipe for finnan haddie needed to be in this book. Most of the old cookbooks I looked in recommended cooking finnan haddie in a cream sauce, so that was the avenue I pursued. The result is the breakfast dish I call Creamed Finnan Haddie (page 314), which is served with Johnny-cakes (page 313). It then occurred to me that smoked haddock might be a fine substitute for the salt cod in *brandade de morue*, a garlicky French fish spread. It worked like a charm.

Combine the onion, celery, parsley, and peppercorns in a large saucepan. Pour in 2 cups water and bring to a boil over high heat. Reduce the heat to medium and add the finnan haddie. Simmer until the fish is softened and flaky, about 10 minutes. Transfer to a bowl and cool. Strain and reserve the cooking liquid.

Place the potato in a small saucepan and pour in cold water to cover. Add salt and bring to a boil. Reduce the heat to medium and cook until the potato is very tender, about 20 minutes. Drain well and put through a ricer or food mill to puree. You should have about $1/2$ cup.

When the fish is cool enough to handle, remove and discard any skin and bones. Break the finnan haddie into large chunks. Place in a food processor and add the olive oil, garlic, and $1/4$ cup of the reserved cooking liquid. Puree until very smooth, stopping and scraping down the sides often. (This will take a while.) Blend in the half-and-half and lemon juice. You should have about 2 cups.

Stir the potato puree with the finnan haddie puree in a large bowl until well blended. Season with salt and pepper. Turn out into a serving bowl and top with parsley, olives, and strips of red pepper as desired. Serve warm or at room temperature with toasts on the side.

Chicken Liver Pâté with Port

9 tablespoons unsalted butter, softened

1 large onion, finely chopped

1 pound chicken livers, trimmed and halved

2 teaspoons kosher salt

1/2 teaspoon freshly ground black pepper

1 1/2 tablespoons minced fresh thyme or 1 1/2 teaspoons dried

1 1/2 teaspoons minced fresh sage leaves or 1/2 teaspoon crumbled dried

1 cup tawny port

Additional kosher salt and freshly ground black pepper to taste

2 teaspoons fresh lemon juice or to taste

Several fresh watercress sprigs for garnish

SERVES 6 TO 8

A couple of years after I graduated from cooking school I apprenticed at a one-star restaurant in Chartres, France. My apprenticeship lasted for only two months, but it was pretty intense nonetheless. (Certainly it didn't help that I was the only woman in the kitchen.) Still, I learned a ton, the most important thing being that the French do not waste anything. When I returned to my job as a restaurant chef in the States, my food cost went down dramatically.

In France we worked six days a week from ten in the morning until three in the afternoon and then from five in the afternoon until ten in the evening. I started going to Paris on Mondays (our day off), on a mission to eat lunch at restaurants where I might learn something new and not have to spend a mint for the privilege. One day at a lovely little place on the Ile St. Louis whose name I don't remember, I ordered the chicken liver mousse as a first course. It was heavenly, silky smooth (nearly as rich as foie gras, in fact) and served with thin slices of toasted brioche. I vowed to reproduce it when I got back to America. Here is the result.

This is a great hors d'oeuvre for an elegant party. Unmold it onto a round platter, then garnish it with grapes and a basket of Bette's Melba Toast (page 29) or a sliced baguette.

Heat 3 tablespoons of the butter in a large skillet over medium heat. Add the onion and cook, stirring often, until softened, about 5 minutes. Transfer to a food processor. Increase the heat to medium-high and add 3 more tablespoons of the butter to the skillet. Add the chicken livers and cook, stirring constantly, until the exteriors are no longer pink, about 2 minutes. Add the salt, pepper, thyme, and sage. Cook until the livers are lightly browned and firm but still slightly pink inside, about 1 minute longer. Add the contents of the skillet to the food processor with the onions.

Remove the skillet from the heat and pour in the port. Return the skillet to the stove and bring to a boil over high heat, scraping up the browned bits from the bottom of the pan. Boil until slightly thickened and reduced to about 2 tablespoons. Pour into the food processor with the liver and onions. Process until smooth. Pass the mixture through a fine-mesh sieve, cool to room temperature, and whisk in the remaining 3 tablespoons butter. Season with salt and pepper.

Line a 3-cup bowl that measures about 6 inches in diameter with plastic wrap. Add the lemon juice to the strained liver puree, pour into the lined bowl, and smooth over the top. Chill, covered, for at least 3 hours or overnight. Invert onto a platter and carefully remove the plastic wrap. Run a warm knife around the sides and top to smooth. Surround with sprigs of watercress.

Oven-Baked Rosemary Potato Chips

Extra virgin olive oil for brushing

1 medium russet potato, peeled

Kosher salt to taste

**1 teaspoon crumbled dried
rosemary**

SERVES 4

In the late eighties, when I left *Gourmet*'s test kitchen to become chef of *Gourmet*'s dining room, I walked into the ideal situation for a chef. The dining room was small—I never had to make lunch for more than 16 people at a time—and I had no budget restrictions. I could make sure that every dish was just so, and—because the dining room wasn't a for-profit restaurant but a showplace for the magazine—I didn't have to pinch pennies. I immediately started putting out the best food I had made in my life.

Instructed to "make the magazine come alive," I was mainly supposed to reproduce *Gourmet*'s recipes, but I could also contribute my own ideas and recipes. These rosemary potato chips were one of my earliest contributions. Everybody who loves potato chips also wishes they were less caloric. These delicious chips, baked, not fried, definitely fit the bill. Today you can find oven-baked potato chips everywhere, but at the time I thought they were sort of original.

I have to be honest: I hate to have anyone buy a special piece of equipment, but for this recipe you really need a mandoline. A mandoline is a slicing machine that looks like a washboard with different blades that can be adjusted according to the task at hand. The Cadillac of mandolines, used by all the French chefs, costs about $200. The Honda of mandolines, a Japanese model made by Benriner, costs about $35 and works equally well. Once you buy it and get used to it, you will pull it out all the time.

Even though you slice them the same, these potato chips all cook at slightly different rates, which means that they require a little bit of baby-sitting. But they keep for days at room temperature, and I have never met anyone who wasn't wild for them. If you're throwing a dinner party and you want to get fancy, cook up homemade mashed potatoes and then top each portion with four or five rosemary potato chips, stuck in like a porcupine's quills.

Preheat the oven to 375°F. Brush 2 large baking sheets lightly with oil. Use a mandoline or hand-held slicing machine to cut the potatoes lengthwise into $1/8$-inch-thick slices. Arrange the slices in one flat layer on the baking sheets. Brush the slices lightly with oil and bake until golden throughout, 15 to 20 minutes, checking often since they brown at different rates. Transfer to paper towels and sprinkle with salt and the rosemary while hot.

Chorizo Chicken Wings

2 pounds chicken wings

1 tablespoon extra virgin
  olive oil

2$\frac{1}{2}$ ounces chorizo sausage,*
  casing removed and very
  finely chopped

2 cups Rice Krispies

$\frac{1}{4}$ cup freshly grated Parmigiano-
  Reggiano

2 teaspoons sweet or hot
  paprika

1 teaspoon ground cumin

$\frac{1}{4}$ teaspoon kosher salt

Freshly ground black pepper to
  taste

$\frac{1}{3}$ cup mayonnaise

2 garlic cloves, minced

2 teaspoons sherry vinegar

*Available at many supermarkets or see
Mail Order Sources.

SERVES 4 TO 6

Several years ago we invited the viewers of "Good Morning America" to compete in a "Cut the Calories" contest. The winning entree was Oven-Fried Chicken with Andouille Sausage by Sandy Greene of Wayne, Pennsylvania. It was completely delicious, even though it was low-fat, low-calorie, and low-salt. The secret ingredient was Rice Krispies. Sandy's little secret was part of my inspiration for this dish. I fattened up the recipe after that.

Cut off the very tip of the chicken wings, known as the *wing tips,* and reserve for stock. Find the joint where the remaining two parts of the wing are joined and cut through the joint to halve.

Preheat the oven to 400°F. Heat the oil in a small skillet over medium heat. Add the chorizo and cook, stirring, until lightly browned, about 3 minutes. Drain on paper towels. Cool to room temperature.

Place the Rice Krispies in a plastic bag with a resealable closure and roughly crush with a rolling pin. Transfer to a large bowl and stir in the cooked chorizo, Parmigiano-Reggiano, paprika, cumin, salt, and pepper.

Combine the mayonnaise, garlic, and vinegar in a large bowl. Add the chicken wings and toss well to coat. Roll the wings in the Rice Krispies mixture until well coated. Arrange in one layer on a lightly oiled baking sheet and bake until golden, 30 to 35 minutes. Serve hot.

chorizo

Chorizo is a kind of sausage popular in Mexico and Spain. It is usually made from pork (but it can also be made from beef or other meat) flavored with garlic and chiles. The Mexican chorizo is made with ancho or pasilla chiles, and the Spanish is made with paprika. Mexican chorizo is a fresh sausage, which must be cooked completely, while the Spanish chorizo is a smoked, dry-cured, ready-to-eat sausage. You can use either in this recipe.

Crispy Zucchini Sticks with Olive Dip

1¹/₂ cups all-purpose flour

1 cup beer, plus more as needed for thinning

1 cup mayonnaise

¹/₂ cup chopped pitted Kalamata olives

1 tablespoon fresh lemon juice

2 medium zucchini

Vegetable oil for deep frying

Kosher salt and freshly ground black pepper to taste

MAKES 50 TO 60 PIECES
WITH 1¹/₄ CUPS DIP

In the early eighties I worked as *chef tournant* at La Tulipe, a three-star temple of French gastronomy in New York's Greenwich Village. One of our best-loved—and most unlikely—appetizers was fried zucchini. I know it sounds déclassé: fried zucchini at a three-star restaurant? But Chef Sally Darr took this typical Italian dish and transformed it according to her own refined and unerring taste. She started with a recipe that was simple and delicious, then had the finished product delivered to the table in a beautiful little woven basket. The key to the flavor was the batter: equal parts beer and flour, period. This batter has since become my all-time favorite. It creates the crispiest crust, which is, after all, the point of deep frying.

This is a great dish for entertaining because you can throw it together so quickly and/or prepare some of it ahead. The zucchini can be cut and the mayonnaise mixed the day before, and then all you have to do is prepare the batter and heat the oil. Don't forget to season the fried zucchini the moment you pull it out of the oil. The salt will stick better when the zucchini is piping hot.

Whisk 1 cup of the flour with the beer in a large bowl until smooth. Pour through a strainer into another bowl and let stand for 1 hour. Thin with additional beer just before frying if thicker than pancake batter.

Meanwhile, mix the mayonnaise with the olives and lemon juice in a small bowl. Thin with 1 to 2 tablespoons water, if you like. Keep covered in the refrigerator until ready to serve the zucchini.

Cut the zucchini into sticks that measure ¹/₄ inch wide and 2 inches long. Heat 2 inches of oil in a large deep saucepan until a deep-fat frying thermometer reaches 375°F. Combine the remaining $^1/_2$ cup flour with salt and pepper in a shallow bowl or pie plate. Add the zucchini and toss to cover in flour. Transfer to a strainer and shake to remove excess flour. Working in batches, dip in the batter, letting the excess drip off. Fry in batches until golden brown and crisp, about 3 minutes. Drain on paper towels and sprinkle with salt. Serve the olive mayonnaise on the side for dipping.

mayonnaise

Some folks turn up their nose at mayonnaise, but I love it. Mayonnaise is just so useful. It can star as the main ingredient in a recipe (such as in Crispy Zucchini Sticks with Olive Dip) or play a supporting role, such as the glue for rosemary scallion crust on a rack of lamb (page 105).

I'd love to pass on a recipe for homemade mayo, but it would call for a raw egg, and the threat of salmonella—minuscule though it is—prevents me. No problem. There are a few supermarket brands that are pretty good. All you need to do is add some flavoring, thin down the mayo a little bit, or add sour cream or yogurt, and you have a sauce. That's how I came up with the olive mayo; I thought the fried zucchini was crying out for a little dipping sauce. People love this one; they can't believe it has only three ingredients and is based on commercial mayo.

Mushroom Rolls

8 tablespoons (1 stick) unsalted
  butter

2 medium shallots, minced

10 ounces cultivated white
  mushrooms, finely chopped

2 teaspoons finely chopped fresh
  thyme or ³/₄ teaspoon dried

¹/₄ cup dry sherry

¹/₄ cup sour cream

Kosher salt and freshly ground
  black pepper to taste

24 slices homemade-style white
  bread, crusts removed

MAKES 48 ROLLS

This is a recipe for the pastry-challenged—or for anyone who doesn't feel he or she has the time to make homemade dough. I've adapted it from one of my aunt Jean's recipes, and it is brilliant because she uses "homemade-style" white bread as a stand-in for pastry. ("Homemade-style" white bread is a legit alternative to that no-flavor, no-texture stuff you can smush into a spitball.) Aunt Jean makes a batch of these rolls, lathers them up with a ton of melted butter, and then parks them in the freezer for future cocktail parties or unexpected last-minute guests. A fairly decadent appetizer—they look elegant and they taste rich—these mushroom rolls don't actually require much work.

Indeed this bread-as-pastry concept works for virtually any stuffing, savory or sweet. Just remember that if the filling is too wet it will sog up the bread. For example, if you've chosen something like mushrooms or apples as stuffing, cook them first. The liquid will evaporate, and you'll concentrate the flavor. I used regular old button mushrooms here, but you could get wild and go with any variety, from chanterelle to shiitake to portobello. (And maybe finish it off with some truffle oil, aka Mushroom Helper.)

Heat half the butter in a large skillet over medium heat. Add the shallots and cook, stirring often, until softened, 3 to 5 minutes. Stir in the mushrooms and cook, stirring often, until all the liquid has evaporated. Add the thyme and the sherry. Increase the heat to medium-high and cook until the mixture is almost dry. Remove the skillet from the heat, stir in the sour cream, and season with salt and pepper. You should have 1 cup of filling.

To make the rolls, preheat the oven to 350°F and melt the remaining butter. Roll out the bread with a rolling pin until very thin. Place about 2 teaspoons of the filling on each slice of bread. Roll up the bread to enclose the filling and form a cylinder, and brush all over with melted butter. (At this point the rolls can be placed in a zipper-type plastic freezer bag and frozen for future use. Frozen rolls take a few extra minutes in the oven.) Cut the rolls crosswise into 2 pieces, place on a baking sheet seam side down, and bake for about 15 minutes or until crisp. Serve warm.

My aunt Jean Moulton, 1982

Miniature Jalapeño Soufflés

1 tablespoon unsalted butter,
plus extra for buttering the
tins

2¹/₂ tablespoons all-purpose flour

2 tablespoons very finely
chopped pine nuts

1 small jalapeño, seeded and
minced

6 tablespoons whole milk

¹/₄ cup grated Gruyère cheese

¹/₄ teaspoon kosher salt

¹/₈ teaspoon freshly ground black
pepper

¹/₂ teaspoon Dijon mustard

1 large egg, separated

MAKES 12 SOUFFLÉS

The beauty of these little soufflés is their resilience. You can make them a day ahead, toss them in the fridge, and then just reheat them when your guests arrive. People aren't usually served mini-soufflés, so they will be charmed. Indeed you might find yourself reaching frequently for those mini-muffin tins. Besides this recipe and the Miniature Goat Cheese Cakes (page 28), you can minimize just about any cake or muffin.

If your jalapeño lacks bite (as so many do these days), just reach for a pickled jalapeño, either your own homemade version (page 345) or your favorite store-bought brand. I always keep a jar on the door of the fridge to toss into those dishes that need a little perking up.

Preheat the oven to 400°F. Butter a nonstick mini-muffin tin with twelve ¹/₈-cup wells that measure 1³/₄ inches in diameter and ³/₄ inch deep. Mix 1 tablespoon of the flour with half the pine nuts in a small bowl. Dust the tins with the flour and nut mixture. Tap out the excess.

Melt the 1 tablespoon butter in a small saucepan over medium-high heat. Stir in the remaining 1¹/₂ tablespoons flour and the jalapeño. Cook, stirring, for about 2 minutes. Whisk in the milk, bring to a simmer, and cook, stirring constantly, for 3 minutes. Transfer to a bowl and add the cheese, salt, pepper, mustard, and egg yolk. Stir until the cheese has melted and the sauce is well blended. Cool to room temperature.

Beat the egg white until firm but not stiff. Stir a fourth of the white into the cheese sauce. Gently fold in the remaining white. Spoon into the prepared tins, sprinkle with the remaining pine nuts, and bake until puffed and golden, 7 to 10 minutes. Cool in the tins on

wire racks. When cool, run a small knife around the edge of each soufflé to loosen. (The soufflés will fall as they cool.) They can be prepared up to a day in advance and refrigerated. Bake in the muffin tins
in a preheated 400°F oven for 5 to 7 minutes before serving.

seeding jalapeños

One night on "Cooking Live" when I was removing the seeds and ribs
from a jalapeño without the protection of surgical gloves, a viewer
called in to say that at least I could make my job easier by using a
grapefruit spoon. If you happen to have one kicking around the house,
try it. It works nicely.

Smoked Salmon and Salmon Roe on Crispy Potato Pancakes with Horseradish Cream and Pickled Onions

1 large baking potato

2 tablespoons unsalted butter

2 tablespoons vegetable oil

Kosher salt to taste

$1/2$ cup crème fraîche

1 tablespoon fresh lemon juice

1 tablespoon grated fresh or drained bottled horseradish

Freshly ground black pepper to taste

2 ounces smoked salmon, julienned

1 tablespoon caviar or salmon roe

$1/2$ cup Pickled Red Onions (page 346)

MAKES ABOUT 12 PANCAKES, SERVING 4

This is a recipe I often make for special occasions when it's just the four of us at home, because you can dress it up or down. Sam leaves the salmon and caviar alone in favor of the unadorned potato pancakes. Ruth also favors the pancakes but adds a shmeer of sour cream to hers. Bill and I load them up with the works.

Assuming you also want the works, you'll appreciate the way that the crisp and salty potato pancakes complement the richness of the salmon and caviar. (The pancakes should be almost as thin as potato chips. To get them that thin, spread them out in the nonstick pan and press them down.)

The pickled onions (page 346), by the way, are a wonderful addition not only to this recipe but to all sorts of recipes. I like to put them on sandwiches, in salads, and on grilled meats. They are simple to make, and they keep in the fridge for at least a week.

Peel and coarsely grate the potato. Working in batches, heat 2 teaspoons of the butter with 2 teaspoons of the vegetable oil in a large nonstick skillet over medium-high heat until very hot. Sprinkle 2 tablespoons of the potatoes into the pan, pressing into a 3-inch diameter with a spatula to create lacy, flat rounds of potato. Don't be concerned if you can see the bottom of the pan through gaps in the potatoes. Cook until well browned, pressing down firmly, 5 to 7 minutes per side. Season with salt while hot. (The cakes can be made several hours in advance and crisped in a hot oven before serving.)

Combine the crème fraîche, lemon juice, and horseradish in a small bowl and season with salt and pepper. Arrange 3 pancakes per serving on small plates. Top the pancakes with equal amounts of smoked salmon, a spoonful of horseradish cream, and a spoonful of caviar. Top with a few pickled onions and serve.

homemade crème fraîche

If you want to make your own crème fraîche, whisk together 1 cup heavy cream and $1/4$ cup buttermilk and transfer to a glass jar with no lid. Cover the top of the jar with a piece of paper towel and a rubber band to hold the paper towel in place and let the mixture stand for 24 hours. Remove the paper towel, cover with plastic wrap, and chill.

Cheesy Popcorn

2 tablespoons unsalted butter

¹/₂ teaspoon fresh lemon juice

2 tablespoons vegetable oil

¹/₄ cup popcorn kernels

Kosher salt and freshly ground black pepper to taste

¹/₄ to ¹/₃ cup freshly grated Parmigiano-Reggiano

MAKES ABOUT 4 CUPS

I loved popcorn as a kid and still love it as a so-called grown-up—especially the homemade stuff. Whenever my kids invite a friend to stay overnight, I casually volunteer to whip up a batch of popcorn to go along with their rented movie. (I say *whip up* because we don't have a microwave, so I actually have to cook it on top of the stove.) In fact, sneaky me, I always end up eating as much as they do. And I'm talking about "plain" popcorn, popcorn tossed with melted butter and a little salt and nothing more. *Gourmet* ran a "Last Touch" column on flavored popcorn many years ago that opened my eyes to how versatile it could be—popcorn as croutons in a soup or a salad or all by itself as an appetizer. Oh, sure, there are companies that make and ship six different kinds of flavored popcorn, but none of them will be as tasty as your homemade version. So here is cheesy popcorn—for kids of all ages.

Preheat the oven to 300°F. Melt the butter with the lemon juice in a small skillet over medium heat. Keep warm.

Heat the oil in a large saucepan over medium-high heat until almost smoking. Add the popcorn, cover, and reduce the heat slightly. Shake the pan constantly until the popping subsides. Pour into a large bowl and drizzle on the lemon butter. Toss well and season with salt and pepper. Turn out into a large baking pan and bake until crisp and hot, about 12 minutes. Sprinkle on the cheese and toss.

Michael Green says:
champagne and popcorn: a perfect match

While I'm not advocating sneaking a bottle of your favorite bubbly into the local multiplex, while at home with the latest video rental, consider serving a glass of Champagne with your popcorn. Seriously! The elegant effervescent bubbles and lively acidity are a welcome contrast to the dry, salty crunch of popcorn. And with cheese or butter on your popped kernels, the result is divine—crisp bubbles refreshing your palate and leaving it ready for the next cheesy bite!

Michael Green says:
blushing: the joy of rosé wine

Rosé is a home-run wine for many first courses and light lunch dishes. Rosé (the French word for "pink") is usually made by keeping the skins of the red grapes in contact with the fermenting juice just long enough to achieve a blush color. The resulting colors will vary from light pink to deeper salmon and cherry. The styles and flavors of these wines can also vary, from still to sparkling, from dry to off dry and even quite sweet. The most elegant versions tend to be fermented totally dry—striking a wonderful balance of fruit, alcohol, and acidity—and the most famous of these hail from the southern French regions of Provence and the Languedoc. Try it with the Miniature Goat Cheese Cakes (page 28). Drink these wines young and with a good chill.

Miniature Goat Cheese Cakes

1 tablespoon unsalted butter, melted, plus extra for buttering the tin

$^1/_2$ cup fresh bread crumbs (page 347)

$^1/_2$ cup very finely chopped toasted walnuts

$^1/_2$ teaspoon kosher salt

$^1/_2$ teaspoon freshly ground black pepper

5 ounces fresh goat cheese, softened

$^1/_4$ pound cream cheese, softened

1 large egg, lightly beaten

1 tablespoon snipped fresh chives

MAKES 18 CAKES

These are great make-ahead hors d'oeuvres because they reheat so beautifully. They require mini-muffin tins (also known as *gem tins*), and if you don't already own some, you may want to buy them. They're really a worthwhile investment. Suddenly everything you used to make big you will think about making mini.

You can line the tins with any kind of chopped nuts, with bread crumbs, or even with your favorite cracker, crushed. These mini goat cheese cakes are a delicious addition to a tossed green salad, like an elegant crouton.

Preheat the oven to 350°F. Butter a nonstick mini-muffin tin with eighteen $^1/_8$-cup wells that measure $1^3/_4$ inches in diameter and $^3/_4$ inch deep. Mix the bread crumbs, walnuts, and butter in a small bowl with half the salt and half the pepper. Stir with a fork until thoroughly combined. Place 2 teaspoonfuls of the mixture in each cup and press down into the bottom to form a crust.

Beat the goat cheese and cream cheese in the bowl of an electric mixer until smooth, light, and fluffy. Beat in the egg, chives, and remaining salt and pepper. Divide between the wells and smooth the tops with a knife. Bake until puffed, about 15 minutes. Cool on a wire rack for 5 minutes, then run a knife around the rim of each cake and carefully unmold. Note: These can be baked a day ahead and kept covered and chilled in the refrigerator. Reheat in a 350°F oven until hot.

Bette's Melba Toast

15 very thin slices homemade-style white sandwich bread

2 tablespoons unsalted butter, melted

MAKES 60 PIECES

Bette Cohen is one of my parents' oldest and best friends. She and her husband Bill used to tear around the country in a red convertible with the top down. They were wild and wonderful and took it upon themselves to introduce my sheltered New England parents to the cultural delights of New York City.

Bette also happens to be a great cook and was one of the main influences on my mom's culinary development. Here is Bette's version of Melba toast, which is miles away from the boring low-fat stuff that comes in a box. Hers is delicious and buttery, a perfect foundation for such hors d'oeuvres as Chicken Liver Pâté with Port (page 12), Finnan Haddie Brandade (page 10), and Herbed Yogurt Cheese (page 9). Store it in a tightly sealed plastic container and it will stay fresh for a week.

Preheat the oven to 300°F. Remove the crusts from the bread slices and cut each slice into 4 triangles. Arrange in one flat layer on 2 large baking sheets. Place in the oven and bake until golden brown, 20 to 25 minutes. Remove from the oven and brush lightly with butter while warm. Keeps for up to 1 week in an airtight container.

Bill Cohen

Bette Cohen

Soups

Chilled Two-Melon Soup with Balsamic-Marinated Strawberries and Sour Cream

1 small very ripe cantaloupe, peeled, seeded, and coarsely chopped (about 6 cups)

2 tablespoons fresh lemon juice or to taste

1/2 very ripe honeydew melon, peeled, seeded, and coarsely chopped (about 6 cups)

3 tablespoons fresh lime juice or to taste

2 teaspoons finely chopped fresh mint, plus several sprigs for garnish

1 cup strawberries, hulled and quartered or cut into sixths if very large

1 tablespoon sugar or more to taste

1 tablespoon balsamic vinegar, preferably aged

1 teaspoon cracked black peppercorns

1/2 cup sour cream

SERVES 6

This totally refreshing summertime soup is a breeze to make if you have a blender. The key is to find really ripe melons and be sure that the soup is served very cold. It looks great, too, because the two purees don't mix when you pour them into the bowl—they hang out together side by side in a happy little yin-yang pattern. The strawberry mixture and sour cream are like the cherry on top.

Working in batches, puree the cantaloupe with the lemon juice in a food processor or blender until smooth. Transfer to a bowl and cover with plastic wrap. Refrigerate for at least 3 hours or overnight. Puree the honeydew in batches with the lime juice and mint. Transfer to a bowl and cover with plastic wrap. Refrigerate for at least 3 hours or overnight. Chill 6 large soup bowls.

Combine the strawberries, sugar, vinegar, and peppercorns in a small bowl and toss. Ladle equal amounts of the soup simultaneously into the bowls, keeping them separate. Spoon a small amount of the strawberries in the center and garnish with a spoonful of the sour cream and a sprig of mint. Serve cold.

chilling soup

When you don't have enough time to chill a soup or drink in the fridge, the best alternative is to pour it into a metal bowl and then set the metal bowl right over another bowl of ice and water. The soup should be plenty cold in about 30 minutes.

Gingery Chicken Broth with Wonton Ravioli

This soup combines two of my favorite recipes—Eileen Yin-Fei Lo's gingery Chinese chicken broth and Jacques Pépin's chicken breast stuffing—with one of my favorite techniques, the wonton as ravioli.

Eileen introduced me to Chinese-style chicken broth when she appeared on my show to make recipes from her book *The Chinese Way*. In the comfort category, it is right up there with the Jewish version. In the healing category, how can you miss with not one but two major restoratives: old-fashioned chicken soup and fresh ginger?

The stuffing is based on the kind that Jacques Pépin used to put under the skin of chicken breasts when he was a guest chef at La Tulipe in the early eighties. He would take the little flap of meat underneath the chicken breast, the part called the *filet* or *tenderloin,* and grind it up with cream and flavorings. It was mousselike and delicious. Here I have substituted a chicken breast for the tenderloin because you can't find tenderloins all by themselves in the supermarket.

I learned what a great stand-in wontons are for homemade ravioli from an article entitled "Wonton Ravioli" that was published years ago in *Gourmet.* They are definitely an important item to have in the freezer. You can stuff wontons with just about anything, and your guests will be impressed because they will think you made pasta from scratch. They are available in the frozen food section of many supermarkets these days.

Speaking of frozen, both the soup and the ravioli (uncooked) freeze well. Just keep it all wrapped tightly in

8 scallions

2 quarts chicken stock, preferably homemade (page 338)

One 4-inch-long piece fresh ginger, peeled and thickly sliced

5 garlic cloves, peeled and smashed with the side of a knife

1 boneless, skinless chicken breast half, about 6 ounces, cut into 1/2-inch cubes

1 tablespoon crushed ice

6 tablespoons heavy cream

1/2 teaspoon freshly grated lemon zest

3/4 teaspoon kosher salt

Cornstarch as needed

36 round wonton skins, preferably Japanese gyoza skins

Chopped fresh cilantro for garnish

Kosher salt and freshly ground black pepper to taste

SERVES 6

the freezer. That way you will always be prepared for the day you wake up feeling a little under the weather.

Trim off all but 1 inch of the scallion greens, chop the greens, and reserve for garnish. Cut each of the scallions into 4 pieces. Combine the stock, scallion pieces, ginger, and garlic in a large pot. Bring to a boil over high heat. Reduce the heat to medium and simmer for 20 minutes or longer. Strain and discard the solids. (The broth can be made a day ahead. Keep refrigerated until ready to serve.)

Place the chicken in a food processor and pulse several times to grind finely. Add the ice and process until the ice is absorbed. With the blade in motion, add the cream. Pulse in the lemon zest and salt to blend. Chill for 1 hour. Sprinkle a sheet pan with cornstarch to hold the wontons before cooking.

Working with a few wontons at a time and keeping the remaining wonton skins covered, mound 1 tablespoon of the chicken mixture in the center of each skin. Moisten the edges with water and place another wonton on top. Press on the edges to seal completely. Repeat until the entire filling is used. As they are done, transfer to the sheet pan.

Just before serving, bring a large pot of salted water to a boil over high heat. Working in 2 batches, drop the ravioli into the boiling water, reduce the heat to medium, and simmer until tender and the chicken mixture is thoroughly cooked, 3 to 5 minutes. Bring the water back to a boil before proceeding with the final batch. Remove the wontons with a slotted spoon and arrange 3 in the center of each serving bowl. (The wontons are best if used just after boiling. Place them right into the serving bowls. If they cool, the hot broth will warm them.)

Reheat the broth almost to boiling, season with salt and pepper to taste, and ladle over the wontons. Garnish with the cilantro and chopped scallion greens. Serve right away.

Michael Green says:
sipping with soup

Down with those who say no wine with soup! In multicourse meals, lighter soups are often served as palate cleansers and no wine is really required, but where the soup takes center stage a well-chosen wine can be an ideal match. It is important here to think about the texture of the soup. Lighter soups such as the Gingery Chicken Broth with Wonton Ravioli (page 33) tend to work best with lighter styles of wine—white wines such as Pinot Grigio, Trebbiano, Albariño, or a dry rosé could be delicious. With more richly textured, rustic, or "fork and knife soups," such as the Cauliflower Soup with Caraway and Rye Croutons (page 40), a richer wine can be served. Look to a warm-climate Chardonnay from either California or Australia. Red wines from France's Côtes-du-Rhône region or Spain's Rioja region might be considered.

With Jacques Pépin at the James Beard House, 1993

Creamy Lime Corn Soup
with Cumin-Salted Tortilla Strips

For the soup:

10 ears corn, husks removed

3 cups chicken stock, preferably homemade (page 338)

2 teaspoons whole cumin seeds

2 tablespoons unsalted butter

2 medium onions, finely chopped

3 celery ribs, finely chopped

2 medium jalapeños, chopped

Kosher salt and freshly ground black pepper to taste

For the garnish:

Three 6-inch corn tortillas

1 teaspoon ground cumin

$1/2$ teaspoon kosher salt

Vegetable oil for frying

1 large red bell pepper

2 teaspoons freshly grated lime zest

1 to 2 tablespoons fresh lime juice or to taste

Additional kosher salt and freshly ground black pepper to taste

1 tablespoon finely chopped fresh cilantro

SERVES 6

Here is a luxuriously thick soup that is very low in calories, especially if you leave out the tortilla chips.

You really boost the corn flavor by adding cobs to this broth. Indeed, any time you have leftover cobs kicking around, especially at the end of the summer, you might want to cook up a corn broth and salt it away in the freezer in anticipation of those long cold winter months. Then it's a snap to make this soup using your frozen broth and a box of frozen corn.

If you are not in the mood to fry your own tortilla strips, you can certainly buy some good store-bought chips and just crumble them on top.

To make the soup, cut the corn from the cobs, reserving the cobs. Pour the stock into a large saucepan or soup pot. Add as many of the stripped corn cobs as the pot will hold, discarding the rest. Bring to a boil over high heat. Reduce the heat to medium-low and simmer, partially covered, for 15 minutes.

Place the cumin seeds in a small skillet and toast over medium-high heat, stirring or shaking the skillet often, until slightly darkened and fragrant, about 3 minutes.

Melt the butter in a separate soup pot or kettle over medium heat. Add the onions, celery, jalapeños, and toasted cumin seeds. Cook, stirring often, until the onions and celery are softened, about 5 minutes. Reserve $1^{1}/2$ cups of the corn kernels for garnish and stir the remaining kernels into the onion mixture. Remove the cobs from the stock and pour the stock over the vegetable mixture. Bring to a simmer over medium-high heat. Season with salt and pepper. Reduce the heat to medium-low and cook, covered, stirring often, until the corn is very tender, about 10 minutes. Remove from the heat and cool slightly.

Working in batches, puree the soup in a blender. Strain through a fine-mesh strainer, pushing hard on the solids to extract as much liquid as possible. Pour the soup into a large saucepan and season with salt and pepper.

To make the garnish, cut the tortillas into quarters, then cut each quarter into 1-inch X $^1/_4$-inch-wide strips. Mix the ground cumin with the $^1/_2$ teaspoon salt in a small bowl. Pour enough oil into a deep saucepan to measure about 1 inch. Heat over medium-high heat until almost smoking. Add the tortilla strips, a few at a time, and fry until browned and crisp, about 1 minute. Drain on paper towels. Sprinkle with the cumin salt while hot.

Preheat the broiler to high and adjust the rack so that it is about 6 inches from the heat. Place the red pepper on a broiling pan and broil, turning often, until charred on all sides. Transfer to a resealable plastic bag and seal. Set aside for 15 minutes or until cool enough to handle. (The steam will loosen the skin from the pepper.) Remove the core, skin, and seeds from the pepper and cut into julienne strips.

Just before serving, bring the soup almost to a boil over medium-high heat. Stir in the lime zest and lime juice, season with salt and pepper, and pour into warmed bowls. Garnish with the reserved corn kernels, the tortilla strips, the red pepper strips, and a pinch of the chopped cilantro.

cutting off corn kernels

When you are cutting corn off the cob, do it over a piece of parchment, wax paper, foil, or even one of those flexible cutting boards (see Mail Order Sources). It makes it easy to pick up the corn and add it to whatever recipe you're making. Another good suggestion came from a viewer who recommends using a metal bench scraper to pick any small pieces off a board (such as chopped onions) for easy transport to a skillet or bowl.

Butternut Squash Soup with Gruyère Pesto

For the soup:

2 medium butternut squash

2 tablespoons unsalted butter

2 medium leeks, white parts only, thinly sliced

1 quart chicken stock, preferably homemade (page 338), plus more as needed for thinning

Kosher salt and freshly ground black pepper to taste

For the pesto:

1/4 cup coarsely grated Gruyère cheese

2 tablespoons toasted pine nuts, coarsely chopped

1/4 cup packed fresh basil leaves, shredded

1 tablespoon freshly grated Parmigiano-Reggiano

Kosher salt and freshly ground black pepper to taste

SERVES 4 TO 6

The generic recipe for winter squash soup or puree typically begins by calling for a scary amount of the squash "peeled, seeded, and cubed," and then steamed or boiled. Have you ever tried to peel, let alone cut, even *one* of these hard winter squashes? There may be no easier way to cut yourself in the kitchen. And why bother boiling or steaming a vegetable, which makes it watery, when you can roast it and concentrate the flavor?

My favorite way to cook winter squash is to cut it in half lengthwise, scoop out the seeds (or not—they're even easier to scoop out and discard after the squash is cooked), and bake it, cut side down, on a sheet pan in the oven. Now caramelized, it is delicious straight up. But puree it and add other ingredients and it can go anywhere.

My Gruyère pesto isn't really a classic pesto. I added some Gruyère to the standard recipe, left out the oil, and did not puree the mixture. But whatever you call it, my "pesto" adds a nice crunch and a fresh final touch.

This is a satisfying soup that freezes well. You can concoct alternative versions of it by flavoring it with fresh ginger and lime or garnishing it with sautéed apple, crispy bacon, and Cheddar or with crumbled blue cheese and toasted walnuts.

To prepare the soup, preheat the oven to 375°F. Halve the squash lengthwise, scoop out the seeds, and arrange cut side down on a lightly oiled baking sheet. Bake until very tender, 50 to 60 minutes. Cool to room temperature. When cool enough to handle, scrape out the pulp. You should have about 6 cups.

Heat the butter in a large soup pot or kettle over medium heat. Add the leeks and cook, stirring often, until softened, about 5 minutes. Add the squash and 1 quart of the chicken stock, increase the heat to high, and bring to a boil. Reduce the heat to medium-high and simmer, stirring often, until the leeks are tender, about 10 minutes. Working in batches, puree the soup in a food processor or blender until smooth. Thin with additional stock as needed to reach the desired consistency. Return to the soup pot and season with salt and pepper.

To prepare the pesto, combine the Gruyère, pine nuts, basil, Parmigiano-Reggiano, salt, and pepper in a small bowl. Keep at room temperature until ready to serve.

Serve the soup in warmed bowls. Garnish with a spoonful of the pesto just before serving.

preventing nuts from burning

I learned a great way to avoid burning items like nuts in the oven from Beverly Gannon, chef-owner of the Hali'imale General Store in Makawao, Hawaii, when I had her on my show. To remind herself that she had macadamia nuts in the oven she took my pepper grinder (and it is big!) and held it between her ear and her shoulder! As long as she had the pepper grinder there, she said, she wouldn't forget the toasting nuts. It is sort of like the old string-around-the-finger trick. Seems like an extreme thing to do to remind yourself (why not the kitchen timer? I never remember to set it), but when you are dealing with an expensive ingredient like macadamia nuts in her case, or pine nuts as in this recipe, you can't take a chance.

Cauliflower Soup with Caraway and Rye Croutons

Three ¹⁄₃-inch-thick slices rye bread

2 tablespoons olive oil

Kosher salt and freshly ground black pepper to taste

1 medium head cauliflower

1 medium Yukon Gold potato, peeled

4 tablespoons (¹⁄₂ stick) unsalted butter

1 large onion, thinly sliced

2 teaspoons caraway seeds

1 quart chicken stock, preferably homemade (page 338), plus more as needed for thinning

2 teaspoons fresh lemon juice

2 plum tomatoes, seeded and chopped

2 tablespoons snipped fresh chives

SERVES 4

What I love about vegetable soups like this one is that they boast the soul-satisfying consistency of cream without actually containing any. Cooked and pureed, most vegetables are amazingly creamy all by themselves. (OK, some of them need to be pureed with potato to create the desired effect, but you get my point.) I love cream, but it is heavy, and although it delivers nice mouth feel, it dulls the flavor of whatever you are eating. When you put a spoonful of cauliflower soup into your mouth, the first thing you want to taste is cauliflower.

The rye croutons called for here pick up on the caraway in the soup, but if you don't want to go the extra few yards and make your own, just use good-quality store-bought croutons. The point is to have a contrast in texture: creamy soup/crunchy croutons.

This recipe will freeze beautifully, so make a double batch and keep half of it for a cold or rainy day.

Preheat the oven to 350°F. Remove the crust from the bread and cut the bread into ¹⁄₂-inch cubes. Place in a large bowl and toss with the olive oil. Arrange in one flat layer on a baking sheet and bake in the middle of the oven, stirring often, until lightly browned, about 20 minutes. Season with salt and pepper.

Remove 1 cup florets from the cauliflower and trim into ¹⁄₂-inch pieces. Bring a saucepan of salted water to a boil over high heat. Add the florets and bring back to a boil. Boil rapidly until tender, about 3 minutes. Drain and rinse under cold running water. Set aside to drain on paper towels until just before serving the soup.

Slice the remaining cauliflower and the potato. Heat 3 tablespoons of the butter in a soup pot or kettle over medium heat. Add the onion and caraway seeds and cook, stirring, until the onion has softened, about 5 minutes. Stir in the sliced cauliflower and potato. Pour in just enough of the chicken stock to barely cover the cauliflower. Season with salt and pepper and increase the heat to high. Bring to a boil, reduce the heat to medium, and simmer until the cauliflower is tender, about 20 minutes. Working in batches, puree the soup in a food processor or blender until smooth. (Or puree the soup right in the pot using an immersion blender.) Return the soup to the pot and reheat over low heat. Stir in the lemon juice and season with salt and pepper. Thin to the desired consistency with stock or water if necessary. You should have about 5 cups.

Heat the remaining tablespoon of butter in a small skillet over medium heat. Add the tomatoes, reduce the heat to low, and cook, stirring often, until thick and pulpy, about 5 minutes. Season with salt and pepper.

Add the cauliflower florets to the soup and cook over medium heat just until warmed through. Serve the soup in warmed bowls. Garnish with the croutons, a spoonful of the tomatoes, and the chives.

how to make your soup smooth and creamy without the cream

I remember when the food processor came along and we all tossed out our blenders. Big mistake—they both have a place in the kitchen. The blender wins in the category of achieving the smoothest, finest puree. There are some tricks to know first. It is best to puree the soup while it is still hot, but don't fill more than a third of the blender at a time, and leave a little air hole at the top, or you will end up wearing it (the mixture expands when hot), as I did on one of my first dates with my husband. I had invited him over to dinner to impress him with my great culinary skills, and just as he rang the doorbell I pressed that fateful button on the blender, which was packed with hot soup waiting to be pureed. Not only did I look a mess with all that stuff in my hair, but I was in pain! Stoic to a fault, I mopped myself off, swallowed my humiliation, and carried on . . . lesson learned.

Mini-Pumpkin Soup with Toasted Pumpkin Seeds, Shaved Parmesan, and Fried Sage

16 mini-pumpkins, 3¹/₂ to 4 inches across

2 tablespoons vegetable oil

Kosher salt to taste

3 tablespoons unsalted butter

2 onions, finely chopped

About 5 cups chicken stock, preferably homemade (page 338)

Freshly ground black pepper to taste

Vegetable oil for frying

1 cup fresh sage leaves

Shaved Parmigiano-Reggiano for garnish

SERVES 8

For the longest time I thought those cute little pumpkins—no more than 3 or 4 inches in diameter—were nothing more than happy little fall decorations. There they'd sit on the side of the road at farmers' markets and at well-stocked grocery stores, bright orange banks of mini-pumpkins bearing such ridiculous names as Jack B. Little.

One day I wondered if these little guys tasted as good as they looked. I cooked one up and was delighted. These are among the tastiest pumpkins or winter squashes you will find anywhere. And indeed, because these miniature pumpkins *are* so decorative, you can go ahead and use them as a stylish container for whatever dish you make with them. I serve this soup in them, but you could plate up anything from pumpkin risotto to vegetable chili in miniature pumpkins, too.

The season for these little pumpkins is fleeting—they pop up briefly in the fall and then vanish—so be sure to grab them whenever you see them. If you can't get to them right away, just roast them (as I do in this recipe), scoop out the pulp, and freeze it in a resealable plastic bag for later on.

If you were wondering about alternatives to the Italian flavorings used in this soup, you might try lime and fresh ginger or chipotles in adobo sauce.

Preheat the oven to 350°F. Slice off about ¹/₄ inch of the top with the stems from 8 of the pumpkins. Slice the other 8 in half. Scrape out the seeds with a spoon. Pull the seeds away from the stringy membrane, clean, rinse, and pat dry.

Toss the seeds with the vegetable oil and salt. Arrange in one flat layer on a baking sheet. Bake in the middle of the oven, stirring occasionally, until golden and crisp, about 10 to 15 minutes.

Place the pumpkins and the lids cut side down on lightly oiled baking sheets and bake until tender, 35 to 40 minutes. Cool the pumpkins on wire racks. Scoop out the cooked flesh from the halved pumpkins. Scrape most of the pulp from the remaining pumpkins, leaving just enough in each so that it retains its shape.

Melt the butter in a large pot over medium-high heat. Add the onions and cook, stirring often, until softened, about 5 minutes. Add the scooped-out flesh from the pumpkins. Pour in enough of the stock to cover and season with salt and pepper. Simmer over medium-high heat for 20 minutes.

Puree the soup in a food processor or pass through the fine setting of a food mill. You should have about 8 cups of puree. Return it to the pot and season again with salt and pepper.

Heat 2 inches of vegetable oil to 350°F in a deep saucepan. Add the sage in very small batches and fry until translucent, about 20 seconds. (The oil will bubble up furiously when you add the sage to the hot oil.) Drain on paper towels.

To serve, warm the pumpkin shells in a 350°F oven for 15 minutes. Heat the soup until hot, adding water if necessary to thin it slightly. Put each of the shells into a shallow soup bowl and ladle some of the soup into the shell. Top with a few fried sage leaves, some Parmigiano-Reggiano shavings, and a few of the toasted pumpkin seeds. Place the lid slightly askew on top and serve at once.

Spanish-Style White Bean, Kale, and Chorizo Soup

1/2 pound dried white beans, such as Great Northern, rinsed and picked over

8 1/2 cups chicken stock, preferably homemade (page 338)

1 bay leaf, preferably Turkish

Kosher salt to taste

Pinch of saffron threads

2 tablespoons extra virgin olive oil

3 Spanish chorizo sausages (see page 17), about 3/4 pound, cut into 1/2-inch dice

1 large onion, finely chopped

4 garlic cloves, minced

1 large red bell pepper, finely diced

1 tablespoon sweet paprika

1 small bunch kale, about 3/4 pound, tough stems removed, washed well, and coarsely chopped

Freshly ground black pepper to taste

Sherry vinegar to taste

SERVES 6

In the early nineties I went on a weeklong press trip to Spain. Other than learning everything there is to know about olive oil—the stated purpose of our trip—all we did for a week was eat ourselves silly and drink many bottles of beautiful Spanish wine. Not surprisingly, I fell in love with Spanish cuisine. Based on impeccably fresh ingredients, it is gutsy, flavorful, and simple.

Place the beans in a large pot or soup kettle. Pour in 2 quarts of the stock and bring to a boil over high heat. Reduce the heat to medium and add the bay leaf and a pinch of salt. Cook, partially covered, stirring often and adjusting the heat to keep it at a slow steady simmer, until the beans are tender, about 2 hours. Remove and discard the bay leaf.

Soak the saffron in the remaining 1/2 cup chicken stock.

Heat the oil in a large skillet over medium-high heat. Add the chorizo and cook, stirring often, until lightly browned, about 5 minutes. Use a slotted spoon to transfer to a plate. Add the onion, reduce the heat to medium, and cook, stirring often, until softened, about 5 minutes. Add the garlic and cook 1 minute longer. Stir in the red pepper and the paprika. Cook for 2 minutes longer, then transfer the contents of the skillet to the bean pot. Stir in the saffron with the soaking liquid, the chorizo, and the kale. Bring back to a simmer and cook just until the kale is wilted, about 5 minutes. Season with salt and pepper, stir in the vinegar, and serve hot in warmed soup bowls.

soaking beans

For years I soaked my dried beans overnight, or if I forgot I would do the famous quick-soak method. (Combine beans with cold water to cover, bring to a boil, simmer for 2 minutes, and let sit for 1 hour. Drain and proceed with the recipe.) And then I read in a great little book called *Full of Beans* by Brooke Dojny that you didn't really need to soak them. They took only 30 minutes longer if you didn't soak them. Her revelation came from an article by Russ Parsons in the *Los Angeles Times*. He had debunked not only this myth but also the one that you shouldn't add salt to the beans while they are cooking or they will toughen. I had to try out these two heretical theories for myself, and he is right. The beans take only a little longer to cook (when you think about planning a day ahead or soaking for an hour ahead, 30 minutes is peanuts), and the addition of salt to the cooking liquid makes the beans 10 times more flavorful without toughening them at all or extending the cooking time. The one rule that remains valid is not to add any acid (tomato, lemon, wine, vinegar, etc.) to the beans until they are tender. Acid *will* extend their cooking time and make them tough.

Smoky Salmon Chowder with Lemon Pepper Crackers

For the crackers:

1 cup all-purpose flour

1¹/₂ teaspoons freshly ground black pepper

2 teaspoons freshly grated lemon zest

4 tablespoons (¹/₂ stick) unsalted butter, chilled and cut into small pieces

2 tablespoons sour cream

1 tablespoon fresh lemon juice

Kosher salt for sprinkling

For the chowder:

4 tablespoons (¹/₂ stick) unsalted butter

1 medium onion, finely chopped

1 pound large boiling potatoes

3 tablespoons all-purpose flour

5 cups whole milk, heated

Kosher salt to taste

1 pound salmon fillet, skinned

¹/₄ pound smoked salmon, finely chopped

¹/₄ cup chopped fresh dill

2 tablespoons fresh lemon juice

Freshly ground black pepper to taste

SERVES 4 TO 6

This hot and hearty chowder is a great dish for a winter weeknight. Made with milk, not cream, it's healthier and lighter than a classic chowder, although it feels plenty substantial going down. (The downside is that this recipe may end up looking a little curdled. Made with cream, it wouldn't curdle.)

The crackers provide the chowder with a tangy counterpoint. I had never made crackers before, but they turn out to be surprisingly easy—a simple variation of pie dough rolled out thin and baked. (Substitute good crusty country bread if you like.) Add a tossed green salad and you have a complete and satisfying meal.

To prepare the crackers, combine the flour, pepper, lemon zest, and butter in a large bowl. Blend with fingertips or a pastry blender until the mixture resembles coarse meal. Stir in the sour cream, lemon juice, and 1 tablespoon cold water. Toss to form a stiff dough. Turn out onto a floured work surface and knead briefly into a ball. Add a teaspoon or two of cold water if the dough appears to be too stiff. Wrap the ball in plastic and refrigerate until well chilled, at least 15 minutes. (The dough can be made up to a day in advance.)

Preheat the oven to 400°F. Cut the ball in half and, working with one half at a time, roll the dough out ¹/₁₆ inch thick. Use a 2-inch cookie cutter to make 16 rounds. Repeat with the other half of the dough. Gather the scraps, reroll, and cut them into rounds. Transfer to an ungreased cookie sheet and sprinkle with salt. Bake in the middle of the oven for 8 to 10 minutes or until golden. Cool on wire racks for 5 minutes before serving. You should have about 32 crackers.

To make the chowder, melt the butter in a saucepan over low heat; add the onion and cook, stirring often, until softened, about 5 minutes. Meanwhile, peel the potatoes and cut into $1/3$-inch cubes. Whisk the flour into the onion and cook for about 3 minutes. Increase the heat to medium-high, pour in the hot milk, and bring to a boil, whisking constantly. Add the potatoes, season with salt, and reduce the heat to medium-low. Cook until the potatoes are almost tender, 10 to 12 minutes. Add the salmon and cook until slightly firm to the touch, about 5 minutes. Transfer the salmon to a plate and break into chunks. Add the chunks, the smoked salmon, the dill, and the lemon juice to the hot chowder. Season with salt and pepper and simmer until just heated through, about 2 minutes. Serve hot with the crackers on the side.

Escarole Soup with Meatballs

1/2 pound lean ground beef, veal, or turkey

1/2 cup freshly grated Parmigiano-Reggiano

1/4 cup finely chopped fresh parsley

1/3 cup fresh bread crumbs (page 347)

3/4 teaspoon kosher salt

1 large egg, lightly beaten

Freshly ground black pepper

1/4 cup extra virgin olive oil

1 medium onion, finely chopped

1 garlic clove, minced

8 cups packed chopped escarole

1 quart chicken stock, preferably homemade (page 338)

Additional kosher salt and freshly ground black pepper to taste

SERVES 4 TO 6

I was working at the Harvest Restaurant in Harvard Square in the late seventies when Peter Vezan, one of the managers, steered me to a little trattoria in Boston's North End. It wasn't much more than a hole in the wall, but it boasted some of the best down-home Italian food in the city. My favorite dish on the menu was an escarole soup with meatballs. It was very old-hat to Italian-Americans—the equivalent of matzo ball soup to American Jews—but it was new and delicious to me and very comforting.

I can't tell you if the place still exists. I don't even remember its name or the name of the street it was on. For that matter, I lost touch with Peter Vezan, that underground gourmet, when he moved to France 20 years ago. But I never forgot that soup. I re-created it for a column that used to run in *Gourmet* called "In Short Order," which featured recipes you could whip up in 45 minutes or less. The meatballs in the restaurant's original recipe were made of veal, but I suspected that it might be hard for home cooks throughout America to get their hands on ground veal, so I changed it to ground beef. Ground turkey would work nicely, too. Round it out with some crusty country bread and a tossed green salad and you have a soul-satisfying dinner.

Combine the ground beef, half the cheese, the parsley, bread crumbs, salt, egg, and black pepper in a large bowl. Use damp hands to form into 24 walnut-size balls.

Heat 2 tablespoons of the oil in a large, heavy soup pot or kettle over medium heat. Add the meatballs and cook, turning often, until firm to the touch and well browned on all sides, about 5 minutes. Transfer to a large plate or platter.

Add the remaining 2 tablespoons oil and the onion to the pot. Cook, stirring often, until the onion is softened, about 5 minutes. Stir in the garlic and cook for 1 minute longer. Add the escarole, cover, and reduce the heat to medium-low. Cook, stirring occasionally, until the escarole is wilted, 4 to 5 minutes. Pour in the stock, return the meatballs to the pot, increase the heat to medium-high, and simmer for 3 minutes. Season with salt and pepper. Ladle into warmed bowls and sprinkle with the remaining cheese just before serving.

Salads

Fried Green Tomatoes with Ranch Dressing and Yellow Cherry Tomato Salad

For the salad:

12 to 15 yellow cherry tomatoes, quartered

1/2 teaspoon kosher salt

2 teaspoons chopped fresh mint leaves

3 fresh basil leaves, cut into thin strips

1 tablespoon chopped fresh parsley

2 teaspoons fresh lemon juice

1 tablespoon extra virgin olive oil

Additional kosher salt and freshly ground black pepper to taste

For the dressing:

1 garlic clove, peeled

1/4 teaspoon kosher salt

1/2 cup mayonnaise

3/4 cup buttermilk

2 tablespoons fresh lemon juice

2 scallions, white part only, minced

1 tablespoon chopped fresh parsley

1 tablespoon snipped fresh chives

1 tablespoon extra virgin olive oil

Additional kosher salt and freshly ground black pepper to taste

For the tomatoes:

3 medium green tomatoes, cut into 1/4-inch-thick slices

Kosher salt to taste

1/2 cup yellow cornmeal

1/2 cup all-purpose flour

Tomato lovers, it doesn't get much better than this. You start with a base of breaded and fried green tomato slices, top it off with a little salad of cherry tomatoes, and spoon on some homemade ranch dressing. Done. Just make sure all the tomatoes are fresh and in season.

Begin with the salad. Sprinkle the tomatoes with the salt and drain in a large strainer for 10 to 15 minutes. Stir the tomatoes gently with the mint, basil, and parsley. Add the lemon juice and olive oil. Stir again and season with salt and pepper to taste. You should have about 1 cup.

To prepare the dressing, mince the garlic, then crush it with the flat side of a large knife. Add the salt and work into a coarse paste. Transfer to a small bowl and add the mayonnaise, buttermilk, lemon juice, scallions, parsley, and chives. Whisk in the olive oil, season with salt and pepper, and blend. You should have about 1 1/4 cups. Keep refrigerated until ready to serve.

For the green tomatoes, sprinkle with salt on both sides, drain in a colander for 10 to 15 minutes, and pat dry. Stir the cornmeal, flour, salt, and pepper together in a large bowl. Working in 3 batches, heat 1 tablespoon butter with 1 tablespoon oil in a large heavy skillet over medium-high heat. Dip 6 tomato slices, one slice at a time, in the cornmeal mixture and gently shake off the excess. Cook slices in one layer until lightly browned, 2 to 3 minutes per side. Drain slices on paper towels and wipe the skillet clean with a paper towel. Make two more batches with the remaining butter, oil, tomatoes, and cornmeal mixture in the same manner, wiping out the skillet between batches.

To serve, decoratively arrange 3 or 4 of the tomato slices overlapping on a plate. Drizzle with a small amount of the dressing and garnish with a spoonful of the salad. Serve at room temperature.

refrigerating tomatoes

Never put a tomato in the fridge unless you have already cut into it. You will kill its flavor. The best way to store a tomato is at room temperature, out of direct sunlight.

1 teaspoon kosher salt

$^1/_2$ teaspoon freshly ground black pepper

3 tablespoons unsalted butter

3 tablespoons vegetable oil

Additional freshly ground black pepper to taste

SERVES 6 TO 8

Arugula Salad with Aged Gouda, Savory Praline, and Whole-Grain Mustard Dressing

For the praline:

1/3 cup pecans, coarsely chopped

1/2 teaspoon kosher salt

1/8 teaspoon cayenne pepper or more to taste

3 tablespoons sugar

For the dressing:

1/2 teaspoon grainy Dijon mustard

2 tablespoons red wine vinegar

Kosher salt and freshly ground black pepper to taste

6 tablespoons extra virgin olive oil

For the salad:

8 cups loosely packed arugula

3/4 cup coarsely grated aged Gouda, Manchego, Asiago, or Parmigiano-Reggiano cheese

1/3 cup dried cranberries

SERVES 6

This is a guests-are-coming-for-dinner salad, fancier and more labor-intensive than most, but the extra effort really pays off. My husband, the salad hater, scarfed it down so enthusiastically that I added extra arugula to the recipe to stretch it. All the parts can be made ahead. Just toss them together at the last moment.

By the way, I tend to prefer so-called bitter greens like arugula to standards like romaine and Boston lettuce—they taste more peppery than bitter to me—but they are not for everyone. If you don't like bitter greens, just substitute your lettuce of choice.

To make the praline, lightly oil a large baking sheet. Toss the pecans with the salt and cayenne in a small bowl. Place the sugar in a heavy skillet or saucepan and cook over medium heat, stirring gently, until the sugar starts to melt. Stop stirring and continue cooking, swirling the skillet or pan often, until the sugar cooks to a dark golden caramel. Add the pecan mixture and carefully stir to coat the nuts with caramel. Pour onto the baking sheet and spread evenly with a knife. Cool completely. Crack the praline into pieces, then finely chop on a cutting board.

To prepare the dressing, whisk the mustard, vinegar, salt, and pepper in a small bowl. Slowly whisk in the olive oil to form a smooth dressing.

Arrange the arugula in the center of a large serving bowl. Sprinkle on the cheese, cranberries, and praline. Toss with just enough of the dressing to thoroughly coat the leaves.

my favorite way to make caramel

The praline in this recipe is a dry caramel, meaning that you cook the sugar without water. I think you get into less trouble. When you start a caramel with sugar and water, the idea is to dissolve the sugar in the water over low heat and then turn the heat up to evaporate the water and caramelize the sugar. The sugar can crystallize on the side of the pan, which is why the instructions always tell you to "wipe down the sides of the pan with a brush dipped in water." If the sugar crystallizes, it can cloud the whole caramel. I used to just put the lid on the pan so the water would condense on the lid and wash down the sides. But this is so much easier. Take the plunge and try it.

Chopped Salad with Feta, Chickpeas, and Pita Croutons

³/₄ cup extra virgin olive oil

1¹/₂ teaspoons ground cumin

1¹/₂ teaspoons sweet or hot
  paprika

Three 6-inch pita breads with
  pockets

Kosher salt to taste

3 tablespoons sherry vinegar

1¹/₂ teaspoons Dijon mustard

Freshly ground black pepper to
  taste

6 cups loosely packed arugula

6 cups loosely packed mesclun

2 large red bell peppers,
  coarsely chopped

2 large yellow bell peppers,
  coarsely chopped

1 pound cherry tomatoes,
  quartered

1¹/₂ cups cooked or drained,
  rinsed, and dried canned
  chickpeas

1¹/₂ cups crumbled feta cheese

1¹/₂ cups diced dill pickle

SERVES 6

Maybe it's just because I'm a girl, but I love almost any kind of salad—and the more ingredients, the better. "Chopped salad," a catchall for any salad boasting a rich variety of chopped vegetables, is my favorite.

This recipe was inspired by a low-fat dish I first encountered several years ago in *Gourmet*. Created by Chef Ed Brown of New York's Sea Grill Restaurant, its most interesting ingredients were chickpeas and diced dill pickles. As a big fan of crunch, I transported those two items to my everyday chopped salad and then, for good measure, piled on some feta cheese and pita croutons.

If you find feta cheese too strong or too salty, substitute ricotta salata, an aged ricotta cheese that has a texture similar to feta but a notch or two less sharpness. As for the pita croutons, use them in any salad, as a garnish for soup, or as a partner to a dip.

Preheat the oven to 400°F. Mix ¹/₄ cup of the olive oil with the cumin and paprika in a small bowl. Split each pita bread horizontally into 2 rounds and brush the rough sides with equal amounts of the oil mixture. Cut the rounds into small triangles or 1-inch pieces and arrange in one flat layer on a large baking sheet. Bake until golden and crisp, about 5 minutes. Sprinkle with salt when just out of the oven.

Whisk the vinegar, mustard, salt, and pepper in a large serving bowl until blended. Slowly pour in the remaining olive oil, whisking to form a smooth dressing.

Just before serving, pile the arugula and mesclun in the center of the bowl on top of the dressing. Surround with the peppers, tomatoes, chickpeas, feta, and pickles. Add the pita croutons, toss, and serve.

Michael Green says:
on wine and salad

Years ago it was a sin even to suggest serving wine with salad, and in theory the combination can present a challenge. Salads, which often contain high-acid ingredients such as vinegar or lemon juice, can make wines taste flat, devoid of acidity, and accentuate their alcohol. But many of today's salad preparations are different, containing fruit, herbs, and protein elements that balance the acidity and make them very wine friendly. The elements of Chopped Salad with Feta, Chickpeas, and Pita Croutons make this salad very wine friendly. Look for wines that are fresh and vibrant with requisite acidity to stand up to the acidity in salad. The Loire Valley whites—Muscadet, Vouvray, and Pouilly-Fumé—are excellent examples of wines that partner well with salad. If you're looking to serve a red, seek out wines with low tannin and high acidity such as the wines of France's Beaujolais region or the Italian grapes Dolcetto, Barbera, and Sangiovese.

Summer Salad

6 ears corn, husks removed

1 small onion, finely chopped

3 to 4 medium tomatoes

Kosher salt to taste

1 large firm ripe Hass avocado, halved, pitted, and peeled

2 tablespoons fresh lemon juice

Lettuce leaves for garnish

1 cup cooked or drained, rinsed, and dried canned black beans

1/2 cup Once-a-Week Vinaigrette (see page 344)

1/2 cup fresh basil leaves, chopped

Freshly ground black pepper to taste

Corn chips or homemade tortilla strips (page 36), if desired

SERVES 6

I think of this recipe as the perfect backyard-cooking-for-a-crowd summertime salad because it features three of the shining stars of summer—corn, tomatoes, and basil—and because all the parts can be prepared ahead of time and tossed together at the last minute. When I'm in the country and find a roadside stand selling just-picked corn, I cut it off the cob raw, straight into the bowl, and don't even bother with the quick-boiling step. Raw fresh corn is perfect as is, wonderfully sweet and crunchy. Try it and see for yourself.

If you have a little extra time, do make the tortilla strips and sprinkle them on top of the salad like little southwestern croutons. I love crunchy food in my salads. It adds a contrast in texture.

Cook the corn in a large pot in 3 inches of boiling water for 2 minutes. Drain, cool, and cut the kernels off the cob. You should have about 4 cups. Soak the onion in ice water for 20 minutes. Drain and pat dry.

Cut the tomatoes in half horizontally and remove and discard the seeds. Finely chop the tomato, transfer to a large strainer, sprinkle with salt, and let drain for 10 to 15 minutes. Cut the avocado into 1/2-inch dice and toss with the lemon juice in a small bowl.

Just before serving, line a serving platter with lettuce leaves and drain the avocado. Combine the corn, tomatoes, avocado, and beans in a large bowl. Add the vinaigrette and basil, stir gently to blend, and season with salt and pepper. Turn onto the serving platter, and serve at room temperature.

Garnish with corn chips or homemade tortilla strips (page 36), if desired.

Endive and Roquefort Spirals
with Creamy Walnut Vinaigrette

This recipe transforms the classic Waldorf salad into a really elegant-looking appetizer. It is not a hard dish to make, but it sure will impress your guests.

Combine the Roquefort, butter, and cream cheese in a food processor and blend until smooth. You should have about $3/4$ cup.

To make the salad, cut $1/4$ inch from the bottom of the endives and peel away the outer leaves. (Reserve the inner core for another use.) Spread each leaf with a $1/4$-inch-thick layer of the Roquefort mixture and press the leaves back together to reconstruct the shape of the whole endive. Wrap in plastic wrap and refrigerate until well chilled, about $1^1/2$ hours.

To prepare the dressing, whisk the mustard with the vinegar, salt, and pepper in a small bowl. Add the oils in a slow stream, whisking constantly until thick and emulsified. Stir in the shallots.

Spoon about $1^1/2$ tablespoons of the dressing over the bottom of each of 4 chilled salad plates. Cut the endive into $1/2$-inch-thick slices. Arrange 3 slices overlapping on each plate. Sprinkle with walnuts and garnish with a sprig of watercress. Cut the apple lengthwise into thin slices. Garnish each plate with 3 of the slices. Drizzle with a small amount of the remaining dressing just before serving.

For the salad:
$3/4$ cup Roquefort cheese

3 tablespoons unsalted butter, softened

3 ounces cream cheese, softened

2 large Belgian endives

For the dressing:
1 teaspoon Dijon mustard

2 tablespoons white wine vinegar

Kosher salt and freshly ground black pepper to taste

2 tablespoons walnut oil

$1/4$ cup vegetable oil

1 small shallot, minced

For the garnish:
2 tablespoons finely chopped toasted walnuts

4 fresh watercress sprigs

$1/2$ McIntosh apple

SERVES 4

heating and chilling plates

One of the rules that was repeated over and over when I was at the Culinary Institute of America was "Serve hot food on hot plates and cold food on cold plates." It really makes a difference in keeping your food the temperature you want it to be. It also makes an impression on your guests. So for this dish, put your plates in the fridge at least 30 minutes before you are ready to serve.

The Ultimate Spinach Salad

1/4 cup mayonnaise

1/4 cup sour cream

1/4 cup crumbled blue cheese,
preferably Roquefort, Stilton,
or Cabrales

1 tablespoon white wine vinegar

1 teaspoon Dijon mustard

1 garlic clove, minced

1/2 teaspoon Worcestershire
sauce

Kosher salt and freshly ground
black pepper to taste

2 to 3 tablespoons whole milk

1 1/2 pounds trimmed spinach
leaves

3 hard-boiled eggs (see page 4
for boiling procedure), peeled
and sliced or coarsely chopped

3 to 4 medium cultivated white
mushrooms

1 1/2 cups Parmesan Croutons
(page 62)

Spiced Bacon Bits (page 62) or
1/2 pound bacon, cooked until
crisp and crumbled

SERVES 4 TO 6 AS A MAIN
COURSE, 8 AS AN APPETIZER

I just love salad. When I'm in the city, I eat salad every day for lunch. When I'm on the road for business, I often order salad from room service for dinner. Of course, I understand that not everyone shares this leafy passion (take my husband, please), so when I make a salad at home or for guests in the *Gourmet* dining room, I try to dress it up.

I think of this as the ultimate spinach salad because all of the elements—other than the spinach and mushrooms—are special. The blue cheese dressing is prepared from scratch with good blue cheese. The croutons are homemade from rustic Italian bread. The bacon bits are spiced. And the lowly hard-boiled egg is cooked with extra love to eliminate the green line dividing the yolk and the white and to keep the white tender. Try it and see if you don't agree that this salad is the ultimate.

Combine the mayonnaise and sour cream in a small bowl. Stir until blended and smooth. Fold in the cheese, vinegar, mustard, garlic, and Worcestershire sauce. Season with salt and pepper. Stir well and thin with milk as needed to reach the consistency of heavy cream. Cover and refrigerate for several hours or overnight. Stir well before serving.

Rinse the spinach leaves and dry them in a salad spinner or use paper towels to remove as much moisture as possible from the leaves. Tear the leaves into bite-size pieces and pile into a very large salad bowl. Arrange the eggs and mushrooms on top. Sprinkle with croutons and bacon bits. Spoon a large dollop of the dressing in the center. Toss well just before serving and serve the remaining dressing on the side.

egg slicer

If you have one of those old-fashioned egg slicers, use it not only to slice the eggs but also to chop them. Here is how you do it: Lay the egg on its side vertically in the slicer and slice it. Then holding it carefully so all the slices stay together, lay it on its side horizontally and slice it. Here comes the hard part: Carefully stand it straight up and give it one last slice. You will end up with a nice chopped egg. You can also use the egg slicer to slice the mushrooms.

mushrooms

When you are planning to eat cultivated mushrooms raw, make sure they are fresh, fresh, fresh. If you have ever had a spinach salad at a restaurant that arrived with slimy dark mushroom slices, you know what I am talking about. When cultivated mushrooms are harvested, they are very firm, very white, and very tight—meaning you will not be able to see the gills underneath the lid. As the mushroom loses its moisture, the cap shrinks, exposing the gills. The mushroom becomes flabby, and the texture is unappealing to eat raw (older mushrooms are fine for cooking, though). Store cultivated mushrooms in a loose paper bag or in a container with air holes in it. They will sweat and get slimy if they are kept too tightly wrapped.

Parmesan Croutons

2 tablespoons extra virgin olive oil

1 garlic clove, minced

1/2 teaspoon dried oregano, crumbled

1/2 teaspoon dried basil, crumbled

1/2 teaspoon dried thyme, crumbled

1/4 teaspoon kosher salt

1/4 teaspoon freshly ground black pepper

1/2 loaf rustic Italian bread, about 6 ounces, cut into 3/4-inch cubes (3 to 4 cups)

2 tablespoons freshly grated Parmigiano-Reggiano

Additional kosher salt and freshly ground black pepper to taste

MAKES ABOUT 3 CUPS

Preheat the oven to 350°F. Mix the oil, garlic, oregano, basil, thyme, salt, and pepper in a large bowl. Add the bread and toss well. Spread out on a jelly roll pan and bake in the middle of the oven until lightly browned, about 15 minutes. Sprinkle the croutons with the cheese and bake until golden brown, about 7 minutes longer. Season with salt and pepper and cool. The croutons will keep in an airtight container for 1 week.

Spiced Bacon Bits

1 tablespoon Worcestershire sauce

1 1/2 teaspoons firmly packed brown sugar

1/8 teaspoon cayenne pepper or more to taste

1/8 teaspoon ground allspice

Freshly ground black pepper to taste

1/2 pound lean bacon, cut into 1/4-inch squares

MAKES ABOUT 3/4 CUP

Combine the Worcestershire sauce, sugar, cayenne, and allspice in a small bowl. Season with pepper. Add the bacon and toss until the bacon is well coated.

Place the bacon in a large skillet over medium-low heat. Cook, stirring often, until the bacon is crisp, about 10 minutes. Transfer to paper towels to drain. This will keep covered in the refrigerator for 3 days.

Poultry

Chicken Under a Brick

2 teaspoons freshly grated
   lemon zest

Juice of 1 lemon, about $1/4$ cup

1 tablespoon finely chopped
   fresh rosemary or 1 teaspoon
   dried

$1^{1}/_{2}$ teaspoons finely chopped
   fresh oregano or $1/2$ teaspoon
   dried

$1^{1}/_{2}$ teaspoons finely chopped
   fresh thyme, preferably lemon
   thyme, or $1/2$ teaspoon dried

$1/2$ cup extra virgin olive oil, plus
   more for rubbing

One $3^{1}/_{2}$- to 4-pound chicken

Kosher salt and freshly ground
   black pepper to taste

SERVES 4

Chicken under a brick? A *real* brick?! Why on earth would someone *do* that to a chicken? Because for some mysterious reason when you take a butterflied, marinated whole chicken and grill it skin side down with a heavy weight pressing on it from above—a real brick, for example—you end up with the moistest, most delicious chicken meat and the crispiest smoky skin imaginable. The process can get a little tricky, because the chicken is wet after all that marination and tends to stick to the grill. Just make sure you pat it dry before you rub it with the oil for grilling and that your grill is properly hot and scrubbed clean. Serve with Grilled Potato and Corn Salad with Chipotle Mayonnaise (page 253) and sliced beefsteak tomatoes on a bed of arugula drizzled with Once-a-Week Vinaigrette (page 344).

Combine the lemon zest, lemon juice, rosemary, oregano, and thyme in a small bowl. Whisk in the olive oil. Transfer to a plastic bag with a resealable closure.

Place the chicken breast side down on a work surface. Position a heavy knife or poultry shears inside the cavity and cut through the ribs along one side of the backbone. Make a second cut through the ribs along the other side of the backbone. Remove and discard the backbone (or freeze and reserve for stock). Turn the chicken over and with the heel of your hands press down on the ribs and flatten. Place in the plastic bag and marinate, turning often, refrigerated for 3 hours, or at room temperature for 1 hour.

Prepare a charcoal fire and allow to burn to a gray ash. Lightly oil the grill. (Alternatively, preheat a large well-oiled stovetop grill until very hot over high heat.) Remove the chicken from the marinade and pat very dry with paper towels. Rub the skin side with plenty of oil and season with salt and pepper. Push the coals to the edges of the grill to create a cooler area for grilling. Place the chicken skin side down over this cooler area. Put a metal pie plate or half sheet pan directly on the chicken and weigh down with 2 bricks or 2 heavy weights such as large cans of tomatoes. Grill, covered, for 30 minutes. (Cook over medium heat if using a stovetop grill.) The chicken is done when there are no traces of pink when pierced in the thigh. Using a metal spatula, very carefully pry the chicken loose from the grill. (The skin tends to stick.) Transfer to a large platter and cover loosely with foil. Let rest for 10 minutes and cut into serving pieces.

Blasted Chicken

**One 3¹/₂-pound chicken, trimmed
of excess fat**

**Kosher salt and freshly ground
black pepper to taste**

**Extra virgin olive oil for
brushing**

SERVES 4 TO 6

Everyone who works in a restaurant looks forward to that fleeting moment fancifully called "family dinner." That's the meal served to the whole staff at around 5 o'clock, just before service starts. Family dinner is important for two reasons. First, it gives you a chance to slow down and take the first break you've probably had since you arrived at noon and started cooking your buns off in preparation for the dinner menu. Second, there's no discounting the *family* in family dinner—the staff that eats together tends to work well together.

One of the dishes we all loved at La Tulipe in the early eighties was roasted chicken. It boasts that winning combination of crispy skin and moist meat. The preparation couldn't have been simpler: season the birds, drizzle them with a little extra virgin olive oil, put them in a shallow roasting pan, and throw them into the oven. No racks, no trussing, no fussing.

As at most restaurants, the ovens at La Tulipe during service were always blazing away at about 500°F. Accordingly, that was the temperature at which we cooked—or, more accurately, blasted—our chickens. It was the easiest dish to prepare, but there was one sacred rule: let the birds rest for 15 minutes before carving. That way the meat had a chance to relax and the juices to redistribute. If you don't let the chicken rest, the juices will come streaming out and the meat will be inedibly dry.

I adapted the recipe for my family when I retired from restaurants. It has since become a staple at our house. The good news is that it takes only an hour from start to finish, and if you remember two numbers, you can make it successfully every time. The numbers are $3^1/_2$ (the weight of the chicken) and 45: You blast a $3^1/_2$-pound chicken for 45 minutes in a preheated 450°F oven (at which point the leg/thigh joint almost always reaches the required internal temperature of 170°F). Pull it out of the oven and let it rest for 15 minutes, and you will have the tastiest roast chicken. Of course, it really helps if you start with a minimally processed chicken, such as a kosher chicken or a free-range chicken or even an organic chicken (see Mail Order Sources). As usual, the rule is "Read the label." Serve with Roasted Lemon Potatoes (page 252) and Sautéed Spinach with Garlic Chips (page 232).

Preheat the oven to 450°F. Season the chicken all over with salt and pepper, brush with the oil, and place breast side up in a heavy roasting pan. Roast, uncovered, until the juices run clear when the thigh is pierced with a skewer, about 45 minutes. (A meat thermometer inserted into the leg-thigh joint should register 165–170°F.) Transfer the chicken to a cutting board, cover loosely with foil, and let stand for 15 minutes before carving.

how to make pan gravy

Anytime you cook a roast you are going to end up with delicious bits of concentrated meat juices sticking to the bottom of the roasting pan. They are a great base for a sauce. If you want to take advantage of them, transfer your roast to a platter and cover it loosely with foil. Then calculate how much gravy you want to end up with. I generally plan on $1/4$ to $1/3$ cup of sauce per person (more at Thanksgiving where so many dishes require a gravy topping—the mashed potatoes, the stuffing, etc.). For each cup of medium-consistency sauce you will need 1 cup of broth and 1 to 2 tablespoons each of fat and flour. Pour all the fat from the roasting pan into a bowl. Measure the correct amount and put it back into the pan. Add the flour and cook over low heat, stirring frequently for a few minutes. Meanwhile, heat your broth in a separate pan. Add the broth to the fat/flour mixture in a stream, whisking, and continue whisking until you see no more lumps. Bring the mixture to a boil and simmer it for as many minutes as there are tablespoons of flour in the gravy. Also use this procedure to make gravy for Roast Turkey with Sauerkraut (page 84).

There is a wonderful wire whisk on the market that makes this task so much easier. Unlike the usual balloon whisk, it is flat, enabling you to reach into the corners of the pan with the tip and loosen all the flour that gets stuck in there.

Esther's Chicken Fricassee

Esther Adler, my mother-in-law, gave birth to three sons in less than three years (yikes!) and a daughter three years later. All four kids had hearty appetites, and all four turned out to be fairly strapping individuals. I'll confess that I've often wondered how in the world she managed to feed them. This recipe is one answer.

Esther's wonderful chicken fricassee was a relatively rare treat. She served it only about once a month, because that's how long it took to assemble the parts. Every Friday night she'd cook two chickens, roasting one and making soup out of the other, while putting aside the packet of giblets that accompanied each bird. After four weeks of this routine she'd finally have enough giblets to make fricassee (as well as enough livers to make chopped liver). Esther thought of her fricassee as a *shidahrein* (Yiddish for "shake into") recipe, meaning that it is put together by feel, not by strict measurement.

Both of my husband's parents grew up on the chicken fricassee cooked for them by their mothers. As Susan R. Friedland, author of *Shabbat Shalom*, has noted, "For the Jewish housewife, fricassee was the ultimate thrifty dish: every part of the bird was used." (This genius for spinning straw into gold reminds me of the similar wonders worked by African-American cooks. In fact, *Dori Sanders' Country Cooking* contains a recipe for Chicken Fricassee with Meatballs that is very much like Esther's. Its genesis? "One day when there was just a little chicken and even less ground beef in the house, Aunt Vestula decreed that the two should

2 tablespoons vegetable oil

2 medium onions, finely chopped

4 chicken necks, trimmed and cut crosswise into 4 or 5 pieces

1 pound chicken gizzards, trimmed

6 chicken wings

Kosher salt and freshly ground black pepper to taste

1 pound ground beef

1/2 cup matzo meal

1 large egg

2 1/2 teaspoons kosher salt

1 teaspoon sweet paprika

1/2 cup all-purpose flour

1/2 teaspoon freshly ground black pepper

SERVES 6

be cooked together to make a meal large enough for the family.") Why this dish is called a *fricassee*, however, is a mystery. It has nothing to do with the fricassees created by the French.

But fricassee/shmicassee, Esther's kids loved this dish because it was so tasty and so substantial. She'd put a big basket of fresh challah nearby, and they'd sop up the gravy. Truthfully, it is almost a meal in itself, although Esther treated it like the merest appetizer to the matzo ball soup, roast chicken, and dessert that usually followed. It's a miracle that none of her brood weighs 300 pounds. Other Jewish families apparently made more of their fricassees, serving them as entrees with rice, noodles, potatoes, or couscous. Serve with Mashed Potatoes (page 247), Mashed Potato Cakes (page 249), or buttered noodles along with Borscht Beets (page 220).

Heat the oil in a large casserole over medium heat. Add the onions and cook, stirring often, until softened, about 5 minutes. Add the necks, gizzards, and wings. Season with salt and pepper. Reduce the heat to low and cover. Cook, stirring often, until the chicken has lost all traces of pink, about 30 minutes.

Meanwhile, combine the ground beef, matzo meal, egg, and $1^1/2$ teaspoons of the salt in a large bowl. Pour in $^1/2$ cup cold water, mix well, and form into small meatballs about the size of a walnut. You should have about 3 dozen.

Bring 2 cups of water to a boil and pour it into the chicken parts mixture. Increase the heat to medium-high and bring to a simmer. Add the paprika and season with salt and pepper.

Mix the flour with the remaining teaspoon of salt and the $^1/_2$ teaspoon pepper in a large bowl. Add the meatballs and roll until coated on all sides. Shake off the excess flour.

Drop the meatballs into the simmering liquid in the casserole. Reduce the heat to low, cover, and cook until the chicken is falling off the bones and the broth is slightly thickened and concentrated, about 2 hours.

My mother-in-law Esther Adler, 1977

Jean Anderson's Oven-Fried Chicken

12 tablespoons (1¹/₂ sticks) unsalted butter

3 garlic cloves, minced

2 cups fresh bread crumbs (page 347)

²/₃ cup freshly grated Parmigiano-Reggiano

2 teaspoons kosher salt

Freshly ground black pepper to taste

One 3¹/₂-pound chicken, cut into 10 pieces (or all thighs, wings, or breasts if desired)

SERVES 4 TO 6

When I told my mentor and good buddy Jean Anderson that this book needed her chicken recipe—it's become one of the most requested on "Cooking Live"—she floored me by replying that it wasn't really her recipe. She had learned it when she was working at *Ladies' Home Journal* and then adapted it for *The Doubleday Cookbook*. Still, I learned it from Jean and think of it as Jean Anderson Chicken, and I have never met a chicken lover who wasn't nuts for it, kids and grown-ups alike. It is great served hot, cold, or at room temperature. It'd probably be great if you served it on the moon. A word to the wise: This is a high-calorie recipe, so you might want to save it for special occasions.

All you have to remember is melted garlic butter and a crumb mixture with a ratio of three parts fresh bread crumbs (page 347) to one part freshly grated Parmigiano-Reggiano. Dip the chicken pieces in the butter, then in the crumb mixture, then bake them. You can dress up this recipe by adding herbs to the crumb mixture, but I usually make it plain for the kids. They get nervous when they spot those little green flecks.

By the way, it is essential to use the real Parmigiano-Reggiano and to grate it yourself. Do *not* reach for that pregrated stuff in a can—it tastes like sawdust. If grating the cheese by hand seems like too much work, just cut some into chunks and throw them into the food processor with the metal blade. The result isn't as fine as hand-grated cheese, but it works just dandy for this recipe.

Jean Anderson's chicken is perfect for a crowd. It is a

little messy to make (I usually end up breading my hands, too), but it is worth the mess, and you will become very popular. Serve with Southern Braised Mustard Greens with Ham (page 242) and your favorite coleslaw.

Preheat the oven to 350°F. Combine the butter and garlic in a small saucepan. Heat over medium-high heat until the butter has melted. Pour into a large bowl and cool to room temperature.

Mix the bread crumbs, cheese, salt, and pepper in a large bowl. Dip each chicken piece, one at a time, into the melted garlic butter. Transfer to the bread crumb mixture and turn until coated on all sides.

Arrange the chicken in one flat layer on a large baking sheet. Drizzle on any of the remaining melted butter. Bake until lightly browned and just cooked through, 50 to 60 minutes.

With Jean Anderson on our way to Brazil, 1982

Indonesian-Style Chicken with Spicy Peanut Sauce

For the chicken:

8 large chicken thighs, about 2¹/₂ pounds

Kosher salt and freshly ground black pepper to taste

¹/₄ cup vegetable oil, preferably peanut oil

¹/₄ cup soy sauce

2 tablespoons honey

2 garlic cloves, minced

One 2-inch piece fresh ginger, peeled and minced

1 tablespoon ground toasted coriander seeds*

¹/₄ teaspoon cayenne pepper

¹/₄ teaspoon curry powder

2 tablespoons unsalted butter

For the sauce:

³/₄ cup peanut butter

¹/₂ cup hoisin sauce**

2 tablespoons fresh lime juice

1 tablespoon soy sauce

2 teaspoons Asian (toasted) sesame oil**

One 1-inch piece fresh ginger, peeled and minced

Pinch hot red pepper flakes

*To toast the coriander seeds, spread them over the bottom of a small skillet. Place on top of the stove over medium-high heat and shake or stir until dark brown and fragrant, 3 to 5 minutes. Transfer to cool on a plate.

**Available at most supermarkets or see Mail Order Sources.

SERVES 4

Chicken thighs should be more popular; the meat is much more flavorful than the white meat and almost always cooks up moist, which is not something you can say of chicken breast meat. Yes, the thigh is slightly more caloric than the breast, but I prefer it anyway.

This is a great weeknight recipe for the whole family—although you might want to decrease the amount of hot pepper flakes in the dipping sauce for the kids.

To prepare the chicken, trim the thighs of excess fat and use a sharp knife to score. Cut through the skin, deep into the flesh, at ¹/₂-inch intervals. Season with salt and pepper. Whisk 2 tablespoons of the vegetable oil, the soy sauce, honey, garlic, ginger, coriander seeds, cayenne, and curry powder together in a small bowl. Transfer to a large plastic bag with a resealable closure. Place the thighs in the bag and marinate at room temperature for 1 hour or in the refrigerator for 2 to 3 hours. Shake the bag from time to time to distribute the marinade evenly.

Preheat the oven to 400°F. Remove the chicken from the marinade and pat dry with paper towels. Melt the butter with the remaining 2 tablespoons vegetable oil in a large ovenproof skillet over medium-high heat. Add the thighs and cook until browned, 3 to 4 minutes per side. Pour off the fat, leave the thighs in the skillet, and transfer to the oven. Bake, uncovered, turning once, until a fork inserted near the bone easily enters the flesh, about 25 minutes.

To prepare the sauce, combine the peanut butter, hoisin, lime juice, soy sauce, sesame oil, ginger, and pepper flakes in a blender. Pour in ¹/₂ cup water and blend until smooth.

Arrange the thighs on a large warmed platter. Drizzle on a small amount of the sauce and serve the rest on the side.

four quick chicken recipes

Although none of us wants to devote more than 45 minutes or so to getting dinner on the table during the workweek, we still want to eat well. The following four recipes are designed to fit that bill. The procedure is essentially the same for all four:

1. Pound the chicken to the appropriate thinness.
2. Dust it in seasoned flour.
3. Brown it in a skillet.
4. Remove the chicken and deglaze the pan with liquid (that is, scrape up all those yummy brown bits in the bottom of the pan).
5. Put the chicken back in the pan to reheat it and to thicken the sauce (a benefit of the bird's flour coating).
6. Serve.

Use a rolling pin or an actual meat pounder (available at most kitchenware stores), but whatever you do, try to get that piece of chicken down to $^1/_4$-inch thickness. It cooks faster that way, and you'll have more control over it. Even if it shreds a little as you pound it, it will all come back together in the pan.

If your family doesn't sit down when you call them and the sauce overreduces and gets too thick, just add a little water.

With my brother Peter, 2001

Once you learn the basic procedure, you can change the flavorings at will and invent endless variations.

a note about the Chicken Tarragon: this is a simplified version of a relatively sophisticated dish that used to comprise the whole of my brother Peter's culinary repertoire. Whenever he confided that he was making Chicken Tarragon for dinner, we knew that Things Were Starting to Get Serious with whichever young woman he was dating.

Chicken Piccata

4 boneless, skinless chicken breast halves, about 6 ounces each

¹/₂ cup all-purpose flour

1¹/₂ teaspoons kosher salt

¹/₂ teaspoon freshly ground black pepper

3 tablespoons extra virgin olive oil

1 cup chicken stock, preferably homemade (page 338)

2 tablespoons fresh lemon juice

2 tablespoons unsalted butter, cut into small pieces

1 tablespoon drained bottled capers, rinsed and chopped

Additional kosher salt and freshly ground black pepper to taste

Thin slices lemon and chopped fresh parsley for garnish

SERVES 4

Serve with Sautéed Shredded Zucchini with Lemon and Thyme (page 226) and buttered noodles.

Sprinkle a small amount of water on a large sheet of plastic wrap. Place 2 of the breast halves on top of the plastic and sprinkle again with water. Cover with another sheet of plastic wrap and pound with a rolling pin or meat pounder until about ¹/₄ inch thick. Repeat with the remaining 2 breast halves.

Mix the flour with the salt and pepper in a shallow pie plate. Heat half the olive oil in a large skillet over medium-high heat until almost smoking. Working in 2 batches, place the chicken in the flour mixture and turn to coat on all sides. Shake off the excess flour and add to the skillet. Cook until lightly browned and cooked through, 3 to 4 minutes per side. Transfer to a plate or platter and cover loosely with foil. Repeat with the remaining oil and chicken.

Pour off the fat from the skillet and return the skillet to the heat. Add the chicken stock and lemon juice. Increase the heat to high and bring to a boil, stirring to pick up any browned bits in the bottom of the pan. Simmer for 3 minutes. Return the chicken to the skillet and simmer, turning often, until warmed through and the sauce is thickened, about 2 minutes. Add the butter and the capers. Season with salt and pepper and heat just until the butter has melted. Serve on warmed plates with a spoonful of the skillet sauce, topped with lemon slices and parsley.

working with raw poultry

After working with raw poultry you should wash your cutting board, knives, and hands well with hot soapy water before touching any other food. To avoid putting my fingers in my salt container, I just spill out a little of the salt onto the cutting board and use that for seasoning the chicken. Then when I am all done I throw out the remaining salt on the board.

Chicken Scaloppine with Fresh Tomato or Salsa Sauce

Serve with Mom's Brushed Eggplant (page 228) and Roasted Lemon Potatoes (page 252).

Sprinkle a small amount of water on a large sheet of plastic wrap. Place 2 of the breast halves on top of the plastic and sprinkle again with water. Cover with another sheet of plastic wrap and pound with a rolling pin or meat pounder until about $1/4$ inch thick. Repeat with the remaining 2 breast halves.

Mix the flour with the salt and pepper in a shallow pie plate. Heat half the butter in a large skillet over medium-high heat until hot. Working in 2 batches, place the chicken in the flour mixture and turn to coat on all sides. Shake off the excess flour and add to the skillet. Cook until lightly browned, 3 to 4 minutes per side. Transfer to a plate or platter and cover loosely with foil. Repeat with the remaining butter and chicken.

Add the shallot and garlic to the skillet. Cook, stirring, until fragrant, about 30 seconds. Add the tomatoes or salsa, stir in the stock, and simmer for 8 minutes. Return the chicken to the skillet and simmer, turning often, until the chicken is warmed through and the sauce is thickened, about 2 minutes. Transfer the chicken to warm serving plates. Stir in the basil and season the sauce with salt and pepper. Spoon over the chicken and serve at once.

4 boneless, skinless chicken breast halves, about 6 ounces each

$1/2$ cup all-purpose flour

$1 1/2$ teaspoons kosher salt

$1/2$ teaspoon freshly ground black pepper

3 tablespoons unsalted butter

1 small shallot, minced

1 garlic clove, minced

2 medium seeded and chopped fresh tomatoes or 2 cups store-bought fresh salsa

1 cup chicken stock, preferably homemade (page 338)

1 tablespoon shredded fresh basil leaves

Additional kosher salt and freshly ground black pepper to taste

SERVES 4

Chicken Scaloppine with Mushrooms

4 boneless, skinless chicken breast halves, about 6 ounces each

$1/2$ cup all-purpose flour

$1^1/2$ teaspoons kosher salt

$1/2$ teaspoon freshly ground black pepper

3 tablespoons vegetable oil

2 tablespoons unsalted butter

$1/2$ pound cultivated white mushrooms, thinly sliced

$1/4$ cup dry white wine or marsala

1 cup chicken stock, preferably homemade (page 338)

2 tablespoons sour cream

2 tablespoons snipped fresh chives

Additional kosher salt and freshly ground black pepper to taste

SERVES 4

Serve with Stewed Green Beans with Tomato and Mint (page 238) and baked sweet potatoes.

Sprinkle a small amount of water on a large sheet of plastic wrap. Place 2 of the breast halves on top of the plastic and sprinkle again with water. Cover with another sheet of plastic wrap and pound with a rolling pin or meat pounder until about $1/4$ inch thick. Repeat with the remaining 2 breast halves.

Mix the flour with the salt and pepper in a shallow pie plate. Heat half the oil in a large skillet over medium-high heat until almost smoking. Working in 2 batches, place half the chicken in the flour mixture and turn to coat on all sides. Shake off the excess flour and add to the skillet. Cook until lightly browned and cooked through, 3 to 4 minutes per side. Transfer to a plate or platter and cover loosely with foil. Repeat with the remaining oil and chicken.

Add the butter to the skillet and heat until melted and foamy. Add the mushrooms and cook, stirring often, until almost all the liquid that the mushrooms give off has evaporated, about 5 minutes. Pour in the wine, increase the heat to high, and cook, stirring, until almost all the liquid has evaporated. Add the chicken stock and simmer for 3 minutes. Return the chicken to the skillet and simmer, turning often, until the chicken is warmed through and the sauce is thickened, about 2 minutes. Transfer the scaloppine to warm serving plates. Stir the sour cream and chives into the sauce. Season with salt and pepper and spoon over the chicken.

Chicken Tarragon

Serve with Provençal Tomatoes (page 227) and Roasted
Lemon Potatoes (page 252).

Sprinkle a small amount of water on a large sheet of plastic wrap.
Place 2 of the breast halves on top of the plastic and sprinkle again
with water. Cover with another sheet of plastic wrap and pound with a
rolling pin or meat pounder until about $1/4$ inch thick. Repeat with the
remaining 2 breast halves.

Mix the flour with the salt and pepper in a shallow pie plate. Heat
half the olive oil in a large skillet over medium-high heat until almost
smoking. Working in 2 batches, place half the chicken in the flour
mixture and turn to coat on all sides. Shake off the excess flour and
add to the skillet. Cook until browned and cooked through, 3 to 4
minutes per side. Transfer to a plate or platter and cover loosely with
foil. Repeat with the remaining oil and chicken.

Add the shallots, tarragon, and wine to the skillet. Increase the heat
to high and bring to a boil, stirring to pick up any browned bits in the
bottom of the pan. Boil until the liquid has reduced to 1 tablespoon.
Pour in the cream, bring back to a boil, and boil until reduced by half.
Pour in the stock, reduce the heat to medium-high, and simmer for
3 minutes. Season with salt and pepper, reduce the heat to medium,
and return the chicken to the skillet. Simmer, turning the chicken
often, until warmed through and the sauce is thickened, about 2 minutes. Spoon some of the sauce over each piece of chicken and serve at
once.

4 boneless, skinless chicken
 breast halves, about 6 ounces
 each

$1/2$ cup all-purpose flour

$1^1/2$ teaspoons kosher salt

$1/2$ teaspoon freshly ground
 black pepper

3 tablespoons extra virgin olive
 oil

2 shallots, minced

2 teaspoons dried tarragon

$1/4$ cup dry white wine

$1/4$ cup heavy cream

1 cup chicken stock, preferably
 homemade (page 338)

Additional kosher salt and freshly
 ground black pepper to taste

SERVES 4

Poussin en Cocotte

³/₄ pound pearl onions

12 to 15 baby carrots, about ³/₄ pound, or 4 medium carrots, cut into 1-inch pieces

4 poussins, about 1 pound each

Kosher salt and freshly ground black pepper to taste

1 small lemon, quartered

¹/₄ cup vegetable oil

¹/₂ pound cultivated white mushrooms, halved or quartered if large

6 ounces smoked ham, cut into ¹/₂-inch dice

3 garlic cloves, minced

1 tablespoon minced fresh sage leaves or 1 teaspoon dried

2 teaspoons fresh thyme leaves or ³/₄ teaspoon dried

¹/₂ cup dry red wine

¹/₄ cup finely chopped fresh parsley

SERVES 4

The baby chickens called *poussins* by the French are often tastier than large supermarket chickens because they are not mass-produced. If you cannot find poussins for this recipe (see Mail Order Sources), use Cornish game hens, which are about the same size as poussins but more widely available. (Look for Cornish game hens in the frozen food section of your local supermarket.)

This is really coq au vin, miniaturized. All the same elements are there: bacon, pearl onions, red wine. After browning your ingredients, you must make sure the flavors don't vaporize. Tightly covered cooking is key here. The best pot for the job is an earthenware casserole, the kind you have to soak first. If you are lucky enough to own one of these, do all your browning and deglazing in a skillet and then transfer the ingredients to the casserole. If you are not the happy owner of an earthenware casserole, just make the whole thing in a casserole with a tight-fitting lid. Serve with Creamed Spinach with Crispy Shallots (page 234) and Mashed Potato Cakes (page 249) or Herbed Spaetzle (page 259).

Bring a pot of salted water to a boil over high heat. Add the onions and cook 1 minute. Remove with a slotted spoon and transfer to a bowl of cold water. Let cool 10 minutes and peel. Add the carrots to the pot and boil until slightly tender, about 5 minutes.

Preheat the oven to 350°F. Rinse the poussins and pat dry with paper towels. Season the cavities with salt and pepper. Place a quarter of lemon in each cavity and tie the legs together. Season the exteriors with salt and pepper.

Heat the oil in a large covered casserole over medium-high heat until almost smoking. Add the poussins and cook, turning often, until browned on all sides, 7 to 10 minutes. Transfer to a plate or platter. Add the onions, carrots, mushrooms, and ham to the casserole. Cook, stirring often, until lightly browned, about 5 minutes. Add the garlic, sage, thyme, and red wine. Stir well and add the poussins along with any juices that have accumulated on the plate. Cover with a buttered round of parchment or wax paper and the lid. Transfer to the oven and bake until the juices from the thighs run clear when pierced with a skewer, about 45 minutes.

Transfer the poussins to a large warmed platter and remove the strings. Use a slotted spoon to transfer the vegetables to the platter. Cover loosely with foil. Place the casserole on top of the stove over high heat. Bring the pan juices to a boil and cook, stirring often, until reduced by half. Stir in the parsley and any accumulated juices from the plate. Season the sauce with salt and pepper and pour over the poussins just before serving.

wine recommendation:
poussin en cocotte

With no one flavor or heat sensation taking center stage, this dish is ultra-wine-friendly. From a crisp Pinot Grigio to a rich Chardonnay, from a fruity Gamay to a hearty Cabernet, most picks will work just fine.

Thai-Style Roasted Cornish Game Hens

4 fresh lemongrass stalks, outer leaves discarded and root ends trimmed off, or 2 tablespoons freshly grated lemon zest

¹/₂ cup coarsely chopped fresh cilantro

2 large shallots, coarsely chopped

8 large garlic cloves, peeled and smashed with the side of a large knife

One 2-inch piece fresh ginger, peeled and coarsely chopped

1 jalapeño or serrano chile, coarsely chopped, ribs and seeds removed to reduce heat if desired

2 teaspoons Thai red or green curry paste*

2 tablespoons Thai fish sauce (nam pla)* or kosher salt to taste

2 teaspoons firmly packed brown sugar

2 cups well-stirred canned unsweetened coconut milk*

4 Cornish game hens, about 1¹/₂ pounds each, legs tied together

1 teaspoon cornstarch

Kosher salt and freshly ground black pepper to taste

Lemon slices and fresh cilantro sprigs for garnish

*Available at Asian food stores and some supermarkets or see Mail Order Sources.

SERVES 4

People love it when you serve them their own little mini-version of a soufflé or cake. But it's also true of chicken. Rock Cornish game hen—a cross between a Cornish and a White Rock chicken—gives you a different idea about chicken, transforming it from something ho-hum into something special. Available in many supermarkets, it ranges in weight from 1¹/₂ to 2¹/₂ pounds. At the heavy end of this range, these hens are almost too much for one person. Cut them in half, however, and they lose their mini-chicken look.

Like the game hens, lemongrass is becoming increasingly available. If you can't find any, however, just substitute some freshly grated lemon zest. It's not lemongrass, but it will add lemongrass's sunny flavor.

Coconut milk is key in this recipe. Pick some up in your local supermarket or check out the Mail Order Sources at the back of this book.

This dish would go very nicely with some basmati or jasmine rice and the Stir-Fried Spicy Carrots with Peanuts (page 236).

Thinly slice the lower, lighter-colored 6 inches of the lemongrass stalks, discarding the remaining parts. Combine the lemongrass, cilantro, shallots, garlic, ginger, jalapeño, curry paste, fish sauce, sugar, and 1 cup of the coconut milk in a food processor or blender. Puree until smooth. Divide the mixture between 2 large plastic bags with re-sealable closures. Add 2 hens to each bag, squeezing out the excess air. Put the bags in a large shallow dish and marinate, refrigerated, turning the bags once or twice, overnight.

Preheat the oven to 450°F. Remove the hens from the marinade,

reserving the marinade. Wipe off the excess marinade and lay the
hens on a rack in a shallow roasting pan. Roast until lightly browned
and there are no traces of pink when the thighs are pierced at their
thickest point, 30 to 40 minutes. (A meat thermometer inserted into
the leg-thigh joint should register 170°F.)

Meanwhile, combine the marinade with the remaining 1 cup coconut milk in a small saucepan. Heat over medium-low heat, stirring
often, until bubbling around the edges, about 5 minutes. Strain
through a fine-mesh strainer into a separate saucepan. Mix the cornstarch with 2 tablespoons cold water in a small bowl and stir to blend.
Whisk into the strained sauce. Increase the heat to high and bring to a
boil, whisking constantly. Season with salt and pepper.

Arrange the hens attractively on a large serving platter. Garnish
with lemon and cilantro. Serve the hens with the sauce on the side.

Michael Green says:
turning down the heat—
wine with spicy foods

The more heat in a dish, the more it can alter your perception of a
wine's taste, making even the most delicious wines taste coarse, al-
coholic, and devoid of fruit. With spicy foods, look to a wine that puts
out the fire, one that soothes and refreshes. Look for wines that are
lively in acidity, modest in alcohol, and have a touch of residual sugar.
The next time you pull a Pavlov and reach for a beer, consider popping
open a bottle of sparkling wine, Sauvignon Blanc, Riesling, or a lighter
red such as a Pinot Noir or Beaujolais. If opting for a red wine, consider serving it with a bit of a chill.

Roast Turkey with Sauerkraut

For the turkey:

One 12- to 16-pound turkey, preferably organic, kosher, or minimally processed (see Mail Order Sources)

Two 1-pound loaves homemade-style white bread, ends and crusts removed

1 cup finely chopped fresh parsley

3 medium onions, finely chopped

3 celery ribs, finely chopped

2 teaspoons dried sage

2 teaspoons dried thyme

1 tablespoon celery salt, plus more as needed

1 tablespoon kosher salt

1 tablespoon freshly ground black pepper

8 tablespoons (1 stick) unsalted butter, melted, plus more for brushing

Additional kosher salt and freshly ground black pepper to taste

Sweet or hot paprika to taste

For the sauerkraut:

Two 14$^{1}/_{2}$ ounce cans sauerkraut, drained

$^{1}/_{2}$ cup packed dark brown sugar

$^{1}/_{3}$ cup cider vinegar

2 tablespoons caraway seeds

2 tablespoons unsalted butter

3 medium onions, finely chopped

SERVES 12 TO 15

This recipe comes from Rick Bzdafka, the amiable husband of my cousin Allison. Cooking for the masses at our family farm—and we often have upwards of 20 people for dinner—does not intimidate Rick. He just checks out what's in the cupboard and makes it up as he goes along. Rick likes to cook.

Rick grew up in the Polish community just outside of Cleveland where, among other things, cooking poultry with sauerkraut is common. His grandfather made vats of sauerkraut, as well as homemade pickles, and taught Rick how to cook. They cooked everything, from brains and eggs and oxtail stew to homemade rye bread. No wonder Rick is so adventurous in the kitchen now. I ate his turkey with sauerkraut only once, but it made a lasting impression on me. The sauerkraut plays the same role as the cranberry sauce it replaces, its sweet-and-sourness cutting through the fattiness of the stuffing and gravy. Serve with Baked Acorn Squash with Mustard and Honey (page 246) and Creamed Spinach with Crispy Shallots (page 234).

To prepare the turkey, preheat the oven to 325°F. Rinse the turkey under cold running water and pat dry with paper towels. Tear the bread into small pieces and place in a large bowl. Add the parsley, onions, celery, sage, thyme, celery salt, salt, and pepper and mix well. Stir in the butter.

Lightly fill the cavity of the turkey with some of the stuffing. (A general rule of thumb is $^{1}/_{2}$ cup stuffing per each pound of turkey.) Butter a covered baking dish large enough to hold the remaining stuffing loosely and set aside.

Tuck the wings under and tie the legs together. Brush all over with additional butter and sprinkle with celery salt, salt, pepper, and paprika as desired.

Place the bird in a large roasting pan and roast for 12 to 15 minutes per pound or until it reaches an internal temperature of 165°F on a meat thermometer in the leg-thigh joint. Baste every 30 minutes.

Prepare the sauerkraut while the turkey is roasting. Combine the sauerkraut in a large saucepan with the sugar, vinegar, caraway seeds, and 2 cups water. Bring to a boil over high heat, stirring often. Reduce the heat to low and cover. Simmer, stirring occasionally, until the sauerkraut has absorbed some of the liquid and is very dark, about $1^1/_2$ hours.

Melt the butter in a small skillet over medium heat. Add the onions and cook, stirring, until softened, about 5 minutes.

Remove the cover from the sauerkraut and increase the heat to high. Bring to a boil and cook until most of the liquid has evaporated. Remove from the heat and add the onions. Return the cover and set aside until ready to serve.

About $^1/_2$ hour before the turkey is done, spoon out a small amount of the turkey drippings and spoon over the stuffing in the baking dish. Cover the dish and bake while the turkey finishes cooking.

Transfer the turkey to a cutting surface or large serving platter and cover loosely with foil. Let rest for 20 minutes before carving.

Gently reheat the sauerkraut, stirring to mix in the onions, over low heat until warmed through, 3 to 5 minutes. Serve hot with the turkey and stuffing and pan gravy, if desired, following the directions on page 68.

Rick Bzdafka, 2001

wine recommendation:
roast turkey with sauerkraut

Sauerkraut with turkey?! Why not? It adds salt and acid to what can otherwise be a pretty bland bird. And let's not overlook the substantial sweetness provided by the brown sugar in this recipe. I would choose a fruity, off-dry wine, such as a white Zinfandel or German Riesling.

Turkey Burgers with Tomato Corn Salsa

For the salsa:

12 cherry tomatoes, finely chopped

$\frac{1}{2}$ teaspoon kosher salt

$\frac{1}{2}$ cup cooked fresh corn or thawed frozen corn kernels

1 tablespoon fresh lime juice

1 garlic clove, minced

1 tablespoon chopped fresh cilantro

2 teaspoons olive oil

Additional kosher salt and freshly ground black pepper to taste

For the burgers:

2 tablespoons vegetable oil

1 small onion, finely chopped

$\frac{1}{2}$ small red bell pepper, finely chopped

1 tablespoon store-bought or homemade Creole Spice Mix (page 348)

1 teaspoon kosher salt

1 pound ground turkey

Freshly ground black pepper to taste

SERVES 4

Hamburgers are so central to American cuisine that messing with them can seem almost sacrilegious. And it's kind of perilous to boot. Replace rich beef with low-fat turkey, as in this recipe, and you risk creating a drier, less flavorful burger, a burger unworthy of the name.

Here I've countered the moisture problem with vegetables. The sautéed onion and red pepper in the burger and the salsa on top of the burger make up for any dryness in the turkey. The Creole seasoning, in combination with the salsa, makes up for turkey's relative lack of flavor.

I'm not the kind of diet-conscious eater who reflexively reaches for the low-fat alternative to every dish, but this low-fat burger is really delicious and satisfying. Serve with Ruthie's Summer Camp Zucchini (page 224) and Oven-Baked Rosemary Potato Chips (page 14).

To make the salsa, toss the tomatoes with the salt and drain in a colander for 15 minutes. Combine the tomatoes, corn, lime juice, garlic, cilantro, and olive oil in a large bowl. Season with salt and pepper and toss well.

To prepare the burgers, preheat the oven to 400°F. Heat 1 tablespoon of the oil in a small skillet over medium heat. Add the onion and red pepper and cook, until softened, about 5 minutes. Cool to room temperature.

Combine the onion, pepper, Creole spice mix, salt, and turkey in a large bowl. Season with pepper. Mix well and form into 4 patties. Heat the remaining tablespoon of oil in a large ovenproof skillet over medium heat. Place the burgers in the skillet and cook until well browned, about 5 minutes per side. Transfer to the oven and cook until firm to the touch, about 6 minutes. Serve topped with the salsa.

Crispy Roast Duck with Mustard and Green Peppercorn Sauce

Roast duck is one of my absolute favorites, but it is not easy to get right. If you concentrate on achieving moist meat, the skin might not crisp up. If you concentrate on crisping up the skin, you risk drying out the breast meat. Still, the desired result is so wonderful that I've spent 25 years trying to figure out how to get it done dependably and easily. I've tried very high heat, very low heat, and a mixture of the two. I've tried *everything*, including air-drying the duck for several days as the Chinese do when they make Peking duck. Most of these methods are probably too much work for the home cook. The method I use here works well and is not too scary.

Making a sauce for your delicious duck can also be an ordeal. When I was still working in restaurants, I'd start by slow-roasting my ducks. Then I'd cool and quarter them and remove all the big bones. Next I'd turn the bones into a dark, rich sauce and chill the duck until service. Finally, I'd crisp the duck skin side down in a skillet and serve it with the sauce. But again, this is too much work for the home cook. So I started thinking about Thanksgiving and the bird of honor and about how to make a turkey gravy without the benefit of turkey stock. I use the wings and whatever neck, gizzards, etc., accompany the bird, and while the turkey itself is roasting in the oven, my stock is coming together in a pot on the stove. I have applied that method to the making of a great duck stock.

If you have never before roasted a duck, this recipe may

One 5-pound Long Island (Pekin) duck

Kosher salt and freshly ground black pepper to taste

1 tablespoon vegetable oil

1 small onion, coarsely chopped

1 small carrot, coarsely chopped

2 garlic cloves, smashed with the side of a knife

$1/2$ cup dry red wine

1 small celery rib, coarsely chopped

2 fresh thyme sprigs or $1/2$ teaspoon dried

$1/2$ teaspoon black peppercorns

$1/2$ bay leaf, preferably Turkish

1 tablespoon tomato paste

1 quart chicken stock, preferably homemade brown chicken stock (page 339)

$1 1/2$ tablespoons all-purpose flour

$1 1/2$ tablespoons unsalted butter, softened

2 tablespoons drained bottled green peppercorns

1 tablespoon Dijon mustard

SERVES 4

make you a believer. Serve with Parsnip Puree (page 237) and Stir-Fried Spicy Carrots with Peanuts (page 236).

Preheat the oven to 450°F. Remove the neck and giblets from the cavity of the duck and reserve. Cut the wings off the duck and reserve. Rinse the duck under cold running water and pat dry with paper towels. Using the tip of a sharp paring knife, prick the duck all over, inserting the knife at an angle to pierce just the skin, not the flesh. Season well with salt and pepper. Place on a rack in a shallow roasting pan and roast until browned and crisp, $1^1/4$ hours. Remove the roasting pan at 30-minute intervals, drain off the fat, and again prick the skin.

While the duck is roasting, rinse the neck, giblets, and wings and pat dry. Cut the wings and the neck into several pieces. Heat the oil in a large saucepan over medium-high heat. Add the neck, giblets, and wings. Cook, stirring often, until golden brown, 8 to 10 minutes. Reduce the heat to medium and add the onion, carrot, and garlic. Cook until the vegetables are lightly browned and softened, 5 to 8 minutes. Increase the heat to medium-high and pour in the wine. Bring to a boil, stirring to pick up any browned bits on the bottom. Boil until almost all of the liquid has evaporated. Add the celery, thyme, black peppercorns, bay leaf, tomato paste, and stock. Reduce the heat to medium and simmer, skimming off any scum that rises to the surface, until the duck is ready to come out of the oven.

When the duck is done, transfer to a carving board, cover loosely with foil, and let rest for 15 to 20 minutes.

While the duck is resting, strain the stock and discard the solids. Measure the liquid. If there is less than 1 cup, add water to measure this amount and pour into a small saucepan. If there is more than 1 cup, return to the saucepan and boil until reduced to this amount.

Bring the liquid back to a simmer over medium-high heat. Combine the flour and butter in a small heatproof bowl and use a fork to work it into a smooth paste. Add a little of the stock to the paste and whisk until smooth. Pour the flour mixture into the saucepan and simmer, whisking, until slightly thickened, 2 to 3 minutes. Stir in the green peppercorns. Remove the saucepan from the heat, stir in the mustard, and season the sauce with salt and pepper. Cut the duck into serving pieces. Spoon on a small amount of the sauce and serve warm with any remaining sauce on the side.

wine recommendation:
crispy roast duck with mustard and green peppercorn sauce

The North Fork of Long Island, once known for its humble potatoes, is now making a mark with its sexy wines. Let's match up this recipe's Long Island duck, then, with some Long Island Merlot or Cabernet. If you can't find any where you live, seek out the California brands.

duck fat

Don't throw out that duck fat. Store it in the freezer in little resealable plastic bags. It adds wonderful flavor to potato dishes.

Duck Confit in an Oven Bag

1¹/₂ tablespoons kosher salt

1 tablespoon minced garlic

**1 tablespoon finely chopped
fresh thyme**

³/₄ teaspoon ground allspice

**1 bay leaf, preferably Turkish,
crumbled**

**One 5-pound duck, cut into
8 pieces, all fat and skin
left on**

1 tablespoon all-purpose flour

SERVES 4

I'm crazy about the rich cuisine of southwestern France, where everyone seems to eat his or her fill of duck, geese, foie gras, rillettes, and cassoulet and somehow live to be 90 years old. The only problem is that most of these dishes require a lot of time to prepare, so I tend to indulge my love of them when someone else is doing the cooking, usually in a French restaurant.

That said, my team at "Cooking Live" figured out a way to prepare a "quick cassoulet" for one of my Wednesday night cook-along shows. Cassoulet is one of those dishes that stirs up strong feelings. There are three authentic versions from three different cities in the south of France, and I'm certainly not going to jump into the middle of the eternal battle over which one is "correct." But I will tell you that the most important elements are slow-cooked white beans with some sort of preserved meat product—duck, pork, or lamb and sometimes all three. Our quick cassoulet called for store-bought duck confit. *Confit* means "preserved," and duck confit is duck that has been marinated in a dry spice cure and then slowly cooked in its own fat. It is rare to find a duck that has enough fat, so I usually have to purchase some duck fat from D'Artagnan, one of my favorite companies (see Mail Order Sources).

During the quick cassoulet show a viewer called in and said that he had had great success making duck confit in one of those oven-cooking bags advertised on TV all the time. I was thunderstruck! I'd never thought of it before, but it made perfect sense. Whenever you cook protein in its own little container—whether parchment (see Fish en Papillote, page 143) or earthenware casserole (see Poussin en Cocotte, page 80)—it creates its own juices or, in this case, its own fat. If those oven-cooking bags could indeed turn the trick, we'd all save enough time, labor, and money to make duck confit a viable entree for home cooks. Piercing the mysteries of cooking in an oven bag took several tests and a phone call to Betty—yes, *the* Betty, of Reynold's Wrap's Pat & Betty fame—but I finally did it. I hope that my version of duck confit makes this very delicious dish accessible to you. Serve with Roasted Lemon Potatoes (page 252) and Stewed Green Beans with Tomato and Mint (page 238).

Combine the salt, garlic, thyme, allspice, and bay leaf in a small bowl. Mix well and rub the mixture over all the meaty sides of the cut-up duck. Place in a plastic bag with a resealable closure and marinate in the refrigerator for 12 to 24 hours.

Preheat the oven to 300°F. Spray the inside of an oven-cooking bag with nonstick vegetable spray. Add the flour to absorb the juices from the duck as it cooks. Rub the marinade off the duck with paper towels and place the pieces in a flat layer inside the bag. Follow the bag manufacturer's instructions for providing proper ventilation during cooking. Place the bag in a large baking dish and cook until tender when pierced with the tip of a knife, about $1^3/4$ hours. Set aside until cool enough to handle.

Before serving, heat a large nonstick skillet over medium-high heat. Place the duck skin side down in the skillet and cook until the skin is crispy and the meat is heated through, 3 to 4 minutes. Serve at once.

wine recommendation:
duck confit in an oven bag

As I read about the origins of this dish in southwestern France, my mind drifted to Gascogne and *The Three Musketeers.* Consider the wines of Cahors, then, endowed with deep color and loads of tannin and flavor. A hearty Syrah or Bordeaux would also work just fine.

Meat

Sautéed Pork Loin with Mustard and Grapes

Eight ¼-inch-thick slices
boneless pork loin, about
1½ pounds

½ cup all-purpose flour

1½ teaspoons kosher salt

½ teaspoon freshly ground black
pepper

1 tablespoon unsalted butter

2 tablespoons vegetable oil

1 small onion, finely chopped

1 cup seedless red or green
grapes, halved

½ cup dry white wine

1½ cups chicken stock,
preferably homemade
(page 338)

1 teaspoon firmly packed dark
brown sugar

1½ tablespoons Dijon mustard

Additional kosher salt and freshly
ground black pepper to taste

SERVES 4

When I was in high school, my mom and I threw all kinds of dinner parties. (Actually, she threw the parties and I helped cook.) Our favorite dish was veal scaloppine. I liked it no matter how it was cooked or sauced. It seemed so elegant to us, and there were so many good recipes for it in our favorite cookbook: Craig Claiborne's *The New York Times Cookbook*. In retrospect, I realize that my fondness for veal scaloppine is based on my love of sauce. Veal, in its velvety blandness, is merely the perfect excuse for sauce.

There was a rumor at the time, horrifying to me, that some Italian restaurants were substituting pork scaloppine for veal because it was so much cheaper and the guests never knew the difference. We didn't eat pork at home, so I had no point of reference, but now I have come to appreciate pork in all forms, and I agree that pork scaloppine, cut from the new lean loin and tenderloin, is also a great backdrop for sauces. See for yourself. (As far as I'm concerned, the pork industry has succeeded in its campaign to make pork into the "other white meat.")

This is a really quick weeknight meal, and the kids will probably be open to it because of the grapes. Serve with Rice for the Rice Impaired (page 256) and Sautéed Spinach with Garlic Chips (page 232).

Sprinkle a small amount of water on a large sheet of plastic wrap. Place 2 of the pork slices on top of the plastic and sprinkle again with water. Cover with another sheet of plastic wrap and pound with a rolling pin or meat pounder until about ¼ inch thick. Repeat with the remaining pork.

Mix the flour with the salt and pepper in a shallow pie plate. Heat half the butter and oil in a large skillet over medium-high heat until almost smoking. Working in 2 batches, place the pork in the flour mixture and turn to coat on all sides. Shake off the excess flour and add to the skillet. Cook until lightly browned, 2 to 3 minutes per side. Transfer to a plate or platter and cover loosely with foil. Repeat with the remaining butter, oil, and pork.

Return the skillet to the heat and add the onion and grapes. Reduce the heat to medium and cook, stirring often, until the onions are slightly softened, about 5 minutes. Increase the heat to high, pour in the wine, and bring to a boil. Cook rapidly, stirring to pick up any browned bits in the bottom of the skillet, until reduced to about 1 tablespoon. Add the stock and sugar and boil until reduced by half. Reduce the heat to medium and return the pork to the skillet with any accumulated juices. Simmer gently until heated through, 3 to 5 minutes. Transfer the pork to a large heated platter. Remove the skillet from the heat, whisk in the mustard, and season the sauce with salt and pepper. Pour the sauce over the pork and serve hot.

Slow-Roasted Spiced Baby Back Ribs

6 pounds baby back ribs

¼ cup sweet or hot paprika

2 tablespoons kosher salt

½ cup firmly packed dark brown sugar

¼ cup chili powder

5 to 6 garlic cloves, minced

2 tablespoons ground cumin

1 tablespoon dry mustard

1 teaspoon cayenne pepper or more to taste

1 recipe Rick's Barbecue Sauce (page 343) or your favorite store-bought barbecue sauce

SERVES 6

One of my all-time favorite field trips for "Cooking Live" was to Memphis to cover the huge annual barbecue cook-off there. It is an astounding event that attracts more than 200 teams from all around the country, from funky little crews of like-minded friends to heavily financed corporate outfits. Everyone competes not just for the best ribs but also for the best booth. Some of the so-called booths are two stories high and extremely elaborate.

Although most of the teams party hard for three days straight—the beer flows—everyone also stays *very* focused on the cooking. If I'd never understood it before, I do now: Barbecuing, done right, is clearly an art that takes years to perfect. I have never eaten such great meat *anywhere*.

When it was all over, we had Chris Lilly of Big Bob Gibson's Barbecue, from Decatur, Alabama—one of that year's champs—come onto the show to show us how they make their ribs. Even cooking in an oven instead of on a grill, and without the benefit of the smoking process, Chris's ribs were absolutely delicious. His secret? Slow and low. In Memphis I'd heard this time and again. Everyone has his or her secret rub and marinade and sauce, but there is one thing on which everyone agrees: slow and low.

I decided to develop my own version of oven-baked ribs. Here it is.

(A word to the wise: If you boil your ribs before you grill or roast them, don't even think about going to Memphis. That is a terrible barbecue no-no.) Serve with Couscous

Tabbouleh (page 255) and Ruthie's Summer Camp
Zucchini (page 224).

Use your fingers to pull off and remove the thin papery skin from the
back of each rib. Combine the paprika, salt, sugar, chili powder, garlic,
cumin, mustard, and cayenne in a small bowl and mix well. Rub the
mixture all over the ribs. Cover and refrigerate for 4 hours or
overnight.

Preheat the oven to 250°F. Place the ribs meat side up in one layer
on several sheet pans and bake, turning from time to time, until very
tender, $3^1/2$ to 4 hours. About 30 minutes before the ribs are done,
remove them from the oven and brush liberally on all sides with the
barbecue sauce. Bake until very tender. Serve additional sauce on the
side.

Lorraine's Green Chile Tamales

2 cups masa harina (corn flour),
preferably the Maseca brand*

2 to 2¹/₂ cups warm chicken
stock, preferably homemade
(page 338)

¹/₂ cup lard or shortening

1 teaspoon kosher salt

1¹/₂ pounds boneless pork
shoulder, cut into 1-inch
cubes

Vegetable oil as needed

1 tablespoon all-purpose flour

1 pound green Anaheim chiles*

3 jalapeños, seeded and coarsely
chopped

2 garlic cloves, coarsely
chopped

1 medium plum tomato, seeded
and coarsely chopped

Additional kosher salt to taste

Freshly ground black pepper to
taste

18 dried corn husks*

1 pound Monterey Jack cheese,
cut into 18 sticks

*Masa harina, mild green Anaheim chiles,
also known as California or long green
chiles, and corn husks are available at Latin
markets or see Mail Order Sources.

MAKES 18 TAMALES,
SERVING 6

We put together a "Cooking Live" holiday special called "Sara's Hometown Holidays" for Christmas of 2000. The idea was for me to visit five families in five different parts of the country to get an idea of the various ways Americans celebrate the holidays. All of the families were quite warm and welcoming (they wouldn't have invited us into their homes otherwise), but Christal Meza and her family in La Habra, California, were especially hospitable.

As at several of the other homes, the Mezas prepare an heirloom recipe during the holidays. Their recipe for Green Chile Tamales was handed down to Christal by Lorraine Gallega, the woman who became Christal's grandmother-in-law. In fact, Christal learned it from Lorraine herself over Christmas of 1993, the first Christmas she spent with her future husband, Jason, and his family. The Mezas are of Mexican extraction, and Jason had warned Christal in advance that she'd probably have to make tamales with the women in his clan because that's what the women do at Christmas. "I was kind of nervous about being the white girl there making the tamales for the first time," says Christal, who grew up in Louisiana. She confesses that she wasn't much of a cook to begin with.

Lorraine put her at ease. "It turned out good because Lorraine was a patient teacher," Christal says. "But she wanted you to do it right—so if you didn't, she would tell you to dump it out and start again." In fact, the whole evening turned out to be a smash. "I really bonded with the family that night," she says. "Lorraine and everybody could see that this was something I wanted to learn and to be a part of."

Eight years later Christal and Jason have two kids of their own. Lorraine passed on in 1998. But every Christmas, Christal sits down with the other Meza women, including Yolanda, Laura, and Sally, to make Lorraine's tamales. "It's a tradition no one wants to lose," she says. "As long as we're still doing it, Lorraine's still there. I don't want to forget this recipe, and I don't want my kids to forget it either." Serve with Magda's Cauliflower (page 245) and Sautéed Shredded Zucchini with Lemon and Thyme (page 226).

Place the masa harina in a large bowl and pour in 2 cups of the stock. Beat with a wooden spoon until smooth. Beat in some of the remaining stock a tablespoon at a time if the mixture seems too stiff. The mixture should be firm but not too loose. Place the lard in the bowl of an electric stand mixer and beat at high speed until fluffy, about 3 minutes. With the beaters in motion, add the masa mixture a handful at a time, scraping the sides of the bowl often. Continue until all the masa mixture is absorbed. Add the salt and the remaining stock a tablespoon at a time to get a light and delicate mixture with the texture of buttercream frosting. Transfer to a bowl and keep covered and chilled.

Place the pork in a large skillet and pour in 1 cup cold water. Bring to a boil over high heat. Reduce the heat to medium, cover, and simmer gently until very tender, about 1^1/$_2$ hours. Stir the pork once or twice to distribute the heat evenly but as little as possible to avoid shredding it. Remove the cover, increase the heat to high, and cook until all the liquid has evaporated. Move the pork to one side and add enough vegetable oil to cover the bottom. Move the pork back around the skillet and cook until lightly brown and a crispy coating forms on the bottom, about 5 minutes. Sprinkle on the flour and stir gently to mix. Remove from the heat and set aside.

Prepare a charcoal fire and let the coals burn down to a gray ash. (Alternatively, preheat a large well-oiled grill pan over medium-high heat until almost smoking.) Working in batches if necessary, arrange the chiles on the grill and roast, turning often, until blistered and almost charred, 5 to 10 minutes on a charcoal grill, 10 to 15 minutes on a stovetop griddle. Transfer to a plastic bag with a resealable closure to sweat the chiles and loosen the skins, 10 to 15 minutes. Completely remove all the skins, stems, and seeds.

Combine the peeled Anaheims, half of the jalapeños, the garlic, and the tomato in a food processor. Process until coarsely chopped but still chunky. Taste and season with salt. Add the remaining jalapeños and process again if a hotter sauce is desired. Add the sauce to the pork and stir gently until well mixed. Return the skillet to medium heat and stir, being careful not to shred the pork and scraping the bottom to pick up the browned bits, until thickened and warmed through, about 5 minutes. Stir gently over low heat until well mixed. Season with salt and pepper. You should have about 4 cups.

Take the masa mixture out of the refrigerator. Fill a sink with very hot tap water. Add the corn husks and let stand until soft and pliable, about 20 minutes. Take out of the water and remove the excess corn silk. Drain well.

To assemble the tamales, arrange a corn husk with the pointed end toward you. Spread $2^1/2$ tablespoons of the masa harina mixture thinly and evenly over the inside center of each corn husk to make about a 4-inch square. Mound 3 scant tablespoons of the pork mixture on top of the masa layer and top with a stick of cheese. Fold the bottom pointed end of the husk up to enclose the filling. Fold in the sides and press the top opening to seal in the filling. (The tamales are not folded in on the top side.)

Prepare a large deep steamer, filling the bottom with water. Place the tamales with the open side up in the steamer. Bring the water to a boil over high heat. Reduce the heat to medium-high and steam, covered, until the filling easily pulls away from the husks when the tamale is opened, 1 to $1^1/4$ hours, adding boiling water as needed to the bottom of the steamer. Let the tamales sit for 5 minutes before serving.

green chile tamales

To make sure you have hot water available to add to the steamer as the water boils away, bring a kettle of water to a boil and then turn down the burner to warm. This is a trick that I have also found useful for steaming whole large globe artichokes.

Indian-Style Shepherd's Pie

When I was a kid, my mom made roast lamb for us every couple of weeks. It's a great dish all by itself, of course, but my mom swore by it as a kind of two-meals-for-the-price-of-one special, knowing that she would recycle that night's leftovers as the next night's shepherd's pie. I loved shepherd's pie. Indeed, sometimes the transformed leftovers—consisting of ground or cubed meat and gravy, topped with mashed potatoes, and baked until bubbly on the bottom and golden on top—tasted better to me than the original roast. Apparently, however, some toxic dish misnamed shepherd's pie was served at college campuses all across the country during the eighties and nineties. When I mentioned it to my very youthful "Cooking Live" team, they all said, "Yuck!" They don't know what they're missing.

This recipe is an offshoot of the one that I developed in the *Gourmet* test kitchen when I was pregnant with Ruthie. Alexis Touchet, a fellow test cook, remembers how comical it was watching me with my big belly struggling to get close enough to the casserole dish to pipe out the potato mixture.

This homey one-pot meal requires a little more work than most of the recipes in this book, although the stew part could certainly be made ahead. In fact, any stew or braised dish tastes better when made ahead because the flavor gets deeper as time passes—I recommend this for Sunday dinner or special guests. Serve with a big tossed green salad and crusty bread.

Heat 2 tablespoons of the oil in a 3-quart casserole, preferably enameled cast iron, over medium-high heat until almost smoking. Season the lamb with salt and pepper. Working in batches and adding more

6 tablespoons vegetable oil

3 pounds boneless lamb stew meat, cut into 1-inch pieces

Kosher salt and freshly ground black pepper to taste

2 medium onions, finely chopped

2 garlic cloves, minced

One 2-inch piece fresh ginger, peeled and finely chopped

1½ tablespoons ground cumin

1 tablespoon ground coriander

¼ cup all-purpose flour

2 cups chicken stock, preferably homemade (page 338)

⅓ cup fresh lime juice

Two 2- to 3-inch-long fresh hot green chiles, such as serrano,* seeded and minced

2 cups drained chopped canned Italian plum tomatoes

1 pound spinach, coarse stems discarded

3 cups small cauliflower florets

2½ pounds sweet potatoes

1 russet (baking) potato

2 tablespoons unsalted butter, softened

*Available at specialty food shops and some large grocery stores

SERVES 6 TO 8

oil as necessary, add the lamb and cook, turning often, until browned on all sides, 5 to 7 minutes. Use a slotted spoon to transfer to a bowl. Reduce the heat to medium, add the onions, and cook, stirring occasionally, until softened, about 5 minutes. Add the garlic and the ginger and cook for 3 minutes longer. Add the cumin, coriander, and flour. Cook, stirring often, for 3 minutes. Pour in the stock and increase the heat to medium-high. Simmer for about 5 minutes. Stir in the lime juice, chiles, tomatoes, the lamb with any juices that have accumulated in the bowl, and salt and pepper. Reduce the heat to medium-low and simmer, covered, skimming occasionally, until the lamb is tender, about 1^1/$_2$ hours.

Meanwhile, rinse and drain the spinach, place it in a large saucepan, and season with salt. Steam over medium heat, using only the water clinging to the leaves, until just wilted, 2 to 3 minutes. Drain in a colander and refresh under cold running water. Squeeze dry in a kitchen towel and chop coarsely.

Add the cauliflower to the lamb mixture and simmer for 5 minutes. Stir in the spinach. (The recipe can be prepared in advance to this point. Keep covered in the refrigerator for up to 3 days or freeze for up to 1 month. Thaw in the refrigerator overnight before continuing with the recipe.)

Preheat the oven to 425°F. Prick the potatoes with a fork and bake until very tender, about 1 hour. Let stand until they are cool enough to handle. Peel the potatoes and puree in a food processor. Stir in the butter and season with salt and pepper.

Preheat the oven to 400°F. Fill a large pastry bag with the potato mixture and pipe evenly over the lamb stew or spoon mounds of the potato puree on top. Spread out with a knife, then use a fork to score the top lightly. Bake until heated through and lightly browned on top, 30 to 40 minutes.

wine recommendation:
indian-style shepherd's pie

This shepherd's pie, an exotic variation of the traditional English dish, calls for a substantial red wine. Why not consider one you've never tried before? Pick a Pinotage from South Africa, an Aglianico from Italy, or a Malbec from Argentina.

Moroccan Spiced Leg of Lamb
with Preserved Lemon Relish

Butterflied boneless leg of lamb is a great dish for a crowd.
I have used a Moroccan-style dry rub here, but you could
substitute any chicken or meat marinade, wet or dry. One of
my old favorites is a Jacques Pépin recipe that we ran when
I was in the test kitchen at *Gourmet*. He just threw some raw
onion, garlic, soy sauce, honey, jalapeño, and fresh ginger
into a food processor and then marinated the lamb in it
overnight. Even the kids liked it.

I recommend cooking your lamb medium-rare, which
means taking it off the grill or out of the broiler when it has
an internal temperature of 130°F. (Rare would also be fine
with me, but not everyone likes it that way.) For an accurate
reading, insert your instant-read thermometer into the meat
sideways, not straight down. After you have taken the lamb
off the heat, let it rest for 10 minutes, covered loosely with
foil, so that the juices have a chance to redistribute themselves and don't come streaming out when you slice the
lamb. By the way, one of the beauties of working with a
boneless leg of lamb is that it is a cinch to carve.

My friend and colleague Marie Ostrosky, who used to
work with us on "Cooking Live" but then left to work on
another show (traitor!), turned me on to the recipe for the
preserved lemons in the relish. Preserved lemons are wonderful Moroccan pickles made by combining lemons, salt,
and lemon juice, then letting the mixture cure for three
weeks. Marie's version, which she learned in her previous
life as a caterer, takes only 24 hours to come together. The

For the lamb:

One 3$\frac{1}{2}$- to 4-pound butterflied
   boneless leg of lamb, trimmed
   of almost all fat

$\frac{1}{2}$ cup extra virgin olive oil

$\frac{1}{4}$ cup fresh lemon juice

3 garlic cloves, minced

1 tablespoon sweet or hot
   paprika

1$\frac{1}{2}$ teaspoons ground cumin

1 teaspoon cayenne pepper

1 teaspoon kosher salt

$\frac{1}{2}$ teaspoon dried marjoram

$\frac{1}{2}$ teaspoon ground ginger

Pinch saffron (optional)

$\frac{1}{3}$ cup finely chopped fresh
   cilantro

Additional kosher salt and freshly
   ground black pepper to taste

For the relish:

2$\frac{1}{2}$ preserved lemons (see note)

$\frac{1}{2}$ small red onion, diced

$\frac{1}{4}$ cup coarsely chopped fresh
   parsley

$\frac{1}{4}$ cup coarsely chopped fresh
   cilantro

2 tablespoons chopped pitted
   Mediterranean olives, such as
   Kalamata

$\frac{1}{2}$ teaspoon fresh lemon juice

1 tablespoon extra virgin olive oil

Kosher salt and freshly ground
   black pepper to taste

SERVES 6

relish is salty, but it makes a nice counterpoint to the lamb. Serve with Magda's Sofrito Rice (page 258) and Stewed Green Beans with Tomato and Mint (page 238).

Pound the lamb to a uniform 1-inch thickness using a meat pounder or rolling pin and place in a large plastic bag with a resealable closure. (If the lamb is too large to fit in the bag, place in a nonreactive baking dish large enough to hold it flat.) Combine the olive oil, lemon juice, garlic, paprika, cumin, cayenne, salt, marjoram, ginger, saffron, and cilantro in a small bowl and whisk to combine. Pour over the lamb and seal the bag. Marinate in the refrigerator for at least 3 hours and up to overnight. Turn often to distribute the flavors.

Prepare a charcoal fire and allow the coals to burn down to a gray ash. Lightly oil the grill. (Alternatively, preheat the broiler to medium-high and adjust the oven shelf so that the broiling pan will be about 6 inches from the heat.) Remove the lamb from the marinade and pat dry with paper towels. Season with salt and pepper. Sear well on both sides over high heat, then move to a cooler side of the grill. Cook for 5 to 10 minutes longer or until a meat thermometer registers 130°F for medium-rare. (Or broil for 5 to 7 minutes per side.) Transfer to a cutting board and cover loosely with foil. Let rest for 10 minutes.

To make the relish, very finely chop the lemons. Place in a small bowl and add the onion, parsley, cilantro, olives, lemon juice, and olive oil. Season with salt and pepper. You should have about 1$\frac{1}{2}$ cups.

Thinly slice the lamb on the diagonal and serve each portion topped with some of the relish. Serve the remaining relish on the side.

note: Preserved lemons can be found in many specialty food stores. To make your own quick version, cut 2$\frac{1}{2}$ thin-skinned lemons (preferably organic) into $\frac{1}{8}$-inch-thick slices. Arrange half the lemons over the bottom of a nonreactive pan and sprinkle on 2 tablespoons of salt. Place the remaining lemons on top and sprinkle with another 2 tablespoons of salt. Cover with plastic wrap, making sure the plastic touches the top of the lemons. Leave at room temperature overnight or for up to 48 hours. Rinse the lemons, remove the seeds, and pat dry before using.

Rosemary-Scallion-Crusted Rack of Lamb

Rack of lamb is my favorite cut of lamb. It's always delicious—the bones add so much flavor—and the basic preparation requires little more than popping it in the oven and keeping an eye on it until it's done. It's really almost impossible to mess up.

But it is an expensive cut, so chances are you'll be saving it for special occasions. Butchers will tell you that one rack feeds three or four people—each rack has seven or eight individual chops—but I think you're safer if you figure on one rack feeding two people . . . and then you can count on some choice leftovers.

Get the butcher to french the chops, a process of scraping off all the fat and meat from the end of the bones so that each chop is left with an elegant long bone attached, almost like a carved handle. Also, make sure the butcher removes the chine bones, or you will not be able to slice through the chops. Finally, ask your butcher to trim all the fat from the top of the meat. He or she will be reluctant, because the fat protects the meat from drying out when you roast it. But we replace the fat with a flavorful, protective crust, which serves the same purpose.

This recipe is an adaptation of one that Kempy Minifie, *Gourmet*'s senior food editor, developed for the magazine in the mid-eighties. I have never found a lamb dish I like quite so much. One of the great things about it is that you can prepare all the parts ahead of time and then just toss it in the oven about 40 minutes before you want to eat it. (It requires 25 to 30 minutes to cook and 10 to 15 minutes to

3 tablespoons olive oil

$1/2$ teaspoon hot red pepper flakes

2 garlic cloves, minced

1 small bunch (6 to 7) scallions, white and 1 inch of the green parts, thinly sliced

2 teaspoons dried rosemary

1 cup fresh bread crumbs (page 347)

Kosher salt and freshly ground black pepper to taste

Two $1^1/4$-pound trimmed and frenched racks of lamb, 7 or 8 ribs each

$1/4$ cup mayonnaise

2 teaspoons Dijon mustard

Fresh watercress sprigs for garnish

SERVES 4

rest. This rest period is crucial. It allows all the juices a chance to redistribute themselves evenly throughout the meat.) The crumb crust and mustard mayonnaise can be made a day ahead. The meat can be seared an hour ahead, topped with the mayo and crust, and then parked on the counter until it is time to put it in the oven. Serve with Roasted Lemon Potatoes (page 252) and Quick Sautéed Shredded Brussels Sprouts with Pancetta and Balsamic Vinegar (page 243).

Heat the oil in a large heavy ovenproof skillet over medium-high heat. Add the pepper flakes and cook for 10 seconds. Add the garlic and cook until softened but not brown, about 30 seconds. Stir in the scallions and rosemary and cook until the scallions are slightly softened, about 10 seconds. Stir in the bread crumbs and remove from the heat. Season with salt and pepper.

Preheat the oven to 400°F. Heat an ovenproof skillet over medium-high heat until almost smoking. Season the lamb with salt and pepper and place in the skillet meat side down. Cook, turning often, until well browned on the sides and the ends, about 5 minutes. Pour off the fat from the skillet.

Mix the mayonnaise and mustard together and spread over the meat side of the rack. Pat the crumb mixture evenly on top. Transfer to the oven and roast until a meat thermometer reads 130°F for medium-rare, 25 to 30 minutes. Let rest on a cutting board, uncovered, for 10 minutes. Cut down between ribs or between every two ribs and arrange attractively on a warmed platter. (If the crumb mixture falls off, gently pack it around the round part of the meat before serving.) Garnish with sprigs of watercress and serve.

instant-read thermometer

If you don't already have an instant-read thermometer, I strongly recommend you purchase one. They cost only about $20, and they are invaluable for gauging when your food is properly cooked. The best way to insert it in the roast is sideways, not straight down; you will get a more accurate reading. If you want to check the accuracy of your thermometer, put it in a pot of boiling water and see if it gets to 212°F.

wine recommendation:
rosemary-scallion-crusted rack of lamb

Lamb and rosemary cry out for wines from the Mediterranean. Accordingly, I would reach for wines from the south of France, Greece, and Spain.

Sautéed Shoulder Lamb Chops with Skordalia Sauce

For the marinade and lamb:

1/2 cup extra virgin olive oil

1/4 cup dry red wine

1 garlic clove, minced

1 tablespoon minced fresh rosemary

Kosher salt and freshly ground black pepper to taste

Eight 1/2-inch-thick shoulder lamb chops

3 tablespoons olive oil

For the sauce:

2 slices homemade-style white bread, crusts removed

1 small boiling potato, 2 ounces, peeled, boiled until tender, and drained

1/4 cup ground toasted almonds

3 garlic cloves, minced

1 1/2 to 2 tablespoons fresh lemon juice

1 1/2 tablespoons white wine vinegar

1/3 cup extra virgin olive oil

Kosher salt and freshly ground black pepper to taste

SERVES 4

Shoulder lamb chops are a wonderful bargain. They're a lot cheaper than rib or loin chops, and they cook up at least two different ways: You can grill or sauté them quickly to rare or medium (they get tough if you cook them any longer) or braise them slowly in liquid until tender. They're great marinated, as in this recipe, but they're also delicious simply seasoned with salt and pepper and tossed onto the grill.

Skordalia is a garlicky Greek dip thickened with almonds or other nuts and potato or bread. I thinned it down a little and turned it into a sauce. It goes nicely on top of any grilled or roasted meat, such as Blasted Chicken (page 66) or Seared Hanger Steak (page 112). You could even just use it as a dip for bread or raw vegetables, which is how it's usually served in Greek restaurants. Serve with Perfect Hash Browns (page 250) and Mom's Brushed Eggplant (page 228).

To make the marinade, whisk together the oil, wine, garlic, rosemary, and salt and pepper to taste, add the marinade and the chops to a large plastic bag with a resealable closure, and let them marinate, covered and refrigerated, for at least 2 hours and up to 8 hours.

For the sauce, preheat the oven to 350°F. Place the bread on a baking sheet and toast until dried and barely crisp, about 10 minutes. Cool slightly, then soak in cold water for 1 minute. Squeeze out the moisture and place the bread in a food processor. Add the potato, almonds, and garlic. Process until smooth. With the blade in motion, pour in the lemon juice, vinegar, and oil. Pour in up to 6 tablespoons water, as much as needed to thin the sauce to pouring consistency. Season with salt and pepper. You should have about 1 cup.

Remove the chops from the marinade, pat dry, and season with salt and pepper. Heat the oil in a large skillet over high heat until almost smoking. Add the chops and cook them for 2 minutes on each side for medium-rare. Serve each portion topped with some of the room-temperature sauce.

Michael Green says:
it's greek to me!

Beyond the idea of taste, there is something psychologically satisfying about serving a wine from the area where a dish or cuisine originates—think tapas and Spanish wine or Tuscan food and Chianti. It has been said that the story of wine began in Greece, and this lamb dish with skordalia sauce would partner well with a fine Greek red. Look for the wines from the prolific quality producer Boutari—now readily available in most markets. One of my favorites is the Naoussa Reserve.

Stuffed Zucchini Greek Style

6 medium zucchini

1 teaspoon kosher salt

2 tablespoons extra virgin olive oil

1 onion, finely chopped

1 celery rib, finely chopped

1 red bell pepper, finely chopped

4 garlic cloves, minced

1½ pounds lean ground lamb

¼ cup dry white or red wine

One 16-ounce can whole plum tomatoes, with juice, chopped

1 tablespoon tomato paste

1 tablespoon herbes de Provence*

Kosher salt and freshly ground black pepper to taste

1 cup crumbled feta cheese

½ cup pitted Kalamata olives, chopped

1 cup fresh bread crumbs (page 347)

½ cup grated Parmigiano-Reggiano cheese

*An herb mixture from the south of France consisting of basil, fennel, lavender, marjoram, rosemary, sage, summer savory, and thyme. If you can't find it, use a mixture of any of those herbs.

SERVES 6

Throughout the Mediterranean vegetables stuffed with various fillings, including meat, often fill the role of entree. But when I tried to sell my meathead American husband on this recipe at any early stage in its development—the lamb then thoughtlessly camouflaged by bread crumbs—he squinted at it and, without venturing to take a bite, said, "Where's the beef?" To be fair, neither of us is a big fan of zucchini served straight up, so he was justified in wondering if I'd lost my mind.

But when he reluctantly stuck a fork in this dish and discovered all those other wonderful Mediterranean ingredients—the ground lamb, the olives, the tomatoes, and the cheese—he got happy. The kids liked the stuffed zucchini better minus the cheese and olives, so if you are preparing one dinner for kids and grown-ups, you might take those two items out of half the mixture. You're also welcome to substitute ground beef for lamb.

This is a great dish for entertaining, because you could set up the whole thing a day before, to the point of stuffing the zucchini. Cover it up, refrigerate it overnight, and then just top it with the crumb mixture and bake it when your guests arrive. Be sure to give it a few extra minutes in the oven since it will be cold from the fridge. Serve with Stir-Fried Spicy Carrots with Peanuts (page 236) and Celery Root Rémoulade with Wasabi, Ginger, and Sesame (page 240).

Preheat the oven to 375°F. Slice the zucchini in half lengthwise. With the tip of a sharp paring knife, cut a $^1/_4$-inch border around the flesh. Use a small spoon or a melon baller to scoop out the flesh and seeds, leaving a shell about $^1/_4$ inch thick. Reserve the flesh. Arrange the shells cut side up on an oiled baking sheet. Sprinkle with salt and bake until slightly softened, about 15 minutes. Remove from the oven and flip over to let any juices drain out. Cool.

Heat the oil in a large saucepan over medium heat. Add the onion, celery, and red bell pepper. Finely chop the zucchini flesh and add to the pan. Cook, stirring often, until softened, about 5 minutes. Add the garlic and cook for 1 minute longer. Increase the heat to medium-high. Stir in the lamb and cook until there are no longer any signs of pink, 3 to 5 minutes. Add the wine and simmer until most of the liquid has evaporated. Stir in the tomatoes and their juice, the tomato paste, and the herbes de Provence. Season with salt and pepper. Reduce the heat to medium and cook, stirring often, until almost all of the liquid has evaporated, about 30 minutes. Just before serving, add the feta cheese and olives. Fill each shell with $^1/_4$ to $^1/_2$ cup of the filling, depending on the size of the zucchini. (Reserve any leftover filling for another use. It freezes very well.)

Arrange the filled shells on a lightly oiled baking sheet. Mix the bread crumbs with the Parmigiano-Reggiano and sprinkle it over the top of each zucchini. Bake in the 375°F oven until browned on top, about 15 minutes. Serve hot.

Seared Hanger Steak with Mustard Basil Butter

8 tablespoons (1 stick) unsalted butter, softened

1 tablespoon Dijon mustard

2 tablespoons minced fresh basil

1 tablespoon minced shallot

1 garlic clove, minced

1/2 teaspoon kosher salt

One 2-pound hanger steak, trimmed

Additional kosher salt and freshly ground black pepper to taste

2 tablespoons vegetable oil

SERVES 4 TO 6

Known as *onglet* in French, hanger steak is sometimes called *butcher's tenderloin* in English because there is only one of these delicious cuts per animal and butchers tend to hog it for themselves. In other words, it is not something that is regularly stocked in the supermarket meat case, so make friends with your butcher and see if he or she can get it for you. Like skirt steak and flank steak, two other very flavorful but tough cuts of meat, hanger steak should be cooked no more than medium-rare and then sliced thin across the grain. That way it is tender and juicy.

The flavored butter is a great thing to have in the freezer for a quick finishing touch to any steak or to toss with cooked vegetables or roasted potatoes. You can just slice off as much as you want from the log and stick the rest back in the freezer for another day. Serve with Warm Cabbage with Bacon and Gorgonzola (page 244) and Provençal Tomatoes (page 227).

Combine the butter, mustard, basil, shallot, garlic, and 1/2 teaspoon salt in a small bowl. Mix well with a fork. Transfer to a 9-inch square of parchment or wax paper and roll to form a 1-inch-wide log. Chill until firm, at least 3 hours. (The butter will keep for a week in the fridge or for a month in the freezer.)

Pat the steak dry and season with salt and pepper. Heat the oil in a large skillet over high heat and add the steak. Reduce the heat to medium-high and cook for 8 to 10 minutes per side for medium-rare. Let rest for 5 minutes, covered loosely with foil. Thinly slice at an angle and top with slices of the seasoned butter. Or deglaze the skillet with the juices that come out of the steak while it is resting, whisk in some of the butter over low heat, and spoon the sauce over the sliced steak.

wine recommendation:
seared hanger steak with mustard basil butter

Many full-bodied red wines would work here—wines that are rich in flavor, alcohol, and tannin. My first thoughts were of Cabernet Sauvignon and Zinfandel, but the Dijon mustard in the butter swayed me toward the south of France, where the Syrah grape rules. Look to wines from the northern Rhône Valley or Provence such as Crozes-Hermitage or Bandol.

Japanese Beef Fondue

For the broth and vegetables:

7 cups chicken stock, preferably homemade (page 338)

One 3-inch piece fresh ginger, peeled and thickly sliced

4 garlic cloves, peeled and smashed with the side of a knife

8 scallions, white and 1 inch of the green parts, coarsely chopped

2 tablespoons soy sauce

1 tablespoon Asian (toasted) sesame oil*

1 small napa cabbage, cored and thinly shredded

6 carrots, thinly sliced

2 large red bell peppers, cut into 1-inch pieces

1/2 pound shiitake mushrooms, stems discarded, caps sliced

1 1/2 pounds boneless shell or sirloin steak

1/2 pound sugar snap peas, blanched in boiling water for 30 seconds, drained, and shocked in ice water

For the sauce:

1/2 cup sour cream

1 teaspoon prepared wasabi*

1 tablespoon snipped fresh chives

1/2 teaspoon dry mustard

Kosher salt and freshly ground black pepper to taste

*Available at Asian markets and some super-markets or see Mail Order Sources.

SERVES 6

This recipe is based on a Japanese dish called *shabu-shabu*, but I left out the kombu (dried kelp) and the tofu, then poked it here and pinched it there, so I can't pretend that my version is even remotely authentic. But both recipes are built around poached beef. I'd almost always prefer to sauté, roast, or grill my meats, but this recipe is an exception to the rule. Here's why: First you make a flavored broth, then you poach all the vegetables and meats in it, which creates an even richer broth. You end up with a fairly lean but enormously flavorful dish that smacks of comfort food. The wasabi cream is the perfect counterpoint.

It is a fun dish for entertaining too. You can dust off the old fondue pot, put it right in the middle of the table, and let your guests take turns cooking their own dinner. Serve with Rice for the Rice Impaired (page 256) and Celery Root Rémoulade with Wasabi, Ginger, and Sesame (page 240).

To make the broth, combine the stock, ginger, garlic, scallions, soy sauce, and sesame oil in a large saucepan and bring to a boil over high heat. Reduce the heat to medium and simmer, uncovered, for 20 minutes. Strain, discard the solids, and return the stock to the saucepan. Keeping the heat at medium to medium-low, maintain a slow, steady simmer while preparing the dish. Add the cabbage and simmer for 1 minute. Use a slotted spoon to transfer to a large platter. Do the same for the carrots, peppers, and mushrooms, cooking the carrots and peppers for 3 minutes and the mushrooms for 2 minutes. Arrange each in a separate mound on the platter as they are cooked.

Place the beef in the freezer for about 30 minutes or until slightly stiff. This makes it easier to slice thinly. Cut the beef against the grain into paper-thin slices and arrange decoratively on a different platter. Add the peas to the platter.

To make the sauce, combine the sour cream, wasabi, chives, and mustard in a small bowl. Thin with water as desired. Stir well and season with salt and pepper.

Set the fondue pot in the middle of the table, fill it with the broth, and bring to a simmer. It is up to each of your guests, in turn, to finish cooking this dish. Diners choose the vegetables they want and place them in their empty soup bowls. Then they take as much of the raw beef as they want and cook it in the fondue pot for 2 to 3 seconds. Next they add the vegetables selected, which should warm up in about 1 minute. Finally, using a slotted spoon, diners transfer their beef and vegetables from the fondue pot to their bowls and then ladle on some hot broth and a spoonful of the sauce.

wine recommendation: japanese beef fondue

This dish always makes me smile. Casual and tasty, it really brings the table together as a community. Here my choice of wine is driven by the accompanying sauce, endowed with the heat of wasabi and dry mustard and the richness of the sour cream—qualities that would be nicely matched by a fresh and fruity Sauvignon Blanc or Beaujolais. A crisp lager, such as the famed Pilsner Urquell from Czechoslovakia, would also work nicely here.

what is the best way to store ginger?

Whenever I have Asian chefs on, they tell me they use ginger in so many recipes they just leave it in a basket in a cool dark place in the kitchen, much like garlic. I never go through it that fast, so I put it in the vegetable drawer in a loose plastic bag. Some people freeze it, but I think that dissipates its flavor. Some people store it peeled in sherry, which makes for awfully tasty alcohol and slightly compromised ginger. Nina Simond, a Chinese cookbook author, suggested planting it in a pot of sandy soil, letting it take root, and then just cutting off pieces as you need them.

Korean Beef

1/2 cup soy sauce

1/4 cup rice vinegar

3 scallions, white and 2 inches of the green parts, finely chopped, plus additional chopped scallions for garnish

2 tablespoons firmly packed brown sugar

One 2-inch piece fresh ginger, finely chopped

1 1/2 tablespoons Asian (toasted) sesame oil*

2 teaspoons hot red pepper flakes

1 1/2 pounds skirt steak

Vegetable oil for deep-frying the noodles plus 3 tablespoons for sautéing the beef

1 1/2 ounces cellophane noodles (bean threads)*

Kosher salt and freshly ground black pepper to taste

*Available at Asian markets and many supermarkets or see Mail Order Sources.

SERVES 4 TO 6

You probably already have most of the ingredients for this recipe's marinade in the house. If you can just manage to find yourself a skirt steak, you will really be in business. You may have loved skirt steak and not even known it when it was served to you at a restaurant and called *fajitas*. Now it's becoming much more readily available to the home cook.

Skirt steak is long and thin and has great beef flavor. It is perfect for grilling or a quick sear in the pan. Tough but flavorful (like flank steak and hanger steak), skirt steak should never be cooked beyond medium-rare. Let it rest for a few minutes before you carve it, then slice it very thin and at an angle. If you don't find skirt steak at your supermarket, ask the butcher to get it for you. (You'll be surprised at how much power you can wield as a consumer.)

Cellophane noodles, also called *bean thread noodles,* are made from the starch of mung beans. When they are soaked, they become soft, much like cooked pasta, and when quickly fried, as they are here, they puff up into crispy white strands. They absorb the flavors of the foods they are served with. Here they provide a dramatic-looking backdrop to the beef. If you can't find them, serve the beef on plain rice (page 256) or on the boiled noodles of your choice. Serve with Chinese Fried Eggplant with Pine Nuts (page 230).

Combine the soy sauce, vinegar, scallions, sugar, ginger, sesame oil, and pepper flakes in a bowl. Whisk well to blend. Reserve 1/4 cup and set aside. Pour the rest into a plastic bag with a resealable closure. Add the skirt steak and seal. Marinate in the refrigerator, turning the bag over often, for at least 4 hours or overnight.

Fill a large deep saucepan to a depth of about 2 inches with vegetable oil. Heat over medium-high heat until a deep-fat thermometer reads 375°F. (Alternatively, use an electric deep-fat fryer.) Pull apart the clusters of noodles into clumps of about 10 strands each. Working in batches, fry the noodles, turning once, until they puff up and turn white, about 10 seconds. Use a slotted spoon or a spider (a slotted spoon designed like a spider's web used for deep-frying) to transfer to paper towels to drain.

Remove the skirt steak from the marinade and pat dry with paper towels. (The drier the beef, the better it will sear.) Working in batches, heat half the oil in a large skillet over high heat until almost smoking. Season the meat with salt and pepper. Place in the skillet and reduce the heat to medium-high. Cook until seared on the outside and rare to medium-rare on the inside, 2 to 3 minutes per side. Transfer to a platter, cover loosely with foil, and let rest for 5 minutes. Repeat with the remaining oil and skirt steak. Cut into very thin slices, holding the knife at an angle and cutting against the grain. Toss with the reserved $^1/_4$ cup sauce in a large bowl until well coated.

Crumble the fried noodles and mound on individual serving plates. Top with equal portions of the beef and garnish with chopped scallions.

wine recommendation:
korean beef

Asian dishes often strike a wonderful balance of salty, sweet, and spicy. This dish is a great example, with its soy sauce, brown sugar, rice wine vinegar, and hot pepper flakes. A light crisp ale is a logical candidate here, though wine could also work. Look for wines with lower alcohol, fresh acidity, and a touch of residual sugar. I like Mosel Riesling and Loire Valley Vouvray.

Red-Wine-Braised Beef Brisket with Horseradish Sauce and Aunt Rifka's Flying Disks

For the braised brisket:

1 large head garlic, separated into cloves

1 cup all-purpose flour

2 teaspoons kosher salt

1/2 teaspoon freshly ground black pepper

One 4- to 5-pound beef brisket

2 tablespoons olive oil

2 large onions, thinly sliced

3 cups dry red wine

1/4 cup tomato paste

2 bay leaves, preferably Turkish

1 teaspoon dried thyme

1 quart chicken stock, preferably homemade (page 338)

For the horseradish sauce:

1/2 cup finely grated fresh or drained prepared horseradish

1 tablespoon white wine vinegar

1 cup sour cream

1 tablespoon snipped fresh chives

1 tablespoon fresh lemon juice

Kosher salt and freshly ground black pepper to taste

For the flying disks:

1/4 cup chicken stock, preferably homemade (page 338)

4 large eggs, beaten

2 tablespoons unsalted butter, melted

1 teaspoon kosher salt

1 cup matzo meal

SERVES 8

My husband Bill has been telling me about his aunt Rifka and her asbestos hands for as long as we've known each other. He claims there was no pot so hot she couldn't pick it up barehanded. (This amazing ability seems just slightly less amazing to me since I went to cooking school and developed some heat resistance of my own.) He also used to brag about his aunt's delicious flying disks. I always wondered just what the heck they were and decided to find out when I started on this book.

Rifka Silverberg Mellen was actually Bill's great-aunt—his mother's mother's older sister. She and Uncle Peter lived upstairs from Esther and her folks in Sheepshead Bay in Brooklyn, where the whole family flourished after fleeing Odessa in the first decade of the twentieth century. It turns out that Rifka's flying disks are nothing more exotic than matzo balls formed into silver-dollar-sized disks and served in brisket gravy instead of chicken soup. Contrary to the image called up by their Space Age sobriquet, flying disks are not exactly lighter than air. In truth, they are dense and heavy. It's more accurate (if considerably less glamorous) to call them *sinkers,* which is what Bill's aunt Yetta called hers. Whatever. They're scrumptious. Serve with Baked Acorn Squash with Mustard and Honey (page 246) and Southern Braised Mustard Greens with Ham (page 242).

To make the brisket, preheat the oven to 325°F. Fill a small saucepan with water and bring to a boil over high heat. Add the garlic, bring back to a boil, and cook rapidly until slightly softened, about 1 minute. Use a slotted spoon to transfer the garlic to a bowl of ice water. Peel when cool enough to handle.

Combine the flour, salt, and pepper in a large shallow dish or large platter. Add the brisket and turn to coat on all sides. Shake off the excess. Heat the oil in a large covered casserole or Dutch oven over medium-high heat until almost smoking. Add the brisket and cook, turning often, until well browned, about 6 to 8 minutes per side. Transfer to a plate or platter and pour off all but 2 tablespoons of the fat. Stir in the onions and the peeled garlic. Reduce the heat to medium and cook, stirring often, until golden, about 10 minutes. Pour in the wine and stir to pick up any browned bits on the bottom of the casserole. Stir in the tomato paste and add the bay leaves and thyme. Increase the heat to high and bring to a boil. Cook rapidly, stirring often, until almost all the liquid has evaporated. Pour in the stock and bring back to a boil. Reduce the heat to medium and add the brisket. Cover tightly with a piece of foil, then cover the pot with the lid. Transfer to the lower third of the oven and cook until a fork comes out easily when pierced, 3 to 4 hours.

Meanwhile, make the horseradish sauce. Mix the horseradish, vinegar, sour cream, chives, and lemon juice in a small bowl. Stir well to blend and season with salt and pepper. You should have about 1 cup. Keep refrigerated until ready to serve.

Bill's Uncle Pete and Aunt Rifka on their 50th anniversary

To make the disks, whisk the stock, eggs, and butter together in a small bowl. Stir in the salt and matzo meal to form a soft dough. Cover with plastic wrap and refrigerate until well chilled, about 1 hour. Bring a large pot of salted water to a boil over high heat. Working with 1 tablespoon of the dough at a time, use wet hands to form the dough into disks about 1¹/₂ inches wide and ¹/₂ inch thick. You should have about 18 disks. Drop them into the boiling water and reduce the heat to medium-low. Cover and simmer until the disks are puffy and cooked through, 30 to 35 minutes.

Transfer the brisket from the casserole to a cutting surface and cover loosely with foil. Let rest for 15 minutes. Gently skim the surface of the liquid in the casserole with a spoon to remove as much fat as possible. Remove and discard the bay leaves. Add the disks to the cooking liquid and cook on top of the stove over medium heat, covered, until they've turned dark and have absorbed some of the sauce, about 10 minutes.

Thinly slice the brisket on an angle, cutting against the grain. Arrange the slices on a warmed serving platter or plate and spoon on some of the horseradish cream. Place the disks on the side and ladle on the pan gravy. Serve warm.

wine recommendation:
red-wine-braised beef brisket with horseradish sauce and aunt rifka's flying disks

Aunt Rifka might well have appreciated a white wine with a touch of fruitiness such a Chenin Blanc or a Riesling, though this hearty meat dish would be great with a full-bodied red wine such as Cabernet Sauvignon or Merlot.

a brisket primer

You can buy beef brisket three ways:
1. Whole with deckle (the deckle is a thin layer of meat with a lot of connective tissue and fat that lies on the underside of the brisket; it can be removed easily), weighing in at 8 to 10 pounds. If you remove the deckle, the remaining piece of brisket weighs 7 to 8 pounds.
2. Flat cut, also known as the *first cut* or *thin cut.* This is the leanest of the possibilities and the most popular, and it usually weighs around 4 pounds.
3. Point cut, cheaper and fattier than the flat cut, also 4 to 5 pounds.

Roast Tenderloin of Beef
with Cornichon Tarragon Sauce

When people phone the show and ask for a great, easy-to-prepare entree for a crowd, I always recommend roasting tenderloin of beef. It's expensive, but you get 100 percent yield out of the cut, it slices up easily and elegantly, and it's delicious served hot or at room temperature.

You can even serve it chilled, with horseradish sauce, say, at a backyard party. Whip up the horseradish sauce from scratch by mixing together sour cream, lemon juice, prepared or freshly grated horseradish (soak the freshly grated stuff in a little white wine vinegar first), and salt and pepper to taste.

If you're serving your roast hot, you can still season and sear it about an hour before your guests arrive, then put it in the oven about 50 minutes before you want to eat it.

This recipe's sauce, made in the pan in which the tenderloin was roasted, takes advantage of the roast's succulent drippings. Serve with Mashed Potatoes (page 247) or Mashed Potato Cakes (page 249) and Creamed Spinach with Crispy Shallots (page 234).

Preheat the oven to 450°F and season the tenderloin with salt and pepper. Heat the oil in a large ovenproof skillet over medium-high heat until almost smoking. Add the roast and cook, turning often, until browned on all sides, 5 to 7 minutes. Transfer the skillet to the oven and roast for 25 to 30 minutes or until a meat thermometer inserted into the center registers 130°F for medium rare. Transfer the roast to a warmed platter and cover loosely with foil.

Place the roasting skillet on top of the stove, being careful not to

One 2-pound beef tenderloin roast, trimmed and tied

Kosher salt and freshly ground black pepper to taste

2 tablespoons vegetable oil

1 cup dry white wine

2 medium shallots, minced

2 teaspoons dried tarragon

8 cornichons (French pickles) or dill gherkins, julienned

1 tablespoon heavy cream

3 tablespoons unsalted butter, softened

2 tablespoons Dijon mustard

2 teaspoons minced fresh tarragon

SERVES 4

touch the hot handle with bare hands. Add the wine, shallots, and dried tarragon and bring to a boil over high heat. Cook rapidly, stirring to pick up any browned bits in the bottom of the skillet, until reduced to $^1/_4$ cup. Add the cornichons, cream, and any meat juices that have accumulated on the platter. Simmer for 3 minutes longer. Reduce the heat to low and whisk in the butter, mustard, fresh tarragon, and salt and pepper to taste. Cut the beef crosswise into $^1/_2$-inch-thick slices. Serve on warmed plates and spoon equal amounts of the sauce over each portion.

wine recommendation:
roast tenderloin of beef with cornichon tarragon sauce

A special-occasion dish calls for a special-occasion wine. Match your succulent roast tenderloin with the best medium/full-bodied red in the house. Polish it off with some cheese.

Mini Meat Loaves

I was making individual free-form meat loaves on a cook-along one night when a viewer called in and said she worked from a similar recipe but always mixed up a double batch and then froze half of it in muffin tins. On evenings when there was nothing else in the fridge, she'd just pop some of these muffin meat loaves into the oven and—*voilà*—there was dinner. Admittedly, meat loaf is not the most complicated dish on this earth, but it is more work than plain old hamburgers, and everyone does love it. So why not stockpile some for dinner number two a few weeks or months down the road?

I tested these guys by freezing them both precooked and raw, and I slightly preferred the way the precooked ones turned out. If you are baking meat loaves that were precooked and frozen, they will take about 45 minutes to heat through. If you are baking meat loaves that you froze raw, put them right in the oven from the freezer and give them about 50 minutes or until cooked through.

Why "mini" meat loaves? I just think everyone likes his or her own little individual dish—and when they are this small, they don't take as long to cook as a full-sized loaf. Serve with Parsnip Puree (page 237) and Quick Sautéed Shredded Brussels Sprouts with Pancetta and Balsamic Vinegar (page 243).

For the glaze:
1 cup ketchup
1/4 cup packed light brown sugar
1 1/2 tablespoons cider vinegar

For the mini meat loaves:
1 tablespoon olive oil
2 celery ribs, finely chopped (1/2 cup)
1 medium onion, finely chopped (1/2 cup)
3 garlic cloves, minced
1 cup sour cream
1 cup fresh bread crumbs (page 347)
1 large egg, beaten
1/4 cup whole milk
1/4 cup chopped parsley
2 tablespoons Dijon mustard
2 1/2 teaspoons kosher salt
1 1/2 teaspoons dried thyme
1 teaspoon freshly ground black pepper
1 pound ground chuck
1/2 pound ground pork
1/2 pound ground veal or turkey

MAKES 12 SMALL LOAVES, SERVING 6

To make the glaze, combine ketchup, brown sugar, and vinegar. Set aside.

For the meat loaves, preheat the oven to 350°F. Oil a foil-lined rimmed baking sheet.

Heat the oil in a medium skillet over medium heat. Add the celery, onion, and garlic and cook, stirring until the vegetables have softened, about 5 minutes. Transfer to a large bowl, stir in $1/4$ cup of the glaze and let cool.

Add the sour cream, bread crumbs, egg, milk, parsley, mustard, salt, thyme, and pepper and stir until combined. Add the chuck, pork, and veal and combine well. (To taste for seasoning, fry a pinch of the meat mixture in a small skillet over medium-high heat until browned and cooked through, about 5 minutes. Season with additional salt and pepper if needed.)

Scoop mixture onto baking sheet using $1/2$ cup measure. Shape into ovals.

Divide the remaining glaze over the tops of the loaves. Bake 35 to 40 minutes. The internal temperature should be 155°F when tested with a quick-read thermometer. Serve at once, while warm.

The meat loaves can be prepared in advance and kept frozen until just before baking. Wrap the loaves with plastic wrap, then slip into resealable plastic bags. Increase the cooking time by about 10 minutes for frozen meat loaves.

Mom's Meatball Stroganoff

This was one of my favorite dishes as a kid, a less expensive version of the classic dish created and named for a Count Stroganov in late-19th-century Russia. Very popular in America during the sixties and seventies, the original recipe for Beef Stroganoff called for thin slices of pricey beef filet. Although my mom used meatballs instead, it seemed luxurious to me. Eventually my mom (and my aunt Jean and my grandmother) stopped making it, maybe because it finally seemed too old-fashioned. By the time I wanted to demonstrate it on my show, Beef Stroganoff was so antique that none of my relatives could come up with a recipe—and all I remembered of it were bouillon cubes, tomato paste, and cultivated mushrooms.

When I re-created the recipe, I lost the bouillon cubes (too chemical-tasting to me now) and the tomato paste but kept the cultivated mushrooms—although you would get a more elegant dish if you used such flavorful mushrooms as shiitakes or chanterelles. The ground beef of choice is chuck because it has the most flavor (and the most fat, too, alas). If you want to make a lighter version of this dish, you can substitute ground sirloin or ground round and low-fat sour cream. Serve with Herbed Spaetzle (page 259) or buttered noodles and Stir-Fried Spicy Carrots with Peanuts (page 236).

Combine the chuck, half of the chopped onion, the garlic, salt, pepper, bread crumbs, egg yolks, and $^1/_2$ cup of water in a large bowl. Mix well and form meatballs that measure about 1 inch in diameter.

1 pound ground chuck

1 medium onion, finely chopped

2 garlic cloves, minced

1 teaspoon kosher salt

1 teaspoon freshly ground black pepper

$^1/_2$ cup fresh bread crumbs (page 347)

2 large egg yolks

2 tablespoons extra virgin olive oil

$^1/_2$ pound cultivated white mushrooms, thinly sliced

$^1/_2$ cup dry sherry

2 cups chicken stock, preferably homemade (page 338)

2 tablespoons unsalted butter, softened

2 tablespoons all-purpose flour

2 tablespoons chopped fresh dill

$^1/_2$ cup sour cream

Additional kosher salt and freshly ground black pepper to taste

SERVES 4 TO 6

Heat the oil in a large nonstick skillet over medium-high heat. Add the meatballs and cook, shaking and turning, until well browned, about 5 minutes. Don't crowd the pan; work in batches if necessary. Transfer to paper towels to drain.

Pour off any excess fat from the skillet, leaving 3 tablespoons in the pan and add the remaining onion. Cook, stirring often, until softened, about 5 minutes. Add the mushrooms and cook, stirring, until the liquid they give off has evaporated, 7 to 10 minutes. Pour in the sherry, increase the heat to high, and boil until almost all the liquid they give off has evaporated. Pour in the stock and bring to a boil.

Rub the butter with the flour in a small bowl until it forms a smooth paste. Pinch off pea-size pieces and add little by little to the boiling sauce, whisking constantly for 3 minutes. Add the meatballs, stir in the dill and sour cream, season with salt and pepper, and cook over low heat until the meatballs are just heated through. Serve hot.

making meatballs

When I had the father/son team from the enormously popular Rao's restaurant in New York City (an old Italian restaurant in East Harlem, where it is absolutely impossible to get a reservation—I'm still hoping I might get one someday) on "Cooking Live," I learned two things about mixing ground meat for meatballs. First, mix the raw ingredients as little as possible. Overmixing pushes the air out and leaves you with a meatbrick instead of a meatball. Second, add water to the mixture; it lightens the texture of the meatball.

My mom and me, 1982

four quick meat sautés

This suite of recipes is the fraternal twin of the Four Quick Chicken Recipes on page 75. As before, the organizing principle is what Jacques Pépin has dubbed *la technique*—once you have mastered the technique, you can make up a million new recipes of your own using whatever you happen to have in the fridge that night.

You start by pounding the meat to make sure it is nice and thin—no more than $1/4$ inch thick—which allows it to cook quickly. Then coat it lightly with seasoned flour. (I like to coat all "white" meat in flour before sautéing because it keeps the meat from drying out and thickens the sauce. I think of veal and pork loin or tenderloin as white meats because they are so lean.) After browning the meat in the pan, you remove it, add liquid, and boil to reduce the liquid a little bit. The meat goes back into the pan to reheat it and to thicken the sauce. When planning how much gravy or sauce to produce, I always start with $1/4$ to $1/3$ cup per person. If the sauce becomes too reduced, just add water.

coating scaloppine

Anytime I am going to coat a piece of poultry, meat, or seafood with flour, I put a piece of parchment paper in a pie plate and then mound my flour on top of the parchment. When I add my scaloppine or fish fillet to the pie plate, it is so much neater to pick up the sides of the parchment and toss the scaloppine back and forth in the flour than it is to lift it up with your hands and turn it over. If you are flouring smaller items like scallops or zucchini sticks, put them in a strainer after you have floured them and shake the strainer to get rid of the excess flour.

Pork Cutlets with Spanish Olives

1 pound pork scaloppine cut from the leg or 4 thin boneless chops

¹/₄ cup all-purpose flour

³/₄ teaspoon kosher salt

¹/₄ teaspoon freshly ground black pepper

2 tablespoons extra virgin olive oil

¹/₄ cup dry sherry

1 cup chicken stock, preferably homemade brown chicken stock (page 339)

¹/₃ cup coarsely chopped pimiento-stuffed Spanish green olives

1 tablespoon unsalted butter

Additional kosher salt and freshly ground black pepper to taste

SERVES 4

Serve with Magda's Sofrito Rice (page 258) and Sautéed Shredded Zucchini with Lemon and Thyme (page 226).

Sprinkle a small amount of water on a large sheet of plastic wrap. Place half of the pork slices on top of the plastic and sprinkle again with water. Cover with another sheet of plastic wrap and pound with a rolling pin or meat pounder until about ¹/₄ inch thick. Repeat with the remaining pork.

Combine the flour, salt, and pepper in a shallow pie plate. Heat the oil in a large skillet over medium-high heat until almost smoking. Add the cutlets to the flour mixture and turn to coat on all sides. Shake off the excess and add to the skillet. Working in batches if necessary, cook until no longer pink, about 1 minute per side. Transfer to a plate or platter and cover loosely with foil.

Add the sherry to the skillet and simmer, stirring to pick up any browned bits on the bottom, until almost evaporated. Add the chicken stock and olives. Simmer for 3 minutes longer. Return the pork to the skillet with any juices that have accumulated on the platter and simmer, turning often, until warmed through and the sauce is thickened, 1 to 2 minutes. Transfer to warmed serving plates. Stir the butter into the sauce and season with salt and pepper to taste. Spoon the sauce over the cutlets and serve at once.

Hungarian Pork Cutlets

Serve with Herbed Spaetzle (page 259) and Borscht Beets (page 220).

Sprinkle a small amount of water on a large sheet of plastic wrap. Place half of the pork slices on top of the plastic and sprinkle again with water. Cover with another sheet of plastic wrap and pound with a rolling pin or meat pounder until about $^1/_4$ inch thick. Repeat with the remaining pork.

Mix the flour with the salt and pepper in a shallow pie plate. Heat the oil in a large skillet over medium-high heat until almost smoking. Place the cutlets in the flour mixture and turn to coat on all sides. Shake off the excess flour and add to the skillet. Working in batches if necessary, sauté until golden, about 1 minute per side. Transfer to a plate or platter and cover loosely with foil.

Add the shallot, paprika, and caraway seeds to the pan. Sauté for 1 minute, then add the wine. Simmer, stirring to pick up any browned bits on the bottom, until almost dry. Add the chicken stock and simmer for 3 minutes. Return the pork to the skillet and simmer, turning often, until warmed through and the sauce is thickened, about 1 minute. Transfer to warmed serving plates. Stir the sour cream into the pan juices and season with salt and pepper. Spoon over the pork and serve at once.

1 pound pork scaloppine cut from the leg or 4 thin boneless chops

$^1/_4$ cup all-purpose flour

$^3/_4$ teaspoon kosher salt

$^1/_4$ teaspoon freshly ground black pepper

2 tablespoons vegetable oil

1 large shallot, minced

1$^1/_2$ tablespoons sweet or hot paprika

1 tablespoon caraway seeds

$^1/_4$ cup dry white wine

1 cup chicken stock, preferably homemade (page 338)

$^1/_4$ cup sour cream

Additional kosher salt and freshly ground black pepper to taste

SERVES 4

scaloppine from the leg

When I was first envisioning quick meat sautés, I thought pork loin and tenderloin, always available at the supermarket, would be the best cuts—until I discovered true tender, moist, and affordable pork scaloppine at New York's Jefferson Market, where I buy most of my meat. It turns out the scaloppine came from the leg, just like veal scaloppine. So my new mission is to get consumers to go into their supermarkets and demand pork scaloppine cut from the leg. Believe me, it is much more tender than the loin and much more affordable. If all you can get is the loin, just make sure you don't overcook it; it will be dry.

Veal Francese

1 pound veal scaloppine

6 large eggs, lightly beaten

3 tablespoons freshly grated
Parmigiano-Reggiano

1 cup all-purpose flour

2 teaspoons kosher salt

1 teaspoon freshly ground black
pepper

2 to 3 tablespoons extra virgin
olive oil as needed

Vegetable oil for frying the herbs

1/2 cup mixed fresh parsley
leaves, rosemary leaves, and
small thyme sprigs

Additional kosher salt to taste

3 tablespoons unsalted butter,
softened

1 to 2 tablespoons fresh lemon
juice or to taste

2 tablespoons finely chopped
fresh parsley

Additional freshly ground black
pepper to taste

SERVES 4

About six months after I started doing "Cooking Live," a viewer called in to ask what exactly veal francese was. I shot from the hip—something I don't like to do—and said I *thought* it was veal coated in an eggy batter and then sautéed. The next day I pored through all my favorite Italian cookbooks and found no mention of veal francese. Stumped, I finally reasoned that if Italians from Italy didn't know anything about it, veal francese was probably an Italian-American invention.

Sure enough, when I stumbled across a recipe for it several years later, it was in Gerard Renny's *The Men of the Pacific Street Social Club Cook Italian,* a fun cookbook about the now-vanished Italian community from the Brooklyn neighborhood called East New York. The recipe came from Gerard's cousin's mom, who used to make it when she got tired of the traditional way of frying veal cutlets. It turned out I hadn't steered my caller very far wrong. Veal francese is pretty much what I'd guessed it to be, with the addition of butter and lemon. It is a quick and tasty dish for any night of the week. I have adapted Gerard's recipe slightly and added fried herbs as an optional (but really tasty!) garnish. Serve with Perfect Hash Browns (page 250) and Sautéed Spinach with Garlic Chips (page 232).

Sprinkle a small amount of water on a large sheet of plastic wrap. Place half of the veal slices on top of the plastic and sprinkle again with water. Cover with another sheet of plastic wrap and pound with a rolling pin or meat pounder until about $^1/_4$ inch thick. Repeat with the remaining veal.

Beat the eggs with the cheese in a large bowl to blend. Mix the flour with the salt and pepper in a shallow pie plate. Place the veal in the flour and turn to coat on all sides. Dip into the egg mixture and lift to let the excess drip off. Return to the flour and turn again to coat on all sides.

Heat 2 tablespoons of the olive oil in a large skillet over medium heat. Working in batches, dip the veal one last time into the egg mixture and add to the hot skillet. Cook until golden brown, 2 to 3 minutes per side. Transfer to a large platter, cover loosely with foil, and continue with the remaining scaloppine. Add the remaining tablespoon of oil if needed.

Heat about 2 inches vegetable oil in a small deep saucepan over medium-high heat until a deep-fat thermometer registers 350°F. Working in batches, add the herbs, patted very dry, a small handful at a time and fry until crisp, about 10 seconds. They will bubble up furiously. Drain on paper towels and sprinkle with salt.

Add the butter, lemon juice, and chopped parsley to the skillet and heat until bubbling. Season with salt and pepper. Spoon a small amount of the sauce over each piece of veal, top with the fried herbs, and serve at once.

Veal Scaloppine with Pesto

1 pound veal scaloppine

¹/₄ cup all-purpose flour

³/₄ teaspoon salt

¹/₄ teaspoon freshly ground
   black pepper

2 to 3 tablespoons extra virgin
   olive oil as needed

¹/₃ cup dry white wine

³/₄ cup chicken stock, preferably
   homemade brown chicken
   stock (page 339)

¹/₄ cup homemade or store-
   bought pesto

Additional kosher salt and freshly
   ground black pepper to taste

Fresh basil sprigs and lemon
   slices for garnish

SERVES 4

Serve with Mom's Brushed Eggplant (page 228) and buttered noodles.

Sprinkle a small amount of water on a large sheet of plastic wrap.
Place half of the veal slices on top of the plastic and sprinkle again
with water. Cover with another sheet of plastic wrap and pound with a
rolling pin or meat pounder until about ¹/₄ inch thick. Repeat with the
remaining veal.

Mix the flour with the salt and pepper in a shallow pie plate. Heat
2 tablespoons of the oil in a large skillet over medium-high heat until
almost smoking. Place the scaloppine in the flour mixture and turn to
coat on all sides. Shake off the excess flour and add to the skillet.
Working in batches, if necessary, cook until lightly browned, about
1 minute per side. Add the remaining tablespoon of oil as needed.
Transfer to a plate or platter and cover loosely with foil.

Add the wine to the skillet and increase the heat to high. Cook,
stirring to pick up any brown bits on the bottom, until reduced to
2 tablespoons. Stir in the stock and the pesto. Reduce the heat to
medium-high and simmer for 3 minutes. Return the scaloppine to the
skillet and cook, turning often, until the cutlets are warmed through
and the sauce is slightly thickened, about 2 minutes. Transfer the
scaloppine to warmed plates. Season the sauce with salt and pepper.
Spoon a small amount of the sauce over the scaloppine and garnish
with the basil and lemon.

Fish and Shellfish

Grilled Swordfish with Greek Salad Salsa

2 garlic cloves, minced

2 tablespoons fresh lemon juice

1/2 cup extra virgin olive oil

2 teaspoons minced fresh oregano or marjoram

Four 7-ounce swordfish steaks, about 1 inch thick

1 pound cherry tomatoes, finely chopped

1 teaspoon kosher salt

1/2 small red onion, diced

One 4-inch-long piece English cucumber, diced

1/2 cup finely chopped, pitted Kalamata olives

4 radishes, diced

1/2 cup crumbled feta cheese

1 tablespoon drained bottled capers

1 tablespoon red wine vinegar

Additional kosher salt and freshly ground black pepper to taste

2 tablespoons shredded fresh basil leaves

SERVES 4

When I was 15, my mom took my sister and me to Greece for spring break. Most of the food there was new to me. In fact—big surprise—even the Greek salads in Greece were different from the Greek salads in New York. Theirs consisted of wonderfully ripe tomatoes, cucumbers, feta cheese, and Greek olives. (But no lettuce!)

This dish's Greek Salad Salsa has all of these, as well as other typical Greek ingredients such as radishes and red onion. You have to toss them all together at the last minute so that the salad doesn't get watery, but you can prepare all the parts beforehand and then just finish it when you are ready.

As a rule, I do not like cheese with fish, but this recipe is an exception. The feta cheese in the salsa is sharp and salty, a perfect complement to the bland fish.

This salsa, by the way, would go well with any fish or grilled meat or chicken. You could also turn it into hors d'oeuvres by putting it on top of grilled or toasted slices of country bread rubbed with a cut clove of raw garlic and sprinkled with olive oil. Serve with Roasted Lemon Potatoes (page 252) and Mexican-Style Street Corn (page 222).

Combine the garlic, lemon juice, 6 tablespoons of the olive oil, and the oregano in a large plastic bag with a resealable closure. Add the swordfish and marinate in the refrigerator, turning the bag over once or twice, for 1 to 2 hours.

Toss the tomatoes with the salt and drain in a colander for 15 minutes. Pat dry on paper towels. Soak the red onion in ice water for 20 minutes. Drain and pat dry. Combine the tomatoes, onion, cucumber, olives, radishes, feta, capers, vinegar, and the remaining 2 tablespoons olive oil in a large bowl. Toss well and season with salt and pepper. You should have about 3 cups.

Prepare a charcoal fire and allow the coals to burn down to a gray ash. Lightly oil the grill and set about 4 inches from the coals. (Alternatively, preheat a large well-oiled grill pan or preheat the broiler and set a broiling pan about 4 inches from the heat.) Remove the swordfish from the marinade and pat dry with paper towels. Season on both sides with salt and pepper. Grill or broil until lightly browned and slightly firm to the touch, 4 to 5 minutes per side. Serve on warmed plates topped with a spoonful of the salsa. Garnish each plate with a pinch of the shredded basil. Serve the remaining salsa on the side.

working with raw onions

Whenever I am adding raw onions to a recipe, I soak them first in a bath of ice and cold water for about 20 minutes. Not only does it crisp them up, but it also takes away that nasty onion bite and resulting bad breath that stays with you for hours after eating them. Don't forget to pat them dry before you add them to the recipe.

Blackened Fish

1¹/₂ pounds thin white fish fillets, such as lemon or gray sole

2 cups whole milk

³/₄ cup all-purpose flour

3 tablespoons Creole Spice Mix (page 348) or your favorite store-bought spice blend

1 teaspoon kosher salt

6 tablespoons vegetable oil

Lemon wedges for garnish

SERVES 4

It was Paul Prudhomme, at his K Paul's Restaurant in New Orleans during the eighties, who introduced spiced and "blackened" redfish. Immediately hailed as a classic, it was copied by many restaurants and loved by all. I liked it enough to start making my own version at home, where it quickly entered our regular lineup as a quick and easy weeknight entree for the husband and me.

There are a couple of simple tricks to this recipe. First, make sure you buy the thinnest whitefish fillets possible, which will give you the most satisfying ratio of crunchy crust to moist flesh. Second, make sure the pan is really hot—just beginning to smoke—before you start to cook. (I grab any old heavy-gauge skillet, but if you have cast iron, all the better. The virtue of cast iron—besides its relatively low price—is that once it gets hot it stays hot, searing your fish beautifully.)

These days you can buy Paul's spice mix at specialty food shops nationwide, but this recipe features a spice mix of my own invention. (Paul's wasn't on the market when I first started making this dish.) By the way, I never put sauce on this fish. A squeeze of lemon finishes it off like a dream. Serve with Couscous Tabbouleh (page 255) and your favorite coleslaw.

Place the fish in a large shallow bowl and pour the milk over it. Cover and chill for 30 minutes.

Preheat the oven to 200°F. Mix the flour, spice mix, and salt in a pie plate lined with a piece of parchment paper. Working in batches, remove the fillets from the milk and drain off the excess. Transfer to the flour mixture and, pulling up the sides of the parchment, turn to coat on both sides. Flour only as many fillets as will fit in a large skillet at one time.

Heat 2 tablespoons of the oil in a large skillet over high heat until just smoking. Add the fillets and cook until golden brown, about 2 minutes per side. Transfer to a heatproof plate and keep in the oven while you cook the remaining fillets. Repeat the procedure with the remaining fillets, flour mix, and oil. Serve with lemon wedges.

handling fish with your hands

My boss at *Gourmet* (she hates it when I call her my boss) is Jane Grenier. She grew up in Bethesda, Maryland, but visited her grandmother Meme (pronounced "Mimi") every August in Corpus Christi, Texas. They spent an awful lot of time fishing, crabbing, and eating things from the sea, and their hands would acquire a distinctly fishy aroma, which was sort of hard to lose. Meme, however, had the perfect solution: rub your hands with toothpaste and then rinse them off. It works.

Baked Striped Bass with Sherry Vinaigrette, Olives, and Capers

¹/₄ cup sherry vinegar

2 teaspoons anchovy paste or 2 anchovy fillets, minced

Kosher salt and freshly ground black pepper to taste

¹/₂ cup extra virgin olive oil

³/₄ cup pitted Mediterranean black olives, preferably Kalamata, finely chopped

1 tablespoon drained bottled capers, finely chopped

1 small shallot, minced

1 garlic clove, minced

1 teaspoon dried oregano

6 skinless striped bass fillets, about 6 ounces each

SERVES 6

Back in the early eighties a pioneering new fish restaurant called Le Bernardin opened up in New York as the American outpost of a French original. Under the direction of Chef Gilbert Le Coze, Le Bernardin's revolutionary stroke was to reduce significantly the butter and cream required in classical French fish cookery in favor of the flavors of the fish itself. The sauces were not heavy, and the fish was not cooked through—it was left translucent in the center—and the result was a revelation.

One of my favorite dishes from Le Bernardin is its signature halibut in warm emulsified sherry vinaigrette. My recipe is a simpler Italian-influenced offshoot made with striped bass, sprinkled with flavorings and oil and vinegar, and baked. It is a great dish for entertaining. Everything can be prepped ahead of time, and then all you have to do is throw the fish into the oven 25 minutes before dinner.

How can you tell when the fish is done? Like meat, fish cooks from the outside in. When it is completely cooked through, you can stick a knife through the thickest part of the fish with no resistance. If you want to eat it rare, as they do in France, you can cook it until there is just a little resistance at the center of the fish. Whatever you do, do not cook your fish until it flakes, even though that's what many of the old cookbooks instruct you to do. By the time it's flaky, your poor fish is also dry and tasteless. Serve with Mom's Brushed Eggplant (page 228) and Mashed Potatoes (page 247) or Mashed Potato Cakes (page 249).

Preheat the oven to 400°F.

Combine the vinegar and anchovy paste in a small bowl and add salt and pepper to taste. Whisk until well blended. Whisk in the olive oil. Stir in the olives, capers, shallot, garlic, and oregano.

Arrange the fillets skinned sides down in baking dish large enough to hold the fish fillets in one flat layer. Season well with salt and pepper. Spoon a small amount of the vinegar and oil mixture over each fillet and drizzle the rest around the bottom of the dish. Cover with foil, and bake until opaque throughout and firm to the touch, 25 to 30 minutes. Transfer to warm serving plates and spoon on any juices in the bottom of the baking dish. Serve warm.

wine recommendation:
baked striped bass with sherry vinaigrette, olives, and capers

The Mediterranean ingredients in this dish—olives, capers, and anchovies—suggest a natural matchup with Mediterranean wines. And fish usually calls for white wine. But this particular dish is quite full flavored, which opens up our options. Consider a flavorful smooth red from Spain's Rioja or Navarra region.

what is the best way to pit an olive?

You can go out and buy one of those cool little olive pitters, which doubles as a cool little cherry pitter. It's a useful tool if you want the olive or cherry to stay whole after its pit has been extracted. But if you just need to get the darn pit out and you don't care what the olive or cherry looks like afterward, simply put your victim on a cutting board and lay your knife flat on top of it with the blunt edge facing you. Give your knife a hard whack down with your hand, and if the pit doesn't come flying out, it will slip out easily with just a little assistance from you. This is a very satisfying exercise.

Crisp Sautéed Whole Fish Bahamian Style

Three 1-pound whole fish such as salmon trout, small snapper, or whiting, gutted and scaled

4 Scotch bonnet or habanero chiles, seeded and minced (wear rubber gloves)

2 tablespoons coarse salt

1/2 cup fresh lime juice

Vegetable oil for panfrying

Lime wedges for garnish

SERVES 4

Back in 1995 my husband Bill and I went to a seafood festival in the Bahamas. We enjoyed ourselves at several of Nassau's fancier restaurants but ate the best food of our stay at Kemp & Sons, a little beachside shack specializing in conch. Conch (pronounced "konk") are the shellfish that live in those pink and pearly iridescent shells, the kind you put to your ear to listen for the sea. Fresh conch are hard to find in America, but in the Bahamas they are right at hand. Mr. Kemp and his sons just shucked the meat out of the shells and produced our choice of conch fritters or raw marinated conch salad, both exploding with the flavor of chiles, lime, and cilantro.

We happily scarfed down what felt like a lifetime's supply of conch and figured we were through for the day when another of the beachside cooks handed each of us a whole crispy fish. We were supposed to eat the whole thing, skin, bones, and all. It was absolutely incredible. They'd scored the flesh down to the bone in several places, then rubbed it all over with Scotch bonnet chiles, salt, and fresh lime juice. It was marinated for 30 minutes, then deep-fried until golden.

This business of scoring a fish and seasoning it down to the bone really makes sense. Most fish are so bland that seasoning them on the outside alone doesn't really do the trick. I decided to replicate the whole procedure minus the deep-fat frying, which can be a little difficult for the home cook. It's easier—and less caloric—to sauté your fish in a hot skillet, and the end product is nearly as wonderful as the deep-fried original.

Indeed, once you locate small whole fish, this recipe is a breeze. But be forewarned: It is very spicy. If you are not a hard-core chile head, use fewer Scotch bonnets or substitute chiles that are less ferocious, like jalapeños. Serve with Parsnip Puree (page 237) and Southern Braised Mustard Greens with Ham (page 242).

Rinse the fish well, inside and out, and pat dry. Using a sharp knife, cut diagonal slashes about $1/2$ inch apart into the fish on both sides all the way down to the bone. Rub the chiles and salt into the slashes (wear surgical gloves), sprinkle with lime juice, and let the fish marinate, covered and refrigerated, for 30 minutes. Heat $1/4$ inch oil in a very large skillet over high heat until just smoking. Pat the fish dry and add to the skillet. Cook over high heat until just cooked through, 3 to 4 minutes per side. Remove the fillets from the bone by running a paring knife down the backbone of the fish on either side. Divide among 4 plates and garnish with lime wedges.

Kemp and Sons seafood stand, Nassau, the Bahamas, 1995

preventing fish from sticking

When Ben Barker, the chef-owner of Magnolia Grill in Durham, North Carolina, was on my show, he gave me this tip: Before frying fish with the skin on, scrape the skin with the blunt edge of a chef's knife to remove excess moisture. This will help keep it from sticking to the pan.

scotch bonnets and habaneros

Scotch bonnets and habaneros, related chiles, from the Caribbean and Mexico, respectively, can be used interchangeably. My brother Peter aptly describes their fruity round flavor as a cross between a mango and a very hot chile. And indeed they are a very hot chile; they get the highest score on the Richter scale (in chile language: Scoville units) of chile heat, which is why you cannot be a wimp if you want to eat a dish flavored with these chiles.

If you need to put out their fire, there are two reliable antidotes, one for overconsumption and one for overhandling. If you ingest too much habanero or Scotch bonnet, drink a glass of milk; better yet, eat a bowl of ice cream. Dairy and sugar tame the flames. If you touch too much of the habanero or the Scotch bonnet (you should have worn those surgical gloves!), rub your hands with a cut tomato. I learned this from Suzanne Trilling, a Mexican cookbook author and chef who appeared on my show.

Fish en Papillote with Julienned Vegetables and Truffle Oil

This is an old French technique. Loosely translated, *en papillote* means "in a bag." The point of putting the fish in a bag—usually formed out of parchment paper, but sometimes out of foil—is to keep the juices from escaping. All of the flavorings that go into the bag—the fish, the vegetables, the wine, the butter, the seasonings—mingle and become one in a delicious sauce.

You can apply this technique to any combination of tender (quick-cooking) protein, vegetables, and starch—and if you put enough ingredients in the bag, you'll end up with a veritable upscale TV dinner. Since the protein will cook in just 10 minutes, you must first blanch any vegetable that takes longer to cook. Try this technique on a weeknight to recycle any leftovers in the fridge or use it to impress your guests on a Saturday night. Serve with Mashed Potato Cakes (page 249).

3 tablespoons ($^1/_2$ stick) plus 4 teaspoons unsalted butter

4 carrots, julienned

2 large leeks, julienned

2 celery ribs, julienned

Vegetable oil for brushing

Kosher salt and freshly ground black pepper to taste

4 thin fish fillets, no thicker than $^1/_3$ inch, such as sole, flounder, pompano, or snapper, about 6 ounces each, skin removed

4 teaspoons fresh lemon juice

4 teaspoons white truffle oil*

*Available at specialty food shops or see Mail Order Sources.

SERVES 4

Melt 3 tablespoons of the butter in a large heavy skillet over medium heat. Add the carrots, leeks, and celery. Season with salt and pepper. Cook gently, stirring often, until softened, 5 to 7 minutes. Remove from the heat and cool.

Preheat the oven to 425°F. Cut four 13 X 15-inch parchment paper rectangles. Fold each in half crosswise. Unfold and brush the whole rectangle lightly with some oil. Lay a fillet just to the right of the center, skinned side down, and season with salt and pepper. Drain the vegetables of as much liquid as possible and divide among the fillets. Drizzle with the lemon juice. Top each vegetable mound with 1 teaspoon butter and drizzle each with 1 teaspoon of the truffle oil.

Fold the unbuttered half of the paper over the fillet and, starting with the top, make $1/4$-inch folds all around the perimeters and press to crimp and seal. Close the final crimp with a paper clip. Place the packets on a large baking sheet and cook until puffed and lightly browned, 10 to 12 minutes. Transfer to warmed plates and serve at once, preferably while the packet is still puffed.

wine recommendation:
fish en papillote with julienned vegetables and truffle oil

I love dishes cooked in parchment paper. They're always moist, delicate, and flavorful. The lighter fish fillets recommended for this recipe would all work wonderfully well with Albariño, one of the world's greatest fish whites. Hailing from the remote northwest of Spain, Albariño wines are fresh, lively, and effervescent.

fresh fish

Fish is extremely perishable, which is why you have to be careful where you buy it and how you store it. The best scenario would be to buy it at a store that sells only fish and where you have become best buddies with the fishmonger. But most people buy their fish at a supermarket. You should still try to make friends with the person who sets up the fish counter so he or she will let you know what is really fresh and local. If the fish is not stored on ice, complain bitterly or go elsewhere. If you are buying a whole bunch of groceries, buy your fish last. Get it home fast and place in the coldest part of the refrigerator. Or, better yet, store it in a plastic bag on a bowl of ice. Try to cook fish the same day you buy it.

Mini-Pumpkin Soup with Toasted Pumpkin Seeds, Shaved Parmesan, and Fried Sage, p. 42

Fried Green Tomatoes with
Ranch Dressing and Yellow
Cherry Tomato Salad, p. 52

Jean Anderson's Oven-Fried Chicken, p. 72

Poussin en Cocotte, p. 80

Japanese Beef Fondue, p. 114

Grilled Swordfish with
Greek Salad Salsa, p. 134

Carrot "Fettuccine" with Spicy Shrimp, p. 156

Escabeche (Portuguese Pickled Fish)

This is a wonderful dish to serve to a crowd in the summertime. I adapted it from one of my favorite recipes in Peter S. Feibleman's *The Cooking of Spain and Portugal*, which is part of Time-Life's great "Foods of the World" library. Those books are out of print now, but if you ever see one at a yard sale, snatch it up. Comprising some 30 volumes covering all the world's great cuisines, "Foods of the World" was written and published, volume by volume, throughout the fifties and sixties. The series' consulting editor was Michael Field, and individual authors and consultants included James Beard, Julia Child, Craig Claiborne, Alec Waugh, and Joseph Wechsberg. Although you might imagine that the whole series must be out of date by now, each of these volumes still stands as a great resource regarding its given cuisine. And they *look* great, too.

This recipe is so refreshing and light; you get your entree and your vegetables at the same time. You just have to plan ahead, because this dish is better if it marinates for a day or two. Also, it's very important to season it as you go; if you wait until the end, the dish will be bland. Halibut is my top choice for this recipe, but you could substitute thick fillets of any flaky white fish. Dress it up with some crusty bread and a starchy side dish such as Grilled Potato and Corn Salad with Chipotle Mayonnaise (page 253) and you have lunch or a light supper covered.

Heat one-third of the oil in a large skillet over medium-high heat. Combine the flour, salt, and pepper in a bowl and stir to blend. Cook

$2/3$ cup extra virgin olive oil

$1/2$ cup all-purpose flour

$1 1/2$ teaspoons kosher salt

$1/2$ teaspoon freshly ground black pepper

$2 3/4$ to 3 pounds halibut steaks, about $3/4$ inch thick, boned and skinned

2 medium onions, thinly sliced

5 medium carrots, coarsely grated

1 large red bell pepper, julienned

3 garlic cloves, minced

1 bay leaf, preferably Turkish

1 tablespoon chopped fresh thyme leaves or 1 teaspoon dried

$1/4$ teaspoon hot red pepper flakes

1 cup dry white wine

1 cup distilled white vinegar

Additional kosher salt and freshly ground black pepper to taste

SERVES 6 TO 8

the fish in batches. Dip the fish in the seasoned flour and shake off the excess. Add the fish to the skillet and cook until browned, 3 to 4 minutes per side. Transfer to a large plate or platter. Repeat with some of the remaining oil and the remaining fish.

Add the remaining oil to the skillet and reduce the heat to medium. Stir in the onions and cook until softened, about 5 minutes. Add the carrots, bell pepper, garlic, bay leaf, thyme, and pepper flakes. Cook, stirring often, until the pepper strips are slightly softened, about 3 minutes. Pour in the wine, vinegar, and 1 cup water. Increase the heat to medium-high and bring to a simmer. Cook until the liquid has reduced by half. Season with salt and pepper.

Transfer half the vegetable mixture to a deep casserole or baking dish. Arrange the fish on top in one flat layer. Spoon on the remaining vegetables and any liquid that remains in the skillet. Cover and chill for 24 hours.

Michael Green says:

"Green wine" or young wine is the literal translation of vinho verde. Produced in the northern area of Portugal, vinho verde is a fresh, slightly effervescent white wine—a touch fruity, low in alcohol, and endowed with a piercing acidity. Think of it as a squeeze of lemon on your fish—easy to gulp and perfect with many fish dishes, including the escabeche. Most versions are priced under $10. A great wine for summer sipping.

Roasted Salmon with Warm Lentil Salad

My favorite way to cook salmon when I am in a rush is simply to drizzle it with a little olive oil and lemon and then to roast it in the oven. As long as you don't overcook it, the salmon will invariably turn out so well it doesn't even need a sauce.

French lentils, lentilles du Puy, are tiny green lentils that cook in no time and have a wonderful texture and flavor. I love them with salmon and a light mustard dressing. They are available at specialty food shops or over the Internet (see Mail Order Sources). You're also welcome to use plain old green lentils for this dish, although they might take a little longer to cook than the French kind.

The pancetta or bacon rounds out this recipe nicely, but if you don't eat pork, just leave it out or add some julienned smoked salmon to the lentils with the vinegar and mustard. Serve with Creamed Spinach with Crispy Shallots (page 234).

Place the lentils in a large saucepan and pour in enough cold water to cover by 1 inch. Add the salt and bring to a boil over high heat. Reduce the heat to medium and simmer until tender, 20 to 25 minutes.

Meanwhile, cook the pancetta in a small skillet over medium heat, stirring often, until crisp, 3 to 5 minutes. Remove with a slotted spoon and drain on paper towels. Pour off all but 1 tablespoon of the fat from the skillet and add the onion and garlic. Reduce the heat to medium and cook, stirring often, until softened, about 5 minutes. Remove from the heat and set aside.

Preheat the oven to 400°F. Arrange the salmon in one flat layer in a shallow roasting pan. Drizzle with 2 tablespoons of the olive oil and

1 cup green lentils, preferably lentilles du Puy (small French lentils)

$1/2$ teaspoon kosher salt

2 ounces pancetta* or bacon, finely chopped

1 small onion, finely chopped

1 garlic clove, minced

Four 6-ounce pieces center-cut salmon fillet, skin removed

6 tablespoons extra virgin olive oil

2 tablespoons fresh lemon juice

Additional kosher salt and freshly ground black pepper to taste

2 tablespoons white wine vinegar

2 teaspoons Dijon mustard

2 to 4 tablespoons chicken stock, preferably homemade (page 338)

2 tablespoons chopped fresh herbs, such as chives, parsley, tarragon, or basil

*Italian bacon, cured with salt and spices but not smoked, available at specialty food shops.

SERVES 4

the lemon juice. Season with salt and pepper. Bake until barely cooked through, 10 to 12 minutes.

Drain the lentils well and return to the saucepan. Add the vinegar and mustard and season with salt and pepper. Stir in the pancetta, the cooked onion mixture, the remaining $1/4$ cup olive oil, and 2 tablespoons of the chicken stock. Stir well and add more stock if necessary to make a moist lentil mixture. Stir in the herbs at the last minute. Serve each portion of salmon with some of the lentil salad.

how do you get rid of that fishy odor after cooking fish?

Rob Bleifer, one of the chefs in the Food Network kitchen, suggests this remedy: Add citrus and whole sweet spices such as cinnamon, cloves, and nutmeg to a pot of water and bring the mixture to a boil. Let it simmer on the stove until the fish smell is overcome by the simmering spices.

Michael Green says: throw out the rule book!

The blanket rule of white wine with fish is not only simplistic but also quite limiting. There is a difference between a grilled piece of salmon and a broiled piece of fillet of sole. The texture is different. The salmon is much meatier and oilier. Some fish are so flavorful and rich they are more akin to beef. We have not even taken into account the myriad sauces, side dishes, and accompaniments that may be included in a meal. Here, with the rich and savory preparation of salmon and lentils, a red wine would be a fine combination, though beware of rich red wines, which contain high levels of tannin. When served with fish dishes these wines may create a fishy and metallic taste in your mouth. Stick to reds that are on the lighter side—endowed with more acid than tannin. Categories here would include Pinot Noir, Beaujolais, Cabernet Franc, and Barbera.

Salmon in Phyllo with Peperoncini and Smoked Salmon Stuffing

One of my all-time favorite *Gourmet* hors d'oeuvres is Peperoncini Stuffed with Smoked Salmon and Dill Cream. At first glance the combination of ingredients seems like a crazy mismatch, but it turns out that they make beautiful music together—the cream cheese cuts some of the peperoncini's heat, the salmon contributes its smoke and salt, and the dill and lemon round it all out.

To turn this appetizer into an entree, I have taken a salmon fillet, stuffed it with this magical combo, wrapped it all up in phyllo, and baked it. It is an elegant dish, perfect for entertaining. Serve with Perfect Hash Browns (page 250) and a tossed green salad.

Preheat the oven to 400°F. Combine the cream cheese, smoked salmon, peperoncini, shallot, lemon zest, and dill in a small bowl. Blend well with a fork and season with salt and pepper. You should have about ²/₃ cup.

Cut each salmon fillet horizontally down the center through its thickness, almost to the other edge but not quite through. Open each fillet like a book and flatten. Season with salt and pepper. Place a quarter of the cream cheese mixture in the center of one half and cover with the other side to enclose the filling. Season the outside with salt and pepper. Refrigerate while preparing the phyllo.

Arrange one sheet of the phyllo on a large work surface. Brush with butter and top with another sheet of the dough. Repeat the procedure with the remaining phyllo dough and butter. Cut the stacked slices of phyllo into 4 pieces. Arrange a piece of the filled salmon in the center of each piece. Drizzle the salmon with equal amounts of the olive oil and lemon juice. Fold in the sides of the phyllo to enclose the

2 ounces cream cheese, softened

¹/₂ cup finely chopped smoked salmon, about 1 ounce

6 peperoncini (Tuscan pickled peppers),* stemmed, seeded, and finely chopped

1 large shallot, minced

1 teaspoon freshly grated lemon zest

1 teaspoon chopped fresh dill

Kosher salt and freshly ground black pepper to taste

Four 6-ounce pieces center-cut salmon fillet, skin removed

Three 13 x 16-inch sheets phyllo dough, thawed

4 tablespoons (¹/₂ stick) unsalted butter, melted

2 tablespoons extra virgin olive oil, plus more for brushing

1 tablespoon fresh lemon juice

*Peperoncini, the pickled peppers you find in Greek salads, are available at many supermarkets.

SERVES 4

fillet. Place the packages seam side down on a baking sheet. (The recipe can be prepared up to 4 hours ahead at this point. Keep refrigerated, covered with plastic wrap, until ready to bake.)

Lightly brush the top of the packages with olive oil. Bake until lightly browned, 18 to 20 minutes.

wine recommendation:
salmon in phyllo with peperoncini and smoked salmon stuffing

In pursuit of contrast, we begin by matching a crisp white wine with the dry flakiness of the phyllo dough. Then we factor in the recipe's spicy peperoncini, a product of Italy's Tuscan Valley. *Presto!* We've settled upon Vernaccia di San Gimignano, a celebrated Tuscan white that is crisp and clean with a distinct almond quality.

wild vs. farmed salmon—which is better?

There are two issues here—flavor and sustainability of the fish population. For the sake of flavor, try to get wild salmon whenever you can. If you cannot get it fresh, there is FAS (frozen at sea) line-caught wild salmon. Another alternative is closed-pen farm-raised salmon. It is tasty fish and better for the environment than farmed-raised salmon from open-net pens. Make friends with your fishmonger and find out where all your fish comes from and how it was raised. Fifty percent of the world's salmon is now coming from aquaculture open-net pens, and there are environmental issues with fish farming that you should be aware of. For more information, see "Fish" on page xv.

Sofrito Clams or Mussels with Prosciutto

Getting to know Jean Anderson in the early eighties was one of the most important breaks in my life. The fabulously knowledgeable cookbook author and food and travel writer began to mentor me about 10 minutes after we first met, quickly hiring me as her assistant on foreign assignments to Brazil, Holland, and Portugal. Once on the ground, Jean did just about all the work herself: She researched and wrote the articles, found and tested the recipes, styled the food, and shot the photographs. All I had to do was lug around the lights, help with the food styling, soak up the local culture, and eat very, very well. It was nice work if you could get it.

I was with Jean in Portugal when I first tasted the brilliant Portuguese equivalent of surf and turf, namely, clams and pork. The pork in question—either fresh pork or *presunto*, an aged-pork product like the Italian prosciutto—is combined with wine and clams. The clams open up as they steam, and the liquid that runs out of the shell contributes to the beautiful broth. The sofrito part of this dish is a recipe from our Guatemalan housekeeper, Magda Alcayaga. It is the vegetable-and-herb base in which she cooks her rice (page 258). You will definitely want to have some crusty bread at hand to mop up all the sauce. Add a big salad to the proceedings and you've put together a delicious and satisfying meal.

By the way, it was Jean Anderson who wrote *The Food of Portugal*, the definitive book on that country's cuisine. I highly recommend it.

1 small onion, coarsely chopped

$1/2$ large red bell pepper, coarsely chopped

4 garlic cloves, coarsely chopped

1 small tomato, coarsely chopped

$1/2$ cup packed fresh cilantro

2 tablespoons extra virgin olive oil

One $1/4$-inch-thick slice prosciutto, about $1/4$ pound, cut into $1/4$-inch dice

1 cup dry white wine

4 dozen cherrystone clams or 4 pounds cultivated mussels, scrubbed clean

$1/2$ lemon

2 scallions, white and 2 inches of the green parts, thinly sliced

SERVES 4

Combine the onion, bell pepper, garlic, tomato, and cilantro in a blender or food processor. Add 2 tablespoons cold water and process or blend until smooth. You should have about 1 cup sofrito.

Heat the olive oil in a large pot over medium heat. Add the prosciutto and cook, stirring 3 minutes. Stir in the sofrito and cook until blended and fragrant, 1 to 2 minutes. Add the wine and the clams or mussels and increase the heat to high. Cover the pan tightly and cook, shaking or stirring often, just until the shells open, about 5 minutes. Remove and discard any that do not open. Turn out into a large serving bowl, squeeze the lemon over them, and sprinkle with the scallions. Serve warm with crusty bread.

Seared Sea Scallops with Celery Root Puree, Parsley Oil, and Lemon-Caper Brown Butter

My cousin Josh Moulton is also a chef and an incredibly talented one. Until the happy day that he opens up his own restaurant, we get to enjoy Josh's food only when we all get together on vacation or during holidays. Greedy me, I take advantage of these opportunities to try to finagle him into cooking most of the meal. He really doesn't require much persuasion, and he always cooks up something completely delicious—even if it does take hours afterward to wash up the massive amount of pots, pans, and dishes he presses into service. And indeed this is a complicated recipe, but it is well worth the extra effort.

Josh was the first one to tip me off to the unfortunate manner in which scallops are usually harvested. To retard their perishability, many scallops are shucked at sea and put into a liquid solution that contains preservatives and keeps them moist. These poor little guys can then spend up to 10 days at sea on their way to us. Obviously, not only are these specimens not at their peak of freshness, but they are also so wet that you can't sauté and put a crust on them.

This is why Josh's recipe calls for "dry" scallops. "Dry" means the scallops are freshly caught and have never been soaked. If your fishmonger doesn't have them, ask him or her to get them. Serve with Magda's Cauliflower (page 245) or Stewed Green Beans with Tomato and Mint (page 238).

Place the celery root in a small saucepan and pour in enough cold water to cover. Season with salt and bring to a boil over high heat.

1 medium celery root, about 2 pounds, peeled and cut into 1-inch cubes (5 cups)

Kosher salt to taste

12 tablespoons (1 1/2 sticks) unsalted butter

Freshly ground black pepper to taste

1 1/2 cups parsley leaves

3 tablespoons extra virgin olive oil

2 tablespoons vegetable oil, plus more for frying parsley

1 1/2 pounds sea scallops, preferably dry-packed, trimmed and patted dry

3 tablespoons drained bottled capers, rinsed

2 teaspoons finely grated lemon zest

3 tablespoons fresh lemon juice

SERVES 4 AS A MAIN COURSE, 8 AS AN APPETIZER

Reduce the heat to medium-high and simmer until very tender, about 20 minutes. Drain well and puree in a food processor or food mill fitted with the finest blade. (The food mill will give a bit rougher texture). Stir in 4 tablespoons of the butter and season with salt and pepper. Cover and set aside until ready to serve the scallops.

Combine $^1/_2$ cup of the parsley leaves and the olive oil in a blender. Stopping and forcing the mass of leaves into the oil frequently with a rubber spatula, puree until smooth and set aside.

Heat about 2 inches of vegetable oil in a small deep saucepan over medium-high heat until a deep-fat thermometer registers 350°F. Working in batches, add the remaining 1 cup parsley leaves, patted *very* dry, a small handful at a time and fry until crisp, about 10 seconds. They will bubble up furiously. Drain on paper towels and sprinkle with salt.

Working in batches, heat the 2 tablespoons vegetable oil in a large skillet over medium-high heat until it starts to ripple and is almost smoking. Season the scallops with salt and pepper. Add the scallops to the skillet and cook for about 30 seconds, moving them slightly to help make an even crust. Continue cooking until golden brown, 2 to 3 minutes. Turn and cook for 1 minute longer or until firm to the touch. Transfer to a warmed plate. Pour off the excess oil from the skillet and add the remaining butter. Cook over medium-high heat until the butter turns brown and the foam begins to recede. Add the capers, lemon zest, and lemon juice. Season with salt and pepper.

To assemble, reheat the celery root puree and spoon equal amounts into the center of warmed serving plates. Top with scallops and use a teaspoon to decoratively dot the parsley oil around the sides of the plates. Spoon on 1 to 2 tablespoons of the butter sauce, being sure to include some of the capers and zest. Top with the fried parsley.

wine recommendation:
seared sea scallops with celery root puree, parsley oil, and lemon-caper brown butter

It is the creamy celery root puree that makes this recipe special. It would go great with the creamy round texture of a medium-bodied Chardonnay from California or Australia.

With my cousin Josh Moulton, 1985

Carrot "Fettuccine" with Spicy Shrimp

2 tablespoons olive oil

2 tablespoons unsalted butter

1/2 pound medium shrimp, peeled with tail intact, deveined, rinsed, and patted dry

2 large shallots, minced

1 garlic clove, minced

One 1-inch piece fresh ginger, peeled and finely chopped

1/4 teaspoon hot red pepper flakes

10 large carrots, about 1 1/2 pounds, cut into ribbonlike strands with a vegetable peeler, tough core discarded

3/4 cup dry white wine

2 cups heavy cream

1 cup chicken stock, preferably homemade (page 338)

1 cup thawed frozen peas or blanched fresh peas

Kosher salt and freshly ground black pepper to taste

SERVES 4

This recipe is the happy result of an unhappy incident. My friend and fellow chef Sandy Gluck was trying out for a job at a very fancy cutting-edge restaurant in New York City in the early eighties. One of the many reasons she decided she wouldn't work there was that the staff meal was so awful. Their Dickensian idea of a vegetable was carrot and asparagus peelings.

But peelings made from the carrot's luscious inner meat, instead of its tough outer skin, taste and look great. They're long and slender, and if you turn your head and squint at them for a while, they begin to remind you of fettuccine. Or at least that's what they reminded me of when I developed this recipe for *Gourmet*. Indeed, these peelings not only look like fettuccine but take to quick cooking like fettuccine, especially if you leave them al dente. They're delicious this way, with the side benefit that you might bamboozle some child to eat cooked carrots because this time they don't look like carrots but like orange pasta.

Leave out the shrimp if you want to make this recipe vegetarian. Serve with Southern Braised Mustard Greens with Ham (page 242) or Stewed Green Beans with Tomato and Mint (page 238).

Heat the oil and butter in a large skillet over medium-high heat until hot but not smoking. Add the shrimp and cook, stirring, for 1 minute. Add the shallots, garlic, ginger, and pepper flakes and cook until the shrimp just turn pink, about 2 minutes more. Transfer to a bowl. Add the carrots to the skillet and cook over high heat, stirring, until barely tender, about 5 minutes. Transfer to the shrimp bowl.

Add the wine to the skillet and boil until it is reduced by half. Add the cream and stock. Bring back to a boil and boil until the liquid is reduced by half. Add the shrimp, carrots, and peas to the pan and simmer until they are just heated through, about 2 minutes. Season to taste and serve hot.

wine recommendation:
carrot "fettuccine" with spicy shrimp

This one is tricky. The carrots are sweet, the cream is rich, and the ginger and pepper are spicy hot. A wine with too much tannin, red or white, would create a fishy and metallic taste in the mouth. Opt instead for one of the crisp but not overly dry whites of northern Italy. Beyond the popular and prolific Pinot Grigio, consider Pinot Bianco and Tocai Friulano.

Tequila Lime Shrimp with Mango Salsa and Cumin Chili Chips

1¹/₂ pounds medium shrimp, peeled and deveined

Kosher salt and freshly ground black pepper to taste

¹/₄ cup orange marmalade

¹/₄ cup silver or white tequila

¹/₄ cup plus 3 tablespoons fresh lime juice

1 garlic clove, minced

¹/₂ teaspoon hot red pepper flakes or to taste

¹/₄ cup vegetable oil, plus extra for brushing the tortillas

¹/₂ teaspoon kosher salt

¹/₂ teaspoon ground cumin

¹/₂ teaspoon chili powder

Three 6-inch corn tortillas

1 small mango, peeled, pitted, and cut into ¹/₄-inch dice

1 small shallot, minced

1 jalapeño, stemmed, seeded, and minced

2 tablespoons finely chopped fresh mint

SERVES 4 TO 6

Here's some weird food science: Alcohol in a recipe heightens the flavor of the other ingredients even if you don't end up tasting the alcohol itself. Shirley Corriher, a food scientist, cookbook author, and frequent guest on my show, has explained to me more than once why this is so. I still don't understand the science of it, but it is demonstrably true. How else to explain the superior flavor of penne alla vodka? Vodka itself *has* no flavor. Another example is my housekeeper Magda's chicken fricassee, which she makes for us occasionally. It is a quick sauté with boneless chicken and tomatoes, and usually it is delicious. But one night it just wasn't as good as usual. The next day Magda told me she couldn't find any white wine, so she'd made it without. What a difference! I didn't know she'd ever put wine in the dish, but I sure missed it when it was gone.

Unlike vodka, tequila has flavor, although you won't taste it in this recipe. You will taste the shrimp, mango, and salsa, and the flavors will be booming—thanks to the otherwise undetectable tequila.

This is a sunny summer dish, but you could serve it in the dead of winter and be happy. (Mangoes are available almost all year round.) Serve with Grilled Potato and Corn Salad with Chipotle Mayonnaise (page 253).

Pat the shrimp dry and season with salt and pepper. Combine the marmalade and tequila in a small saucepan. Stir over low heat until the marmalade has dissolved. Remove from the heat and cool to room temperature. Stir in the $1/4$ cup lime juice, the garlic, pepper flakes, and 1 tablespoon of the vegetable oil. Transfer the marinade to a plastic bag with a resealable closure. Add the shrimp, seal the bag, and marinate in the refrigerator for 30 minutes, turning over once or twice.

Preheat the oven to 400°F. Mix together the $1/2$ teaspoon salt, the cumin, and the chili powder. Brush the tortillas with a thin coating of oil and sprinkle with the seasoned salt mixture. Cut the tortillas into 6 wedges each and place on a baking sheet. Bake until golden and crispy, 7 to 9 minutes.

Combine the mango, shallot, jalapeño, mint, and remaining 3 tablespoons lime juice in a small bowl. Mix well and season with salt and pepper. You should have about $1 1/4$ cups salsa.

Remove the shrimp from the bag and pat very dry with paper towels. Place the marinade in a small saucepan and bring to a boil. Boil until reduced by half. Heat $1 1/2$ tablespoons of the remaining oil in a large skillet over high heat. Add half the shrimp, season with salt and pepper, and cook, stirring often, until the shrimp are light pink, 3 to 5 minutes. Transfer the shrimp to a bowl, add the remaining oil and shrimp to the skillet and sauté, 3 to 5 minutes. Add the reduced marinade and shrimp from the bowl and toss to coat.

Divide the shrimp among plates. Arrange some of the tortilla chips around each portion and top with a spoonful of the salsa. Serve any remaining salsa on the side.

wine recommendation:
tequila lime shrimp with mango salsa and cumin chili chips

A dish this hot and spicy is beautifully balanced by a cool, crisp white wine. As an alternative to the popular Italian Pinot Grigio, consider the Spanish whites made from the Albariño grape. If you crave beer, look for a crisp and refreshing lager.

Crispy Soft-Shell Crabs with Country Ham Butter

8 small soft-shell crabs, cleaned

About 1 quart whole milk

6 tablespoons unsalted butter

2 small shallots, minced

One ¼-inch-thick slice country ham, about 2 ounces, julienned

4 to 5 small cherry tomatoes, halved or quartered

½ cup dry white wine

2 tablespoons vegetable oil, plus more as needed

½ cup all-purpose flour

½ teaspoon kosher salt

¼ teaspoon freshly ground black pepper

2 tablespoons snipped fresh chives

Additional kosher salt and freshly ground black pepper to taste

SERVES 4

The first time I ate soft-shell crabs was at the New York World's Fair in 1964. Looking back, I can't imagine where I found the nerve to try them. I didn't even like *fish*. But try them I did, and I was knocked out by the sweet crabmeat and that crispy edible shell. Unfortunately, soft-shell crabs were a rarity in the Northeast in the sixties, and years went by before I got to try them again. I didn't really begin to get my fill of them until I started working at La Tulipe in the early eighties, where the menu featured softshells in season.

Soft-shell crabs should still be alive and wriggling when you buy them at the fishmonger or supermarket. Have the fishmonger clean them for you while you wait and then be sure to cook them that night. With soft-shells as with lobsters—which are also extremely perishable—the fresher, the better.

Finally, soak them in milk to take out any overly fishy taste. (Soaking *anything* in milk—anchovies, game, fish fillets—pulls out strong unwanted flavor. It is a good trick to know.)

One last note: Soft-shell crabs spit like crazy when you cook them, so use a long pair of tongs to turn them and be sure to stand back from the stove when you do. Serve with Sautéed Shredded Zucchini with Lemon and Thyme (page 226) and your favorite coleslaw.

Place the crabs in a large shallow bowl and pour on enough milk to cover. Refrigerate for 30 minutes.

Meanwhile, melt 2 tablespoons of the butter in a small skillet over medium heat. Add the shallots and cook, stirring often, until softened,

2 to 3 minutes. Stir in the ham and cook until softened, about 3 minutes. Add the tomatoes and cook until softened, about 2 minutes. Pour in the wine and increase the heat to medium-high. Cook, stirring, until the liquid has reduced by half.

Heat the vegetable oil a large nonstick skillet over high heat until almost smoking. Combine the flour, salt, and pepper in a large bowl and mix well. Flour and cook the crabs in batches (or cook them in 2 skillets). Remove the crabs from the milk and dip into the seasoned flour. Turn to coat on all sides, shake off the excess flour, and add to the skillet. Cook, turning once, until golden, about 3 to 5 minutes per side. Continue until all the crabs are cooked, adding more oil as needed. Transfer to a large platter.

Heat the sauce over medium heat until just warmed through, 2 to 3 minutes. Whisk in the remaining butter, add the chives, and season with salt and pepper. You should have about 1 cup of sauce. Pour the sauce over the crabs and serve at once.

wine recommendation:
crispy soft-shell crabs with country ham butter

The wine of choice here should act like a squeeze of lemon. A crisp light to medium-bodied white would do the trick. No oak required! Just fruit and acidity. France's Loire Valley offers up these elements in abundance in the wines of Sancerre and Pouilly-Fumé.

how to clean soft-shell crabs

If you get brave and decide to clean your soft-shell crabs yourself at home, here is how you do it.

First, lay the crab down flat on a cutting board with the head facing up. Cut off the top part of the crab, the part with the eyes. (I know this sounds brutal, but you want to put it out of its misery fast.)

Next, turn it over and pull off the "apron," the little flap on the underside. (In female crabs it is rounded and in males it is pointy—some things don't change.) Last, turn it over again and lift up either side of the shell one side at a time to expose and pull out the spongy lungs.

Crab Cakes with Red Pepper Rémoulade

For the sauce:

¹/₂ **large red bell pepper, cut in half**

¹/₂ **cup mayonnaise**

2 **teaspoons drained bottled capers, finely chopped**

6 **cornichons (French pickles) or dill gherkins, finely chopped**

1 **to 2 teaspoons fresh lemon juice or to taste**

1 **shallot, minced**

1 **small garlic clove, minced**

Pinch of cayenne pepper

Kosher salt and freshly ground black pepper to taste

For the cakes:

4 **tablespoons (¹/₂ stick) unsalted butter**

3 **scallions, white parts only, finely chopped**

1 **celery rib, finely chopped**

¹/₄ **large red bell pepper, finely chopped**

1 **pound fresh lump crabmeat, picked over**

2 **tablespoons mayonnaise**

³/₄ **cup fresh bread crumbs (page 347)**

2 **tablespoons fresh lemon juice**

Kosher salt and freshly ground black pepper to taste

1¹/₂ **cups panko* or additional fresh bread crumbs for dredging**

2 **tablespoons vegetable oil**

Basil leaves for garnish

*Available at Asian markets or see Mail Order Sources.

SERVES 4

Crab cake is about crab, not "cake." With that goal in mind, I have tried to keep the recipe's binding elements—bread crumbs and mayonnaise—to a minimum and the crab to a maximum.

You can downsize this recipe and make a luxurious appetizer of mini crab cakes. The sauce, which can be made a few days ahead, would also go nicely on top of any sautéed fish or grilled chicken. It's a swell dip for crudités, too. Serve with Provençal Tomatoes (page 227) and Sautéed Spinach with Garlic Chips (page 232).

To make the sauce, preheat the oven to 450°F. Put the bell pepper in a pie plate and roast until the skin is black around the edges and the pepper is tender, 35 to 40 minutes. Remove and cool. Peel off and discard the skin. Combine the pepper with the mayonnaise in a blender and puree. Transfer to a bowl and stir in the capers, cornichons, lemon juice, shallot, garlic, and cayenne. Season with salt and pepper.

To make the cakes, heat 2 tablespoons of the butter in a large skillet over medium heat. Add the scallions, celery, and bell pepper and cook, stirring often, until softened, about 5 minutes. Set aside to cool.

Combine the crabmeat, mayonnaise, bread crumbs, and lemon juice in a large bowl. Add the cooled vegetable mixture and stir to combine. Season with salt and pepper. Use wet hands to form 8 cakes about 2 inches in diameter.

Place the Japanese bread crumbs in a large shallow bowl. Working with one cake at a time, roll to coat on all sides.

Melt the remaining 2 tablespoons butter with the vegetable oil in a large skillet over medium-high heat. Working in batches if necessary, add the cakes and cook, turning once, until golden brown, 2 to 3 minutes per side. Serve topped with sauce.

Pasta

Spring Spaetzle

2 cups sifted all-purpose flour

1 teaspoon kosher salt

Pinch of freshly grated nutmeg

2 large eggs, lightly beaten

3/4 pound medium asparagus

1 tablespoon vegetable oil

**Additional kosher salt and freshly
ground black pepper to taste**

**2 cups chicken stock, preferably
homemade (page 338), or
Vegetable Stock (page 341)**

1 cup heavy cream

**3/4 cup freshly grated Parmigiano-
Reggiano**

**1 cup blanched fresh or thawed
frozen peas**

**2 tablespoons finely chopped
fresh herbs, such as chives,
parsley, dill, tarragon, or a
combination**

SERVES 4 AS A MAIN
COURSE, 6 AS AN APPETIZER

Soon after I started making spaetzle as a side dish at home on a regular basis, it occurred to me that you could dress up and sauce this German pasta much as you would any other fresh pasta—an inspiration that automatically promoted spaetzle from side dish to entree. This recipe takes advantage of ingredients available in the spring—asparagus, peas, and fresh herbs—but I want to encourage you to take the basic spaetzle recipe and run with it. Toss it with a tomato sauce, sausage, and freshly grated cheese, combine it with wild mushrooms, whatever. The possibilities are endless. A wonderful comfort food, spaetzle is the perfect backdrop to any sauce.

The right tool for making spaetzle is a spaetzle maker. This specialized but inexpensive tool consists of two parts— a flat metal grater that sits across the top of a pot of boiling water and a cup into which you pour the batter. If you don't have a spaetzle maker, you can pour your batter through a colander with coarse holes. Serve with an arugula and cherry tomato salad and garlic bread.

Bring a large pot of salted water to a boil over high heat. Combine the flour, salt, and nutmeg in a large bowl and stir well. Whisk together the eggs and 2/3 cup water and add to the flour mixture, beating until just smooth. The mixture should be the consistency of thick pancake batter. If too thick, whisk in 2 to 3 tablespoons more water. Set the batter aside.

Preheat the oven to 450°F. Break off the tough ends of the asparagus and discard. Peel the stalks and arrange in one flat layer over the bottom of a roasting pan or baking sheet. Drizzle on the oil and season with salt and pepper. Roast on the middle rack of the oven until just tender, about 10 minutes. Cool and cut into 1-inch pieces.

Pour the chicken stock into a large skillet and bring to a boil over high heat. Boil until reduced by half. Pour in the cream, bring back to a boil, and reduce again by half. Reduce the heat to low.

Working in batches, drop the batter through a spaetzle maker into the boiling water. Simmer until tender, 3 to 4 minutes. Drain but do not rinse.

Stir $1/2$ cup of the Parmigiano-Reggiano, the spaetzle, the peas, and the asparagus into the skillet holding the cream. Add the herbs and season with salt and pepper. Stir until the spaetzle has absorbed some of the sauce and warmed through, about 5 minutes. Serve in individual warmed bowls sprinkled with the remaining Parmigiano-Reggiano.

Penne with Slow-Roasted Cherry Tomatoes and Goat Cheese

2 pounds red and yellow cherry tomatoes

3 tablespoons extra virgin olive oil

2 teaspoons kosher salt

6 ounces fresh goat cheese

1 pound penne

1 cup loosely packed fresh basil leaves, torn into pieces

Additional kosher salt and freshly ground black pepper to taste

SERVES 4 TO 6

Any excuse to eat ripe tomatoes in season is a good one, but the best reason to check out this delicious vegetarian recipe is that it gives you the chance to sample and support some of the wonderful artisanal cheeses—including homemade fresh goat cheese—now being produced right here in the U.S. of A.

Taking a belated cue from the Europeans, small-time entrepreneurs all over America began to produce great local cheeses about 25 years ago. These producers include people like Miles and Lillian Cahn. After making an international name for their Coach leather company, the Cahns sold out and established a brand-new and equally lofty reputation for themselves as producers of goat cheese. Nineteen years later, Coach Farm goat cheese has not only led artisanal America but created jobs for dozens of folks in Columbia County in upstate New York.

A key element in this recipe is the use of pasta cooking liquid, a technique we learned from the Italians. They know that water in which pasta has been cooked is slightly starchy—and that this starch will connect the pasta to the sauce without compromising the flavor of the dish.

This dish is best eaten right away. You can make all the parts—except for the pasta—way ahead of time and just throw it together at the last minute. (The slow-roasted tomatoes are also great in other roles—as part of an antipasto in the summertime, as an omelet filling, or as a topping on grilled bread.)

I know, of course, that goat cheese is one of those foods you either love or hate. I love it, but if you are a hater, just use another soft meltable cheese in its place. Serve with Mom's Brushed Eggplant (page 228) and roasted peppers tossed with olive oil and balsamic vinegar.

Preheat the oven to 250°F and line 2 large baking sheets with parchment paper. Halve each tomato and place cut side up in one flat layer on the baking sheets. Drizzle the tomatoes with 1 tablespoon of the olive oil and sprinkle on the salt. Roast until the tomatoes are dried around the edges but still moist, about 2 hours.

Crumble the goat cheese into large chunks and refrigerate until ready to serve the pasta.

Cook the pasta in salted boiling water according to the package directions. Remove 1 cup of the cooking liquid and reserve. Drain the pasta well and return to the pot. Add the tomatoes, goat cheese, basil, reserved cooking liquid, and remaining 2 tablespoons olive oil. Toss well and season with salt and pepper. Serve warm.

Michael Green says: you say tomato, i say chianti!

When many folks think of pasta, especially with tomato-based sauces, the famed wines of Italy's Chianti region come to mind. And with good reason. Produced primarily from the Sangiovese grape, most versions have great acidity to complement the acid in tomatoes. There are many quality levels of Chianti, depending on where in the region it comes from and how long it has been aged, but for hearty dishes I prefer the simplest, most straightforward versions—usually labeled simply as Chianti rather than those from the more specific districts such as Chianti Classico. During the warmer months and with lighter dishes, I serve these wines slightly chilled.

Crispy Broccoli with Capellini in Broth

Kosher salt to taste

¹/₄ cup extra virgin olive oil

1 large head broccoli, 1¹/₄ to 1¹/₂ pounds, stems removed and florets trimmed into pieces 2 inches long with a stem about ¹/₂ inch thick (4 to 5 cups)

1 quart chicken stock, preferably homemade (page 338)

1 to 2 teaspoons hot red pepper flakes or to taste

¹/₂ pound capellini

1 cup freshly grated Parmigiano-Reggiano

Freshly ground black pepper to taste

SERVES 4

Once you have your pasta water at a boil and your broccoli cut into florets, this dish—a perfect weekday quick-comfort meal—takes no time at all to prepare.

The star here is the crispy broccoli. You create that crispiness by allowing your pan and oil to get a lot hotter than you normally would—to the point where the oil is just about smoking—and then quickly throwing in the broccoli and covering the pan. The broccoli sears around the edges, caramelizes, and develops a real depth of flavor.

The capellini—or angel hair pasta—cooks in 3 minutes, so don't put it in the boiling water until the broccoli/broth part of the recipe is ready. (If you make the pasta wait for the sauce, it will start clumping up.)

Finally, here's a handy tip on how to grate your Parmigiano-Reggiano without scraping your knuckles raw: just cut it into chunks, toss it into the food processor, and let the blades grate it as fine as you like. Serve with crusty bread and a side of Borscht Beets (page 220).

Bring a large pot of salted water to boil for the pasta. Meanwhile, heat the oil in a large skillet over high heat until just smoking. Add the broccoli and season with salt to taste. Cover and cook until just crispy and brown around the edges, about 3 minutes. Remove the cover, stir, and reduce the heat to medium-high. Cover and cook until the florets are crisp but tender, about 5 minutes. Add the chicken stock and pepper flakes.

Add the capellini to the boiling water and cook until al dente, 2 to 3 minutes. Drain the pasta and add to the skillet with the broccoli and stock. Stir in half the cheese and season with salt and pepper. Divide among 4 warmed soup plates and sprinkle with the remaining cheese.

Pasta Pizza

I first learned about "pasta pizza" from Leslie Glover, one of *Gourmet*'s test cooks, who developed it for "In Short Order." It is ridiculously simple and so tasty. Anytime you make angel hair pasta, just cook double the amount you need. The leftover pasta, recast as the star of this recipe, can provide you with the base for dinner the next night.

To make your "pizza," press the pasta into a round in a nonstick pan and crisp it on both sides to form a "crust." Then top it off with anything you have kicking around in the fridge, including leftover meats and vegetables. Just glue down whatever it is with some cheese.

This dish can be dressed up for guests (artichoke hearts, olives, shrimp) or dressed down for kids (plain, with tomato sauce, mozzarella, and Parmigiano-Reggiano). If you don't want to make a tomato sauce from scratch, use your favorite bottled variety. Serve with Summer Salad (page 58) or a simple tossed green salad.

Kosher salt to taste

¹/₄ pound capellini

1 tablespoon olive oil

¹/₂ small green bell pepper, sliced into thin rings

¹/₂ cup Quick Tomato Sauce (page 342) or your favorite store-bought tomato sauce

¹/₄ pound Italian fontina cheese, thinly sliced

2 ounces prosciutto, thinly sliced

Fresh basil sprigs for garnish

SERVES 2 AS A MAIN COURSE, 4 AS AN APPETIZER

Bring a large kettle of salted water to a boil. Add the capellini and cook until tender, 2 to 3 minutes. Drain well. Heat the oil in a 10-inch nonstick skillet over medium-high heat until hot. Add the bell pepper and cook 30 seconds per side. Transfer to a plate.

Add the capellini to the skillet, distributing evenly and pressing down hard. Reduce the heat to medium and cook, covered, until the bottom is golden, about 25 minutes. Invert the "crust" and cook the other side, covered, for 10 minutes longer.

Spread the tomato sauce over the "crust," leaving a ¹/₂-inch border. Arrange the fontina on top, overlapping the slices, and top with the bell pepper rings and prosciutto. Cover and cook until the cheese is melted, 3 to 5 minutes. Cut into wedges and garnish with the basil sprigs.

Baked Orzo and Cheese

Kosher salt to taste

6 tablespoons unsalted butter

3 tablespoons all-purpose flour

3 cups whole milk, heated

**2 cups coarsely grated extra-
sharp Cheddar cheese**

¹/₂ teaspoon kosher salt

**¹/₄ teaspoon freshly ground black
pepper to taste**

¹/₂ pound orzo

**1¹/₄ cups fresh bread crumbs
(page 347)**

**1¹/₄ cups freshly grated
Parmigiano-Reggiano**

SERVES 4 TO 6

I can't tell you how hard I tried when the kids were little to come up with a homemade macaroni and cheese that they would choose to eat over that stuff in the box. They just weren't interested. But now that they are older and have traveled a little bit, they seem to be open to new tastes. Their affection for this dish is proof.

This recipe is really just a blueprint. It is your basic macaroni and cheese baked with a crumb crust. You can use different cheeses, spice it up southwestern style with some corn and chipotles or pickled jalapeños, or add Mediterranean elements such as sun-dried tomatoes, olives, and capers. Get wild—just keep the proportions roughly the same. Serve with Sautéed Shredded Zucchini with Lemon and Thyme (page 226) or Stewed Green Beans with Tomato and Mint (page 238).

Preheat the oven to 375°F and bring a large pot of salted water to a boil for the orzo.

Heat 3 tablespoons butter in a large saucepan over medium-low heat. Whisk in the flour and cook, stirring constantly, for about 3 minutes. Increase the heat to medium-high, pour in the milk, and bring to a boil, whisking constantly. Reduce the heat to low and cook, whisking often, for 5 minutes. Remove from the heat and stir in the Cheddar. Season with salt and pepper.

Add the orzo to the boiling water and bring back to a boil over high heat. Cook until al dente, 7 to 8 minutes. Drain well and stir into the cheese sauce. Transfer to a large shallow buttered baking dish.

Mix the bread crumbs with the Parmigiano-Reggiano in a small bowl and sprinkle over the orzo. Bake in the middle of the oven until bubbling and lightly browned on top, about 20 minutes.

Ants in a Tree

This is a simplified version of a Chinese dish. An uncomplicated and delicious combo of ground pork and noodles, it is called Ants in a Tree because that is supposedly what it looks like. The first time I ate it was when Kempy Minifie, the senior food editor at *Gourmet*, tested Nina Simond's version of it for the magazine. Nina has written many great Asian cookbooks. I recommend them all.

I love this recipe, but it calls for one hard-to-get ingredient: cellophane noodles. Cellophane noodles (also known as bean threads) are made from the starch of mung beans, and you can find them at Asian markets or on the Internet (see Mail Order Sources). But capellini (also called angel hair pasta) is much more readily available, and I thought that that might work just as well. It does. Everybody likes this recipe. Try it yourself and see if it doesn't become a weeknight regular. Of course, if you are antipork, just substitute lean ground beef or turkey. Serve with Chinese Fried Eggplant with Pine Nuts (page 230).

Kosher salt to taste

$^1/_2$ pound cellophane noodles (bean threads)* or angel hair pasta

1 pound ground pork

$^1/_4$ cup soy sauce

1 tablespoon Asian (toasted) sesame oil*

2 teaspoons cornstarch

6 scallions, white and green parts, thinly sliced

3 tablespoons vegetable oil

One 2-inch piece fresh ginger, peeled and finely grated

4 garlic cloves, minced

1 tablespoon Asian chile paste*

2 cups shredded napa cabbage

$^2/_3$ cup chicken stock, preferably homemade (page 338)

Freshly ground black pepper to taste

*Available at Asian markets and many supermarkets or see Mail Order Sources.

SERVES 4 TO 6

Bring a large pot of salted water to a boil over high heat. Add the noodles and bring back to a boil. Boil for 1 minute for cellophane noodles and 2 to 3 minutes for angel hair pasta. Drain in a colander and rinse under running water. Set aside.

Stir the pork with 2 tablespoons of the soy sauce, the sesame oil, the cornstarch, and half the scallions in a small bowl.

Heat the vegetable oil in a wok or large skillet over high heat until almost smoking. Add the ginger, garlic, and chile paste. Cook, stirring constantly, until fragrant, about 30 seconds. Add the pork mixture and cook for 1 minute longer. Stir in the cabbage and the remaining

2 tablespoons soy sauce. Cook, stirring, until the cabbage is almost wilted, 1 to 2 minutes. Add the cooked noodles and cook, cutting them slightly with the side of a spatula, until the pork is no longer pink, about 1 minute. Pour in the chicken stock and add the remaining scallions. Season with salt and pepper and reduce the heat to medium-low. Cover loosely with foil and simmer until the noodles have absorbed some of the stock, about 3 minutes.

Roasted Butternut Squash Lasagne

This is a delicious alternative to the classic meat-and-tomato-sauce lasagne. The squash comes on surprisingly big; roasting it caramelizes it and concentrates its flavor. I made a relatively light "cream sauce"—half milk/half chicken broth—because the two cheeses contribute a ton of richness.

The big news here is that you don't need to precook the lasagne noodles. Cooking lasagne on the show one night, I was demonstrating a relatively new product called "no-boil" noodles, which are somehow processed so that you don't need to precook them. A viewer called in and volunteered that she never needed to cook the noodles for her lasagne so long as she used enough sauce. I was skeptical, but she was right. We tried it for this dish, and it works just fine. Serve with Quick Sautéed Shredded Brussels Sprouts with Pancetta and Balsamic Vinegar (page 243).

Preheat the oven to 450°F. Toss the squash with the oil in a large bowl. Season with salt and pepper and spread out in one flat layer over the bottom of a large shallow roasting pan. Roast, stirring gently or turning once or twice, until almost tender, 15 to 20 minutes.

Meanwhile, combine the milk, stock, rosemary, and sage in a large saucepan. Bring to a boil over high heat. Remove from the heat, cover, and let steep for 10 minutes. Strain, discarding the herbs. Melt the butter in a separate saucepan over medium-high heat. Add the garlic and reduce the heat to medium-low. Cook, stirring often, until the garlic is tender and fragrant, 2 to 3 minutes. Add the flour and cook, stirring, for 6 minutes. Increase the heat to high, whisk in the strained

1 large butternut squash, about 3 pounds, peeled, quartered, seeded, and thinly sliced

3 tablespoons vegetable oil

Kosher salt and freshly ground black pepper to taste

2$\frac{1}{2}$ cups whole milk

2$\frac{1}{2}$ cups chicken stock, preferably homemade (page 338), or Vegetable Stock (page 341)

2 tablespoons dried rosemary

2 teaspoons dried sage

5 tablespoons unsalted butter

2 garlic cloves, minced

$\frac{1}{4}$ cup plus 2 tablespoons all-purpose flour

Nine 7 x 3$\frac{1}{2}$-inch regular or no-boil lasagne noodles

1 cup coarsely grated whole-milk mozzarella

1$\frac{1}{4}$ cups freshly grated Parmigiano-Reggiano

SERVES 6

milk, and bring to a boil. Reduce the heat to medium and simmer for 5 minutes. Season with salt and pepper. Cool slightly.

Reduce the oven temperature to 375°F and butter a 13 X 9 X 2-inch baking dish. Spread a quarter of the sauce over the bottom of the dish. Cover with 3 lasagne sheets, arranging them so that they do not touch. Arrange half the squash slices on top. Spread a third of the remaining sauce over the pasta and sprinkle on half the mozzarella and $^1/_2$ cup of the Parmigiano-Reggiano. Make one more layer in the same manner. Top with the remaining sauce and sprinkle on the remaining $^1/_4$ cup Parmigiano-Reggiano. Cover the dish tightly with foil and bake in the middle of the oven for 30 minutes. Remove the foil and bake for 15 minutes longer or until bubbling. Preheat the broiler to high and set the oven rack about 6 inches from the source of heat. Broil, watching carefully and turning to distribute the heat evenly, until golden, 2 to 3 minutes. Let stand for 5 minutes before serving.

wine recommendation:
roasted butternut squash lasagne

Savory and autumnal, this dish would partner beautifully with Pinot Noir: light to medium-bodied, and often loaded with spice, earth, and acidity. Seek out versions from Burgundy, Oregon, or New Zealand.

cutting squash

Butternut squash are downright dangerous to halve because they roll around on the table, making it hard to get a grip on them. I recommend laying them on their side and inserting the tip of your knife in the middle of the squash with the heel of the knife facing one of the ends. Bring down the heel of the knife, while holding firmly onto the other end of the squash, to cut through half of the squash lengthwise. Then put the tip of your knife in the middle of the squash with the heel facing the end of the squash that has not yet been halved. Bring the knife down to cut the remaining part of the squash lengthwise in half.

Spinach Gnocchi Gratin with Gruyère and Parmigiano-Reggiano

I'd been working in the test kitchen at *Gourmet* for a couple of years when we were joined by a young woman named Amy Mastrangelo. Although she was starting out as the junior member of our team, Amy quickly began creating some of our best recipes. Amy is a soulful cook, the kind who just seems to have it in her blood.

This flour-based gnocchi (which is, I think, slightly easier to make than the equally delicious potato-based kind) is adapted from one of Amy's recipes. If you've done much baking, you'll recognize this as a pâte à choux dough that has been flavored, boiled, and then baked. (Cream puffs and éclairs are made out of pâte à choux.) It is quintessential comfort food, the sort of dish to serve to someone who's had a bad day. Serve with a salad of roasted red and green peppers, marinated artichoke hearts, and Mediterranean olives.

3/4 **pound fresh spinach, large stems removed, leaves washed in several changes of cold water**

1 **cup chicken stock, preferably homemade (page 338)**

1/2 **cup whole milk**

4 **tablespoons (1/2 stick) unsalted butter, cut into small pieces**

1 **cup all-purpose flour**

3 **large eggs**

1 **teaspoon kosher salt**

1/2 **teaspoon freshly ground black pepper**

Pinch freshly grated nutmeg or to taste

1/2 **cup heavy cream**

1/2 **cup freshly grated Parmigiano-Reggiano**

1/2 **cup coarsely grated Gruyère cheese**

SERVES 4 TO 6

Pile the wet spinach into a large nonreactive pot. Place the pot over medium heat and cook, stirring, until just wilted, about 3 minutes. Drain and rinse under cold running water. Use your hands to squeeze out the water. Transfer to a work surface and chop fine.

Combine 1/2 cup of the chicken stock and the milk in a large saucepan. Heat over medium-high heat until bubbles form around the edges. Add the butter and stir until melted. Add the flour all at once. Stir with a wooden spoon until the mixture forms a stiff dough and pulls away from the sides of the pan. Reduce the heat to medium and cook, stirring, for 1 minute. Transfer to a large bowl. Use an electric mixer to beat in the eggs one at a time, beating well after each addition. Stir in the salt, pepper, nutmeg, and spinach.

Preheat the oven to 425°F. Bring a large pot of salted water to a boil over high heat. Working with 10 at a time, drop walnut-size pieces of the dough into the water. Bring back to a boil and boil until they rise to the surface and are cooked through, about 5 minutes. Drain in a colander.

Arrange the gnocchi over the bottom of a buttered $1^1/_2$-quart shallow gratin dish or flameproof baking dish. Stir the cream and the remaining $^1/_2$ cup chicken stock in a small bowl to blend. Spoon evenly over the gnocchi and sprinkle with the cheeses. Bake in the middle of the oven until bubbly, about 10 minutes. Preheat the broiler and arrange the oven rack about 4 inches from the heat. Broil, watching carefully to avoid burning, until lightly browned on top, about 2 minutes.

Pasta Pizza, p. 169

Short Ribs Ravioli with Tomato Sauce
and Ricotta Salata, p. 179

Portobello Burgers with Red
Peppers and Gorgonzola, p. 182

Tomato, Basil, and Cheese Tart
with Pancetta Crust, p. 206

Strawberry-Rhubarb Cobbler with Gingered Biscuit Topping, p. 266

Dried Apple and Cheddar Strudel, p. 270

Dulce de Leche Rice Pudding with Toasted Almonds, p. 287

Ruth Moulton's Spice Balls, p. 292

Giant Chocolate Turnovers with
Orange Custard Sauce, p. 296,
and Chocolate Caramel Peanut
Truffles, p. 298

Ruthie's Chocolate French Toast with Raspberry Sauce, p. 308

(From left): Frozen Café au Lait, p. 332;
Watermelon Screwdriver, p. 330; Fresh
Lemonade, p. 328

Fontina-and-Prosciutto-Stuffed Wonton Ravioli with Porcini Sauce

I've got to be honest with you—this recipe takes some work. That said, it is an outstanding special-occasion dish. Putting aside the Italian fontina and prosciutto—both great agents of flavor—the star of this recipe is the ounce and a half of dried porcini mushrooms in the sauce. The process of rehydrating a superb dried mushroom like the porcino creates an incredibly flavorful liquid, and that flavor then permeates your sauce.

To make your life easier, you could make the sauce ahead of time and even freeze it. Then, on the day of the dinner, recruit a buddy to help stuff the ravioli. Serve with Sautéed Spinach with Garlic Chips (page 232) and Mom's Brushed Eggplant (page 228).

To make the sauce, combine the marsala and 1 cup water in a small saucepan. Bring to a boil over high heat. Remove from the heat and add the porcini. Cover and soak for 30 minutes. After the mushrooms have been soaked, pour them and the liquid into a strainer lined with a damp paper towel set over a small bowl. Reserve the liquid and rinse the mushrooms under cold running water to remove all grit. Squeeze out the moisture and chop fine.

Heat the oil in a small skillet over medium heat and add the onion. Cook, stirring often, until softened, about 5 minutes. Add the cultivated mushrooms and the chopped porcini and increase the heat to medium-high. Cook, stirring often, until all the liquid has evaporated. Add the tomatoes, the strained porcini liquid, and the chicken stock. Simmer until reduced by a third. Season with salt and pepper.

To prepare the ravioli, combine the fontina, ricotta, prosciutto, and chives in a small bowl. Season with salt and pepper. Working with a

For the sauce:

1/2 cup marsala

1 1/2 ounces dried porcini*

1/4 cup extra virgin olive oil

1 small onion, finely chopped

1/2 pound cultivated white mushrooms, trimmed and finely sliced

1 1/2 cups chopped drained canned tomatoes

1/2 cup chicken stock, preferably homemade (page 338), plus more as needed

Kosher salt and freshly ground black pepper to taste

For the ravioli:

1 cup coarsely grated Italian fontina cheese

1/2 cup whole-milk ricotta

2 ounces thinly sliced prosciutto, finely chopped

1 tablespoon minced fresh chives

Kosher salt and freshly ground black pepper to taste

48 round wonton skins**

1/4 cup freshly grated Parmigiano-Reggiano

*Available at specialty food shops or see Mail Order Sources.
**Available in the produce or frozen food section of many supermarkets or at Asian markets.

SERVES 4

few wonton skins at a time, keeping the others covered with plastic wrap, moisten the edges with water. Mound 2 teaspoons of the cheese filling in the center of a wonton and press another wonton skin on top. Press out the air and crimp the edges tightly to seal. As they are filled, transfer to a flour-dusted sheet pan. Repeat with the remaining wonton skins and filling.

Bring a large pot of salted water to a simmer over medium-high heat. Add the ravioli and cook until just tender, 3 to 5 minutes. Drain well and transfer to warmed pasta bowls. Reheat the mushroom sauce if necessary and thin with additional chicken stock as needed. Spoon the sauce over the ravioli and serve sprinkled with some of the Parmigiano-Reggiano.

Short Ribs Ravioli with Tomato Sauce and Ricotta Salata

Chef Mario Batali really has a genius for big flavor. His shows on the Food Network give you a pretty good idea of that genius, but go to his restaurant Babbo in New York and he will knock your socks off. I love just about everything on the menu, but one of the standouts is Beef Cheeks Ravioli. Weird, right? You've probably never thought about the beef's cheeks and don't particularly like thinking about them now. Well, a beef cheek turns out to be the tenderest little nugget of meat you've ever eaten—or at least it is by the time Mario is done with it. The problem is that you're not likely to find beef cheeks kicking around the meat counter at your local supermarket. So I've created an offshoot of his dish using short ribs, which also have a ton of flavor but are nowhere near as hard to acquire.

Why cook meat on the bone if you know you're eventually going to take it off? Because whatever you cook on the bone—meat, fish, or chicken—has more flavor.

This dish is not your basic weeknight dish. It requires a few days of preparation. Braise the short ribs one day; put together the ravioli the next. It is worth it, though. Your guests will be blown away. Serve with Stir-Fried Spicy Carrots with Peanuts (page 236) and a tossed green salad.

3 tablespoons extra virgin olive oil

2 to 2 1/2 pounds beef short ribs

Kosher salt and freshly ground black pepper to taste

1 small onion, finely chopped

1 carrot, finely chopped

4 garlic cloves, minced

1 tablespoon chopped fresh rosemary or 1 teaspoon dried

1 1/2 teaspoons chopped fresh thyme or 1/2 teaspoon dried

1 cup dry red wine

3 cups chicken stock, preferably homemade (page 338)

1 bay leaf, preferably Turkish

1/4 cup freshly grated Parmigiano-Reggiano

72 round wonton skins*

2 cups Quick Tomato Sauce (page 342) or your favorite store-bought tomato sauce

3/4 cup crumbled ricotta salata

1/4 cup shredded fresh basil leaves

*Available in the produce or frozen food section of many supermarkets or at Asian markets.

SERVES 6

Heat the oil in a large covered skillet over medium-high heat until almost smoking. Pat the ribs dry with paper towels and season with salt and pepper. Transfer to the skillet and cook, turning often, until browned on all sides, 5 to 7 minutes. Transfer to a plate or platter and pour off all but 1 tablespoon of the fat. Reduce the heat to medium and add the onion and carrot. Cook, stirring often, until softened, about 5 minutes. Add the garlic, rosemary, and thyme. Cook for 2 minutes longer. Pour in the wine, increase the heat to high, and bring to a boil. Boil until the wine has reduced by half. Return the ribs to the skillet, pour in the chicken stock, and add the bay leaf. Reduce the heat to medium-low, cover tightly, and simmer until the meat is tender and pulls away from the bone, 2 to $2^1/2$ hours. Transfer to a plate or platter and set aside until cool enough to handle. Skim off the fat from the surface of the cooking liquid. (Alternatively, transfer the ribs and the sauce to a bowl, cool, and refrigerate overnight. The next day, remove the congealed fat that rises to the surface of the cooking liquid.) Return the liquid to the skillet and increase the heat to high. Bring to a boil and cook rapidly until the sauce is slightly thickened and reduced to $3/4$ or $1/2$ cup, just enough to lightly bind the meat and cheese. Season with salt and pepper. Remove and discard the bay leaf.

Take the meat off the bones of the ribs, removing all fat and gristle. Chop the meat fine and discard the bones. Add the meat to the reduced sauce and stir in the Parmigiano-Reggiano. Season with salt and pepper.

Working with a few wonton skins at a time, keeping the others covered with plastic wrap, moisten the edges with water. Mound 1 tablespoon of the filling in the center of a wonton and press another wonton skin on top. Press out the air and crimp the edges tightly to seal. Transfer to a flour-dusted sheet pan. Repeat with the remaining wonton skins and filling. (The ravioli may be frozen at this point and kept tightly wrapped in the freezer for up to 1 month. Freeze flat on a sheet pan and, when solid, transfer to resealable plastic bags.)

Bring a large pot of salted water to a simmer over medium-high heat. Heat the tomato sauce in a small saucepan until almost boiling. Add the ravioli to the simmering water and cook until just tender, 3 to 5 minutes. (If frozen, the ravioli will take a few minutes longer.) Drain well and transfer to warmed pasta bowls. Spoon some of the tomato sauce on top of the ravioli and serve the rest on the side. Top with some of the ricotta salata and a pinch of the basil.

wine recommendation:
short ribs ravioli with tomato sauce and ricotta salata

Despite the wonton skins, this is basically a hearty Italian dish. Numerous full-bodied red wines would partner up beautifully with it: Zinfandel, Shiraz, or Nebbiolo.

Vegetarian Main Courses

Portobello Burgers with Red Peppers and Gorgonzola

4 large portobello mushrooms, stems removed

$1/4$ cup balsamic vinegar

3 garlic cloves, minced, plus 1 whole clove, peeled and halved

1 tablespoon chopped fresh thyme

$1/4$ cup extra virgin olive oil, plus more for brushing

2 small red bell peppers

Kosher salt and freshly ground black pepper to taste

$1/2$ cup crumbled Gorgonzola cheese

Eight $1/2$-inch-thick slices rustic country bread, cut from a 6-inch-high loaf

$1/2$ cup mayonnaise

$1/2$ cup shredded fresh basil

SERVES 4

This is an absolutely wonderful meatless summer sandwich. In the center is a marinated and grilled portobello mushroom cap. It is filled with melted Gorgonzola, topped with roasted red peppers, and lathered with just a little mayonnaise, the whole of it pinned down between slices of toasted garlic bread. What could be better? Try adding this item to the menu the next time you're grilling up hot dogs and hambies in the backyard, and I bet you'll win some converts.

Of course, using your trusty grill pan or broiler, you can also enjoy this recipe in the dead of winter. Serve it open-faced and cut into fourths as an appetizer at a dinner party. If you don't love blue cheese, substitute any strongly flavored melting cheese. Whenever and however you make it, no one's going to miss the beef. Serve with Grilled Potato and Corn Salad with Chipotle Mayonnaise (page 253).

Wipe the mushroom caps clean and use a small spoon to scrape out the gills on the underside. Place 3 tablespoons of the vinegar in a small bowl and whisk in the minced garlic, thyme, and $1/4$ cup olive oil. Divide the mixture between 2 large plastic bags with resealable closures. Put 2 mushroom caps in each bag and seal, pressing out the excess air. Marinate the mushrooms at room temperature for at least 1 hour and up to 2 hours, turning the bags often.

Prepare a charcoal fire and let the coals burn down to a gray ash. Lightly oil the grill. Set the peppers on top and grill, turning often, until the skins are blackened on all sides, 10 to 15 minutes. (Alternatively, preheat the broiler to high and place the broiling pan 4 to 5 inches from the source of heat. Set the peppers on the pan and broil, turning often, until blackened on all sides, 12 to 15 minutes.) Place the charred peppers in a large bowl and let stand, covered with plastic wrap, until cool enough to handle. Peel, core, and seed the peppers and then cut into thin strips. Toss the strips with salt and pepper.

Remove the mushrooms from the marinade, pat dry, and season with salt and pepper. Place the mushrooms cap sides up on the grill and cook until dark and slightly softened, 2 to 3 minutes. Turn and grill the other side until tender, 2 to 3 minutes longer. (Alternatively, the mushrooms can be grilled in a hot, well-seasoned ridged grill pan over medium-high heat for about 5 minutes per side, but grill the bread first; see below.) When the mushrooms are almost tender, sprinkle a quarter of the cheese into the cavity of each cap.

While the mushrooms are grilling, brush the bread with olive oil on both sides. Grill until lightly toasted, turning often, 3 to 5 minutes. Rub one side of each slice with the cut garlic clove while hot. (If using a grill pan, grill the bread first and then the mushrooms.)

Add the reserved tablespoon of vinegar to the mayonnaise. Stir well and season with salt and pepper. Spread on the garlic-rubbed side of each slice of bread. Top half the bread slices with a mushroom cap, equal amounts of the peppers, and basil. Place the other bread slices on top. Cut the "burgers" in half and serve.

portobello mushrooms

Did you know that portobello mushrooms are cremini mushrooms all grown up? I prefer portobellos; they develop a lot more flavor when they turn into adults. The only downside is that their gills, when cooked, stain everything they touch a dark brown color, which is why it is important to remove them.

Black-Eyed Pea Cakes with Salsa Mayonnaise

For the cakes:

2 tablespoons unsalted butter

1 small onion, finely chopped

1/2 small red bell pepper, finely chopped

2 garlic cloves, minced

2 jalapeños, seeded and minced

2 cups cooked black-eyed peas, drained and rinsed if canned

1 tablespoon finely chopped fresh cilantro

1 teaspoon ground cumin

Kosher salt and freshly ground black pepper to taste

Tabasco sauce to taste

2 large egg yolks

1 cup fresh bread crumbs (page 347)

For the salsa mayonnaise:

4 plum tomatoes, seeded and finely chopped

Kosher salt to taste

1/2 small onion, finely chopped

1 jalapeño, seeded and minced

1 tablespoon finely chopped fresh cilantro

2 tablespoons fresh lime juice

1/4 teaspoon ground cumin

1 cup mayonnaise

Freshly ground black pepper to taste

For cooking the cakes:

2/3 cup yellow cornmeal

1/4 cup vegetable oil

SERVES 4

Once upon a time *Gourmet* ran a recipe for an appetizer of black-eyed pea cakes with jerk pork. I loved it as it was, but it occurred to me that we could conjure up a great vegetarian entree by losing the pork, making the cakes bigger, and then topping the cakes with a tasty sauce. The use of canned black-eyed peas (they mash up better than the dried and cooked kind) and prepared mayonnaise makes the preparation of this dish a breeze. You could even cheat and use drained store-bought salsa. Suddenly, there it is on the table—a meatless weeknight entree that even the die-hard carnivore will find satisfying. Serve with Couscous Tabbouleh (page 255) and steamed sugar snap peas.

To make the cakes, melt the butter in a small saucepan over medium heat. Add the onion and bell pepper. Cook, stirring often, until softened, about 5 minutes. Add the garlic and jalapeños and cook for 1 minute longer. Remove from the heat and cool slightly.

Place half of the peas in a large bowl and crush them thoroughly with a fork. Stir in the other half of the peas, along with the onion mixture, cilantro, and cumin. Taste the mixture, season with salt and pepper and Tabasco sauce, then stir in the egg yolks. Starting with 1/2 cup of the bread crumbs, add just enough to form a mixture that will hold its shape. Cover and chill the mixture for 2 hours.

Meanwhile, make the salsa mayonnaise. Toss the tomatoes with a pinch of salt and drain in a colander for 15 minutes. Combine them with the onion, jalapeño, cilantro, lime juice, and cumin in a large bowl. Mix in the mayonnaise and season with salt and pepper. Cover and chill until ready to serve. (The salsa mayonnaise can be made up to a day in advance.) You should have about 2 cups.

Working with 1/4 cup of the pea mixture at a time, make 8 to 10

$^1/_2$-inch-thick patties. Coat the patties in the cornmeal and shake off the excess. Heat half the oil in a large nonstick skillet over medium-high heat until hot. Fry the patties in 2 batches, adding the remaining oil for the second batch. Do not flip until a brown crust has formed on the first side, $1^1/_2$ to 2 minutes. Remove the patties from the pan when uniform in color. Drain on paper towels and keep warm in a 200°F oven until ready to serve. Repeat until all the patties are cooked. Serve hot topped with the mayonnaise.

Sweet Potato and Black Bean Burrito

2 sweet potatoes, about 10 ounces each

2 tablespoons vegetable oil, plus more for brushing

1 small onion, finely chopped

2 garlic cloves, minced

1/2 teaspoon ground cumin

1/2 teaspoon chili powder

1 1/2 cups thoroughly cooked black beans or one 15-ounce can black beans, rinsed and drained

1/2 cup vegetable stock (page 341) or water

Kosher salt and freshly ground black pepper to taste

Freshly grated nutmeg to taste

Eight 6-inch flour tortillas

2 to 3 scallions, white part only, thinly sliced

1 cup shredded Monterey Jack cheese

Shredded romaine, sour cream, and chopped Pickled Jalapeños (page 345) for garnish

SERVES 4

A couple of years ago "Good Morning America" ran a low-fat, low-calorie Healthy Eating contest that asked viewers to submit original recipes for Best Entree and Best Dessert. We received hundreds and hundreds of entries, narrowed them down, then flew the winner in each category to New York to make their dish on the show.

Dana Richardson from Durham, North Carolina, submitted a recipe for Sweet Potato Burritos, and although it did not win, I personally liked it a lot, enough to use it as the inspiration for this recipe. I have added a layer of black bean puree and upped the fat content significantly. (It's still pretty healthy.) We all loved it, even the husband, who usually bites into a dish like this and grouses, "Where's the beef?" Not this time. Serve with Celery Root Rémoulade with Wasabi, Ginger, and Sesame (page 240) or your favorite coleslaw.

Preheat the oven to 400°F. Prick the potatoes with a knife in several places and bake in a small baking pan until very tender, 1 to 1 1/2 hours.

Meanwhile, heat 2 tablespoons vegetable oil in a large skillet over medium heat. Add the onion and cook, stirring often, until softened, about 5 minutes. Add the garlic and cook for 1 minute longer. Stir in the cumin and chili powder and cook for 1 minute. Add the beans and vegetable stock, cover, and cook until the beans are very soft and the flavors have blended, about 5 minutes. Use a fork or potato masher to coarsely mash the beans. Season with salt and pepper. You should have about 1 1/2 cups.

Remove the potatoes from the oven and cool. (Keep the oven at the same temperature.) When the potatoes are cool enough to handle, halve and scoop out the flesh. Place the flesh in a small bowl and use a fork to mash coarse. Discard the skins. Add the nutmeg and season with salt and pepper. You should have $1^1/_2$ to 2 cups.

Spread the tortillas with roughly equal amounts of the bean mixture. Top with equal amounts of the potato puree. Sprinkle on equal amounts of scallions and cheese. Roll the tortillas into cylinders and arrange, seam side down, on a baking sheet. Brush the tops with vegetable oil. Place in a baking pan large enough to hold the burritos in one flat layer. For a soft burrito, cover with foil and bake until warmed through, about 20 minutes. Bake uncovered for a crisper burrito. Arrange the garnishes attractively in bowls and let diners garnish their own burritos.

Vegetarian Chili Pie with Monterey Jack Cheese and Corn Bread Crust

For the chili:

3 tablespoons olive oil

1 small onion, finely chopped

1 large carrot, finely chopped

1 celery rib, finely chopped

3 garlic cloves, minced

2 jalapeños, seeded and finely chopped

1 large green bell pepper, finely chopped

1 tablespoon chili powder

$^1/_2$ teaspoon ground cumin

1 tablespoon tomato paste

3 to 4 medium plum tomatoes, seeded and chopped

$^3/_4$ cup Vegetable Stock (page 341) or water

Kosher salt and freshly ground black pepper to taste

$^1/_2$ pound cultivated white mushrooms, halved or quartered

$1^1/_2$ cups cooked kidney beans or one 15-ounce can kidney beans, rinsed and drained

$1^1/_2$ cups grated Monterey Jack cheese

For the topping:

$^1/_4$ cup all-purpose flour

$^1/_4$ cup plus 2 tablespoons cornmeal

$1^1/_2$ teaspoons sugar

$^1/_2$ teaspoon baking powder

$^1/_4$ teaspoon table salt

$^1/_2$ cup whole milk

1 large egg

Vegetable chili, like any stewed dish, is even better the day after you make it, when all the flavorings have had a chance to sink in. Of course, it's also fine if you eat it the same day you make it. But whenever you make it, make a double batch and freeze the second half for another meal. Top it with the cheese and the cornmeal batter right before you pop it into the oven. Serve with Baked Acorn Squash with Mustard and Honey (page 246) and coleslaw.

To make the chili, heat 2 tablespoons of the oil in a large soup pot or kettle over medium heat. Add the onion and cook, stirring often, until softened, about 5 minutes. Add the carrot and celery. Cook, stirring, until slightly softened, about 3 minutes. Add the garlic and cook for 1 minute longer. Stir in the jalapeños and bell pepper. Reduce the heat to low, cover, and cook until the peppers are softened and fragrant, about 5 minutes. Stir in the chili powder, cumin, and tomato paste. Add the tomatoes and pour in the stock. Increase the heat to medium-high and cook, uncovered, stirring often, until slightly thickened, 7 to 10 minutes. Season with salt and pepper.

Meanwhile, heat the remaining tablespoon of oil in a large nonstick skillet over medium-high heat. Add the mushrooms and cook, stirring often, until the liquid they give off has evaporated and they start to brown, about 10 minutes. Season with salt and pepper.

Add the mushrooms to the soup pot and stir well. Pour chili into a 9-inch deep-dish pie plate and cool to room temperature. Sprinkle the cheese on top.

For the topping, preheat the oven to 375°F. Stir the flour, cornmeal, sugar, baking powder, and salt in a large bowl until well blended. Beat the milk with the egg and oil in a small bowl with a fork. Pour into the dry ingredients, add the corn, and stir briefly until the mix-ture forms a soft batter. Pour over the chili, spread evenly, and place on a baking sheet to avoid spillovers. Bake for 35 to 40 minutes or until a toothpick inserted in the center comes out clean. Transfer to a wire rack to cool for 10 minutes before serving.

2 teaspoons vegetable oil

$^1/_4$ cup cooked fresh or thawed frozen corn kernels

SERVES 6 TO 8

Eggplant Rollatini with Four Cheeses

1 medium eggplant, stem end
   trimmed off

3 tablespoons extra virgin olive
   oil

Kosher salt and freshly ground
   black pepper to taste

³/₄ cup freshly grated Parmigiano-
   Reggiano

¹/₂ cup coarsely grated
   mozzarella cheese

¹/₂ cup coarsely grated Italian
   fontina cheese

¹/₂ cup whole-milk ricotta cheese

2 cups Quick Tomato Sauce
   (page 342) or your favorite
   store-bought tomato sauce

¹/₄ cup mixed chopped fresh
   parsley, chives, and basil for
   garnish

SERVES 4

This recipe improves on the traditional eggplant rollatini by calling for roasted, not fried, eggplant. Consequently, it is easier to prepare (no baby-sitting the slices in the pan) and easier on your waistline (roasting requires far less oil than frying).

You're welcome to stuff the eggplant with cheeses other than the ones I list; just make sure whichever ones you choose melt easily. Likewise, if you don't feel like making quick tomato sauce, you can use your favorite store-bought brand. The whole dish can be prepared ahead of time—even as much as a day ahead—and then just popped into the oven at the last minute. Serve with an arugula salad and garlic bread.

Preheat the oven to 375°F. Cut the eggplant lengthwise into 8 slices. Brush both sides of the slices with the oil and season with salt and pepper. Arrange in one layer on 2 large sheet pans lined with parchment. Bake until tender and light golden, about 20 minutes. Remove from the oven and carefully turn the slices over. Cool on the baking sheets.

Combine the cheeses in a small bowl and stir with a fork until well mixed. Season with salt and pepper. Divide the cheese mixture into 8 equal portions. Mound one portion of the mixture on a short side of each eggplant slice. Roll up the eggplant slices to enclose the mixture. Arrange the rolled slices in a shallow casserole or gratin dish seam side down, tightly packed in one layer. Pour on the tomato sauce and bake until the sauce is bubbly and the cheese is melted, about 30 minutes. Top each portion with some of the fresh herbs and serve hot.

salting eggplants

Some people like to salt and drain their eggplant before they cook it. The theory is that the salt helps to remove any bitterness. I believe that the way to avoid bitterness is to get a fresh small eggplant with fewer seeds (see page 229 for buying tips).

I do agree with the second reason for salting, which is that if you salt and drain the eggplant it will absorb less oil when you cook it. I try to cut back on the oil as well by roasting instead of frying.

wine recommendation:
eggplant rollatini with four cheeses

The richness of the cheeses in this dish and the acidity of its sauce call for a red wine with answering flavor and acidity. Any of several light to medium-bodied Italian reds—Dolcetto, Barbera, or Chianti—would be ideal here.

Grilled Polenta with Mushroom Ragout

For the polenta:

1 quart whole milk

1 teaspoon kosher salt

1 cup polenta or yellow cornmeal

1/4 cup freshly grated Parmigiano-Reggiano

For the ragout:

3 tablespoons extra virgin olive oil

2 shallots, minced

2 garlic cloves, minced

1 pound cultivated white mushrooms, cleaned and finely chopped

1 pound assorted wild mushrooms, cleaned and coarsely chopped

2 to 3 plum tomatoes, seeded and chopped

1/2 cup dry white wine

1/2 cup Vegetable Stock, preferably homemade (page 341), or water

2 teaspoons chopped fresh thyme

Kosher salt and freshly ground black pepper to taste

Truffle oil* to taste

2 tablespoons chopped fresh parsley

Additional grated Parmigiano-Reggiano for serving

*Available at specialty food shops or see Mail Order Sources.

SERVES 4 AS A MAIN COURSE, 8 AS AN APPETIZER

It seems to me that mushrooms must mean to vegetarians what steak means to carnivores. They are both stick-to-your-ribs, center-of-the-plate comfort foods. These days our supermarkets always boast a huge selection of mushrooms, many of which were terribly exotic a generation ago. My advice for this recipe is to mix together a few of the exotics and add some button mushrooms for filler. But don't combine too many of the most pronounced in flavor—such as morel and shiitake—because they will cancel each other out.

The real secret ingredient here, to be added at the last minute, is truffle oil. Truffle oil is like vanilla extract or Asian sesame oil; a little goes a long way. For a while in the nineties chefs were putting it in everything, and it quickly became a cliché. But I still think a little truffle oil, used judiciously, can bestow on many dishes a final luxurious pick-me-up. It is one of those secret ingredients that make you look like a genius.

The mushroom ragout is served here on grilled polenta, but it would be delicious tossed with fettuccine, too. Or make it part of an elegant first course by serving it on top of slices of grilled country bread rubbed with a raw garlic clove. Serve with Stir-Fried Spicy Carrots with Peanuts (page 236) and a tossed green salad.

To make the polenta, bring the milk with the salt to a boil in a large saucepan over high heat. Gradually add half the polenta, whisking constantly. Reduce the heat to medium-low and add the remaining polenta in a slow, steady stream, whisking constantly. Reduce the heat to low and cook, whisking often, for about 20 minutes. Remove from the heat and stir in the cheese. Pour into an 8-inch square baking pan lined with oiled aluminum foil and smooth the top. Cool slightly, then cover with plastic wrap. Refrigerate until very well chilled, at least 6 hours or overnight.

Meanwhile, prepare the ragout. Heat the olive oil in a medium saucepan over medium-high heat. Add the shallots and cook, stirring constantly, until slightly softened, about 2 minutes. Stir in the garlic and cook for 1 minute longer. Add all the mushrooms and cook, stirring often, until the liquid they give off begins to evaporate, about 10 minutes. Add the tomatoes and the wine, increase the heat to high, and bring to a boil. Stir until the liquid has evaporated. Reduce the heat to low and pour in the vegetable stock. Add the thyme and season with salt and pepper. You should have about $2^1/_2$ cups.

Just before serving, light a charcoal fire and let the coals burn down to a gray ash. Oil the grates and set the grill about 5 inches from the heat. (Alternatively, place a stovetop grill over medium-high heat.) Turn the polenta out of the pan onto a large work surface. Cut into 4 equal squares, then cut each square in half diagonally to form triangles. Grill the triangles until heated through, 5 to 7 minutes per side.

Reheat the ragout and correct the seasoning with salt and pepper. Overlap 2 triangles on each of 4 serving plates (or serve 1 triangle per person as an appetizer). Ladle on equal amounts of the ragout, drizzle with truffle oil, and sprinkle with parsley and cheese to taste. Serve hot.

baked polenta

When I was on an airplane coming back from a business trip, one of the flight attendants (with the first name of Dobbs) came up to introduce herself and tell me how much she liked my show. She went on to say that she had tried to call in one night when I was making polenta to tell me her technique for making it in the oven. It is brilliantly easy and far less dangerous than having that Vesuvius pot on the stove.

Dobbs's Baked Polenta
SERVES 4 TO 6

1 quart water (less if you want a thicker polenta)
1 tablespoon unsalted butter
1 cup cornmeal
1 teaspoon kosher salt
Freshly grated Parmigiano-Reggiano, crumbled goat cheese, or any favorite grated or crumbled cheese to taste
Additional kosher salt and freshly ground black pepper to taste

Preheat the oven to 350°F. Mix the water, butter, cornmeal, and salt in a 1-quart ovenproof casserole. Bake, uncovered, in the middle of the oven for 1 hour.

Remove from the oven and stir in the cheese. Bake for 10 minutes more and season with salt and pepper.

Tomato Pie

Make this pie during the high tomato season and you just can't lose; those big ripe local tomatoes will do all the work for you. After you slice and salt the tomatoes and roll out the dough, the rest is simple. (If you want to cheat, use a store-bought pie shell instead of homemade dough. Just let it soften enough so you can ease it into the tart tin.)

By the way, feel free to substitute other fresh herbs for the ones I list here. Basil, mint, cilantro, dill, oregano, marjoram, chives, chervil, and tarragon all pair nicely with tomatoes. Serve with Mexican-Style Street Corn (page 222) and a tossed green salad.

Roll the dough into an $1/8$-inch-thick round on a lightly floured work surface. Transfer to a 9-inch tart pan with a removable bottom, cut off any excess dough from the edges, and prick the bottom lightly with a fork. Chill for 30 minutes.

Preheat the oven to 375°F. Line the shell with foil and fill with pie weights, dried beans, or rice. Bake in the lower third of the oven for 20 minutes. Carefully remove the weights and foil. Return to the oven and bake for 10 minutes more or until light golden. Cool in the pan on a wire rack.

Turn up the oven to 400°F. Sprinkle the tomatoes with salt and drain in a colander for 10 to 15 minutes. Spread the mustard over the bottom of the shell and sprinkle the cheese over it. Arrange the tomatoes over the cheese in one overlapping layer. Bake until the pastry is golden brown and the tomatoes are very soft, 35 to 40 minutes.

In a small bowl, stir together the parsley, thyme, garlic, olive oil, and salt and pepper to taste to blend. Sprinkle the pie with this mixture while hot and spread out gently with the back of a spoon. Serve the pie hot or at room temperature.

$1/2$ recipe Basic Pie Pastry Dough (page 351)

3 large tomatoes, about $1^{1}/2$ pounds, peeled and cut into $1/2$-inch-thick slices

Kosher salt for sprinkling

$1/4$ cup Dijon mustard

1 cup coarsely grated Gruyère cheese

1 tablespoon finely chopped fresh parsley

1 tablespoon chopped fresh thyme

1 garlic clove, minced

2 tablespoons extra virgin olive oil

Additional kosher salt and freshly ground black pepper to taste

SERVES 6 TO 8

Roasted Ratatouille Crepes with Goat Cheese

1 medium eggplant, stem end cut off

2 medium zucchini, trimmed

2 teaspoons kosher salt

4 large plum tomatoes, quartered

1 large red bell pepper, quartered

1 large onion, quartered

1 head garlic

3 tablespoons extra virgin olive oil

Additional kosher salt and freshly ground black pepper to taste

2 teaspoons fresh thyme leaves or ³/₄ teaspoon dried

¹/₂ cup shredded fresh basil

One 6-ounce log fresh goat cheese

12 crepes (page 349)

SERVES 6

My mom made ratatouille from the *New York Times Cookbook* all the time when we were kids, and I just loved it. This venerable vegetable stew from the south of France has all the complexity of a meat stew with its many flavors layered together. All the stars of Provençal cuisine play a role—tomatoes, eggplant, zucchini, garlic, onions, and bell peppers. Usually the vegetables in ratatouille are sautéed, but I thought roasting them might intensify the flavor. So I did, and then wrapped them up in a crepe and baked it. I must say I think it turned out very well.

If you don't want to make crepes, you can buy them in the supermarket. If you aren't a fan of goat cheese, substitute any of your favorite melting cheeses. Serve with Celery Root Rémoulade with Wasabi, Ginger, and Sesame (page 240) or a tossed green salad and garlic bread.

Cut the eggplant into 1-inch cubes and the zucchini into ¹/₄-inch-thick slices. Toss with 2 teaspoons salt and place in a large colander. Set a plate on top and place the colander inside a large bowl or in the sink. Set aside at room temperature and drain for 30 minutes. Transfer to a clean kitchen towel and gently squeeze out as much moisture as possible.

Preheat the oven to 450°F. Combine the eggplant and zucchini with the tomatoes, bell pepper, and onion in a shallow roasting pan large enough to fit all of the vegetables in one flat layer. Cut a ¹/₄-inch slice off the root of the head of garlic. (This allows for easy removal of the cloves once the garlic is soft.) Place the garlic in the center of a large square of foil. Drizzle with 1 tablespoon of the oil and season with salt and pepper. Bring up the corners of the foil and crimp to seal tightly. Drizzle the remaining 2 tablespoons olive oil over the vegetables and add the thyme. Season with salt and pepper and place in the oven, with the wrapped garlic on the oven rack next to the roasting pan. Roast, stirring the vegetables often, until the onions are browned around the edges and the peppers are crinkly, about 45 minutes.

Transfer the roasted vegetables to a large bowl and cool. Unwrap the garlic and cool. When cool enough to handle, peel the peppers and cut into thin strips. Use a slotted spoon to transfer the tomatoes to a food processor. Pull the garlic apart and squeeze the pulp from the individual cloves into the processor with the tomatoes. Puree until smooth.

Transfer the zucchini and eggplant to a large work surface. Chop coarsely. Remove the onion and chop finely. Combine all the vegetables in a large bowl and pour on the pureed tomatoes. Add the basil and stir well to blend. Season with salt and pepper. You should have about 4 cups ratatouille.

Place the goat cheese in the freezer for 10 minutes, remove, and cut into twelve $^1/_4$-inch disks. Preheat the oven to 375°F.

Lay a crepe flat on a work surface. Spoon about $^1/_3$ cup of the filling onto the bottom half and roll into a cylinder. Continue until all the filling and crepes have been used.

Butter a large baking dish and arrange the filled crepes seam side down snuggly in one flat layer. Top each crepe with a disk of cheese. Bake until the goat cheese is lightly browned and the crepes are crisp, 30 to 40 minutes. Serve hot.

dental floss as a tool for cutting

When you need to cut something soft and creamy like goat cheese or cheesecake into even neat slices, the best tool for the job is dental floss, unflavored of course.

White Bean, Artichoke, and Tomato Gratin

1/2 pound dried white beans, such as Great Northern, cleaned and picked over

Kosher salt to taste

2 bay leaves, preferably Turkish

1 tablespoon extra virgin olive oil

3 to 4 medium tomatoes, seeded and finely chopped

3 garlic cloves, minced

1 tablespoon chopped fresh thyme leaves or 1 teaspoon dried

1 tablespoon chopped fresh rosemary or 1 teaspoon dried

4 to 6 medium artichokes

3/4 cup Vegetable Stock (page 341)

Additional kosher salt and freshly ground black pepper to taste

1 1/2 cups fresh bread crumbs (page 347)

1/2 cup freshly grated Parmigiano-Reggiano

2 tablespoons melted unsalted butter

SERVES 4 TO 6

Any recipe devoted to artichoke hearts involves the terribly boring and even slightly dangerous job of bending back and pulling off those prickly leaves. After wrestling with some artichokes during the first test of this recipe, Andrea Hagan, the backup recipe tester on this book, said, "Why don't we just steam the whole vegetable and then use only the part we want from now on?" Brilliant. It's so much easier—and less injurious—to pull off the leaves after they've been cooked. And you're also much more likely to recycle cooked leaves than raw ones; cold artichoke leaves with vinaigrette or flavored mayonnaise are delicious. I think I may have performed the classical trim-down of this vegetable for the last time.

The rest of the components of this recipe—white beans, tomatoes, garlic, and olive oil—make a happy Mediterranean marriage with the artichokes. You will love this dish, as an entree or even as a side dish to accompany the Sautéed Shoulder Lamb Chops with Skordalia Sauce (page 108). As an entree, serve with Mom's Brushed Eggplant (page 228) and Sautéed Shredded Zucchini with Lemon and Thyme (page 226).

Place the beans in a soup pot or kettle and pour in enough salted cold water to cover by 3 inches. Add the bay leaves and bring to a boil over high heat, reduce the heat to medium-low, and simmer, partially covered, until tender, 2 to 2 1/2 hours. Drain the beans and discard the bay leaves.

Meanwhile, heat the oil in a small skillet over medium heat until hot. Add the tomatoes and garlic. Cook, stirring often, until softened, about 5 minutes. Stir in the thyme and rosemary and cook for another minute. Remove from the heat.

Place a steamer basket in a large soup pot with a lid. Add 1 inch of water to the pot. Cut the stems off the artichokes and place the artichokes pointed sides up in the steamer. Bring the water to a boil, reduce the heat to low, and cover. Steam the artichokes until the leaves pull off easily, 40 to 45 minutes. Remove the artichokes from the pot and cool to room temperature.

Pull the outer leaves off the artichokes and reserve for another use. Remove and discard the inner leaves until you get down to the tender smallest leaves. Cut the artichokes lengthwise into quarters. Use a spoon to scrape away the hairy chokes. Cut each trimmed artichoke quarter in half.

Preheat the oven to 350°F. In a 2-quart casserole dish, mix the beans, the tomato mixture, the artichoke hearts, and the vegetable stock. Season with salt and pepper. Mix the bread crumbs with the Parmigiano-Reggiano in a small bowl. Sprinkle the bread crumb mixture over the top of the beans and drizzle on the melted butter. Place the casserole in the oven and bake, uncovered, until the top is lightly browned, about 30 minutes.

Michael Green says:
wine warning

Artichokes contain an acid known as *cynarin*. For most of us, eating an artichoke with any beverage, including water, will make the beverage taste sweet. When choosing a wine to go with any dish containing artichokes, there are two schools of thought: 1. Select a wine that is very high in acid such as a Sancerre, vinho verde, or Champagne. While your perception of taste will most likely be fruitier, it will still retain some dry characteristics. 2. Alternatively you can serve a light and fruity wine such as a German Riesling or Beaujolais. Although the wine will taste even fruitier, the combination can also be quite pleasant.

preparing artichokes

I always steam whole artichokes rather than boil them. They lose some flavor and get watery when you boil them. Don't throw out that artichoke stem. Cut it off so the artichokes can sit level on the steamer and set it aside. About 15 minutes before you think the artichokes are going to be done, peel the stems all the way down to the light green core and throw the peeled stems in the steamer along with the artichokes. They will get tender in the time it takes the artichokes to finish cooking, and they will have the same taste and texture as the artichoke heart.

Try serving your kids a whole steamed artichoke with melted butter. Because it is so sweet, many kids (even as young as age 5) just love it. It is also so much fun to take apart leaf by leaf and eat.

Light Lunches

Grilled Eggplant Wraps
with Lemon Aïoli, Feta, and Mint

2 medium eggplants, cut lengthwise into $1/4$-inch-thick slices

$1/2$ cup plus 2 tablespoons olive oil

Kosher salt and freshly ground black pepper to taste

2 medium red onions, cut into $1/4$-inch-thick slices

Four 10-inch flour tortillas

$1/2$ cup mayonnaise

1 small garlic clove, minced

1 tablespoon fresh lemon juice

$3/4$ cup chilled crumbled feta cheese

$1/2$ cup fresh mint leaves

SERVES 4

Many of my favorite flavors from Greece are contained in this one fragrant little wrap. You can make them all summer long using an outdoor grill, but you can also cook them indoors year-round using a grill pan or a broiler. Stick a skewer sideways through the onions to keep them together when you cook them. If feta cheese is too strong for you, substitute ricotta salata, an aged ricotta cheese that is similar in flavor to feta but not as salty.

By the way, this recipe is easily transformed into a delicious vegetarian entree. Just roll the slices of eggplant around the onion, cheese, and mint, bake the rolls, and then top each one with some of the aïoli.

Preheat the oven to 350°F and preheat a charcoal grill and let the coals burn down to a gray ash. (Alternatively, preheat a broiler and lightly oil a broiling pan.) Brush the eggplant slices with the $1/2$ cup oil and season both sides with salt and pepper. Grill or broil on a rack set 5 to 6 inches from the heat, turning once, until tender, about 5 minutes. Transfer to a baking sheet to cool. Brush the onions with the remaining 2 tablespoons oil and season with salt and pepper. Grill or broil until brown and tender, about 5 minutes. Wrap the tortillas in foil and heat in the oven for 5 minutes.

Whisk the mayonnaise with the garlic and lemon juice in a small bowl to make the aïoli. Spread 2 tablespoons of the aïoli over each tortilla. Cover the bottom third of each tortilla with a quarter of the eggplant and a quarter of the onions. Sprinkle on a quarter of the cheese and top with mint leaves. To make the wrap, fold in the two sides of the tortilla. Roll away from you, tucking in the edges to form a tight cylinder. Wrap the cylinder in foil and cut in half diagonally right through the foil. The foil becomes the holder to be peeled away as the wrap is consumed. Serve the wrap hot or at room temperature.

warming tortillas

When I had Rick Bayless, chef-owner of several excellent restaurants in Chicago and an expert on Mexican food, on my show to make some of his delicious dishes, I was shocked when he told me his favorite way to warm tortillas: in the microwave! Most chefs do not reach for the old microwave. But I trust him; he knows what he is doing, and as a cookbook author and TV host he has thought hard about the best way to do things. So here is the procedure: Wrap the tortillas in a damp towel and put them in the microwave on high for 4 minutes. Let them sit in the microwave for 2 to 3 minutes more with the microwave turned off and they will be perfectly warmed and pliable.

Grilled Southwestern Pizza

For the dough:

²/₃ cup lukewarm water (105° to 115°F)

1 envelope (2¹/₂ teaspoons) active dry yeast

¹/₂ teaspoon sugar

2 to 2¹/₄ cups all-purpose flour

2 tablespoons olive oil, plus more for oiling the bowl

1 teaspoon kosher salt

For the pizza:

Olive oil for brushing and drizzling

3 cups grated Monterey Jack cheese

3 scallions, white and 1 inch of the green parts, thinly sliced

1 fresh or Pickled Jalapeño (page 345), seeded and thinly sliced

1 teaspoon ground cumin

1 small garlic clove, minced

1 cup shredded grilled chicken and/or finely chopped cooked chorizo (see page 16)

1 cup grilled fresh corn kernels (page 222)

Pickled Red Onion (page 346) and chopped fresh cilantro for garnish

MAKES 2 MEDIUM PIZZAS

The first time I even sank my teeth into a slice of grilled pizza was at George Germon and Johanne Killeen's wonderful restaurant, Al Forno, in Providence, Rhode Island, the first restaurant in America to offer this Italian original. Of course, homemade oven-baked pizza is also great, but grilling it crisps up the crust so beautifully and makes the whole pie sexy with smokiness.

The hardest part of grilling up a pizza on the rig in your backyard is making part of the grill very hot while keeping the other part cooler. It is sort of like searing a steak and then turning down the temperature.

This is a great recipe for outdoor entertaining and a really nice break from the usual hot dogs and burgers.

To prepare the dough, combine the water, yeast, and sugar in a small bowl. Mix well and set aside until foamy, about 10 minutes. Transfer to a food processor and add 2 cups flour, 2 tablespoons olive oil, and the salt. Process until the mixture forms a ball, adding more water a teaspoon at a time if too dry or more flour a tablespoon at a time if too wet. The dough should be soft but slightly sticky. Continue processing to knead the dough for about 30 seconds.

Oil a large bowl with olive oil. Transfer the dough to the bowl, turning to coat. Cover with plastic wrap and set aside in a warm place until doubled in bulk, about 1 hour. Punch down and divide into 2 pieces.

While the dough is rising, prepare the grill. Open the vents of the lid and in the bottom of a kettle charcoal grill. Place about 25 briquettes on 2 opposite sides of the bottom, leaving the center clear. Oil the rack and light the briquettes. (They will be ready for cooking when burned to a gray ash, about 20 minutes.) Combine the cheese, scallions, jalapeño, cumin, and garlic in a large bowl. On a lightly floured surface, roll each piece of dough $1/16$ inch thick. Oil one side. Working with 1 piece at a time, lift up the dough and put the oiled side down on the cooking grate directly over the heat for approximately 1 minute or until it puffs up slightly and shows grill marks. Brush the other side with oil and flip the dough over. Top the grilled side with half of the cheese mixture, chicken or chorizo, and corn and drizzle it with some olive oil. Place in the center of the cooking grate, over indirect heat. Cover and cook until the cheese bubbles, 6 to 7 minutes. Repeat with the remaining dough and ingredients. Remove the pizza and top with the pickled onion and cilantro. Slice into pieces and serve at once.

Tomato, Basil, and Cheese Tart with Pancetta Crust

For the pastry:

¹/₄ pound pancetta* or bacon

1¹/₄ cups all-purpose flour

¹/₄ teaspoon kosher salt

6 tablespoons unsalted butter,
   cut into small pieces and
   chilled

2 tablespoons chilled vegetable
   shortening

For the filling:

4 large tomatoes, sliced ¹/₃ inch
   thick

1 teaspoon kosher salt plus more
   for sprinkling the tomatoes

1 cup firmly packed fresh basil
   leaves plus 3 sprigs for
   garnish

¹/₂ cup plus 2 tablespoons
   whole-milk ricotta cheese

2 large eggs, lightly beaten

1 cup coarsely grated whole-milk
   mozzarella cheese

¹/₂ cup freshly grated Parmigiano-
   Reggiano

Freshly ground black pepper
   to taste

About 1 tablespoon extra virgin
   olive oil for brushing the
   tomatoes

*Available at the deli counter of many super-
markets, at Italian markets, and at specialty
food shops.

SERVES 6

I developed this tart in the mid-eighties for a column in *Gourmet* called "Gastronomie Sans Argent," which loosely translated means "eating well on a budget." It was for an August issue, and the theme was tomatoes. Not a tough assignment; I can't think of a cheaper and more satisfying way to feel rich than to bite into a locally grown beefsteak tomato in season. I came up with an entree that recruited all of the tomato's usual partners in crime—bacon, mozzarella, and basil. The result was a big hit.

The only problem I had in developing this recipe was that the water in the tomatoes diluted the rest of the filling. Finally I figured out that if I presalted and drained the tomatoes my problem would be solved. I have presalted my tomatoes for almost every recipe ever since.

Here is my original recipe, slightly improved; I replaced the bacon in the crust with Italian pancetta, which is like unsmoked bacon. Of course, if you left out the pork product all together, you'd be left with a great vegetarian main dish. Serve this with a tossed green salad.

To prepare the pastry, finely chop the pancetta. Cook in a small skillet, stirring often, over medium-high heat until lightly colored, 5 to 7 minutes. Drain on paper towels until cooled. Combine the flour, salt, and pancetta in a large bowl. Add the butter and shortening. Blend with a pastry blender or your fingertips until the mixture resembles the texture of small peas. Add 3 to 4 tablespoons ice water or enough to form a dough, tossing the mixture until the water is incorporated. Knead the dough lightly with the heel of your hand against a smooth surface for a few seconds to distribute the fat evenly and form it into a ball. Flatten slightly, dust with flour, and chill, wrapped in plastic wrap, for 1 hour. Roll out into a disk $1/8$ inch thick on a lightly floured work surface. Transfer to a 9-inch tart pan with a removable bottom, cut off excess dough from the edges, and prick the bottom lightly with a fork. Chill for 1 hour and preheat the oven to 375°F. Line the shell with foil and fill with pie weights, dried beans, or rice. Bake in the lower third of the oven for 20 minutes. Carefully remove the weights and foil. Return to the oven and bake for 10 minutes more or until light golden. Cool in the pan on a wire rack.

To make the filling, turn down the oven to 350°F. Sprinkle the tomato slices on both sides with the additional salt and drain in a colander. Combine the basil leaves, ricotta, and eggs in a food processor and process until blended. Add the teaspoon of salt, the mozzarella, the Parmigiano-Reggiano, and pepper. Process until just combined.

Pat the tomato slices dry with paper towels. Line the bottom of the shell with the tomato end pieces and spoon on the cheese mixture. Arrange the remaining tomato slices in one layer, overlapping slightly, over the cheese mixture. Brush the top with olive oil and bake until the cheese mixture is set, 50 to 60 minutes. Cool on a wire rack for 10 minutes. Serve hot or at room temperature, garnished with sprigs of basil.

tart tin

I use a metal tart tin with a removable bottom for this recipe, the Three-Mushroom Tart (page 216), and the Tomato Pie (page 195). It is a worthwhile investment for making open-face tarts and savory pies because it gives your finished pie a lovely fluted edge and because it makes it much easier to remove your tart from its pan.

Crispy Buffalo Chicken Salad and Slaw

4 boneless, skinless chicken breast halves, about 6 ounces each

2 cups buttermilk

2 tablespoons hot sauce

Kosher salt and freshly ground black pepper to taste

1/2 cup mayonnaise

1/2 cup sour cream

1/2 cup crumbled blue cheese

1/2 small head green cabbage, shredded (4 cups)

3 to 4 large carrots, coarsely grated

2 celery ribs, thinly sliced

1 box Triscuit crackers, pulverized in a food processor, or 2 cups fresh bread crumbs (page 347)

1/2 cup vegetable oil

SERVES 4

One of my favorite dishes on this earth is Buffalo chicken wings, that bizarre but irresistible combination of deep-fried chicken wings tossed in hot sauce with a side of blue cheese dipping sauce and celery sticks. I'm also crazy about veal Milanese—veal dipped in egg and Parmesan bread crumbs and then sautéed—especially when it's topped with a green salad.

This recipe combines the ingredients of the first recipe with the concept of the second. Triscuits make a unique crust, and by soaking the chicken in buttermilk first you ensure that the meat remains moist. (A tip of the toque to my southern viewers, by the way, who taught me this trick when I first starting frying chicken on the show.) I threw the celery and the blue cheese into the slaw along with the hot sauce.

This slaw would also go great with any grilled meat or chicken in the summer. But be sure to toss it at the last minute because it gets watery if it sits around. If you are worried about calories, use low-fat mayonnaise and low-fat sour cream. The substitution won't affect the flavor much.

Separate the tenders (the little flap of meat attached to the breast) from each of the breasts. Sprinkle a small amount of water on a large sheet of plastic wrap. Working in batches, place the breast halves and tenders on top of the plastic and sprinkle again with water. Cover with another sheet of plastic wrap and pound with a rolling pin or a meat pounder until about 1/8 inch thick. Whisk the buttermilk and half of the hot sauce in a large bowl. Season with salt and pepper. Add the chicken and marinate, covered, in the refrigerator, for 45 minutes to 1 hour.

Meanwhile, prepare the slaw. Combine the mayonnaise, sour cream, and blue cheese in a food processor or blender and process until smooth. Season with the remaining half of the hot sauce and salt and pepper. You should have about 1 cup dressing. Just before cooking the chicken, toss the cabbage, carrots, and celery with about $^3/_4$ cup of the dressing. Reserve the remaining $^1/_4$ cup dressing for serving.

Put the cracker crumbs in a shallow bowl or plate. Lift the breasts and tenders one at a time and drain off the excess liquid. Dip into the crumbs and turn to coat on all sides.

Heat half the oil in a large skillet over medium-high heat until hot but not smoking. Add half the chicken and cook, turning once or twice, until browned and cooked through, 6 to 8 minutes. Repeat with the remaining oil and chicken.

Divide the chicken among 4 plates, drizzle each with some of the reserved dressing, and top with a spoonful of the slaw. Serve warm or at room temperature with any remaining dressing or slaw on the side.

breading

Anytime you bread something with crumbs, the crumbs will stick better if you give the breaded item a little chilling-out time in the fridge. Put it on a rack if possible so the air can circulate underneath and park it in the fridge for at least 15 minutes before cooking it.

Basil Chicken Salad with Bacon, Lettuce, and Tomato

1 quart chicken stock, preferably homemade (page 338)

2 large whole boneless, skinless chicken breasts, about 1½ pounds total

16 to 20 cherry tomatoes, about 2 cups, halved or quartered

Kosher salt to taste

¾ cup mayonnaise

½ cup packed fresh basil leaves

Freshly ground black pepper to taste

8 slices bacon, about 6 ounces

2 bunches fresh arugula, stems removed, rinsed and spun dry or 4 cups mesclun

¼ cup vinaigrette, preferably homemade (page 344)

SERVES 4

Time and again on my show viewers call in wondering "How do I cook white meat chicken so that it doesn't get tough?" The answer appears to be simple: Don't overcook it. In fact, that's easier said than done these days. The threat of salmonella requires that you cook your chicken until it is well done. However, there is a brief moment, just before it dries out, when your chicken is cooked perfectly. If you poach your chicken breasts according to the method in this recipe, you will capture that moment every time. And if you poach them in chicken broth rather than water, you will also intensify the flavor of the cooking liquid. You can then recycle this liquid for soup or a sauce or throw it into the freezer for another day. Use a blender to make the sauce for this recipe. It will pulverize the fresh basil and get all the flavor out of it.

Bring the stock to a boil over medium-high heat, add the chicken, reduce the heat to medium, and simmer, uncovered, 5 minutes. Remove the pan from the heat, cover, and let stand for 10 minutes. Check for doneness. Simmer for 2 minutes longer if the chicken appears to be undercooked. Transfer to a plate or platter and cool to room temperature. Cut into ½-inch cubes. Strain the cooking liquid and reserve for another use.

Sprinkle the tomatoes with salt and pile into a colander. Set the colander in a large bowl or the sink and allow the tomatoes to drain for at least 15 minutes.

Combine the mayonnaise and the basil in a food processor. Add 1 tablespoon warm water and puree until smooth. Season with salt and pepper.

Preheat the oven to 375°F. Arrange the bacon on a rack in one flat layer on a small rectangular baking sheet with sides. Cook in the oven, turning once, until browned and crisp, 25 to 30 minutes. Drain on paper towels. Cool completely and crumble into small pieces.

Combine the chicken, tomatoes, basil mayonnaise, and bacon in a large bowl. Stir well to mix and season with salt and pepper. Toss the arugula with the vinaigrette and divide among 4 chilled serving plates. Mound each with a large spoonful of the chicken salad.

what is the best way to store basil?

All leafy (as opposed to woody) fresh herbs like the same treatment. Stand them root end down in a glass or measuring cup and fill the glass with water. If your house is cool, you can just keep this pretty bouquet on the counter. If it is not, store the herbs in the glass in the fridge. This is also a great way to resuscitate herbs that look a little haggard when they come home from the supermarket. Herbs that respond well to this treatment are basil, parsley, cilantro, dill, and tarragon. My friend Jean Anderson has kept basil this way on her kitchen counter for weeks.

Spicy Shrimp and Avocado Salad with Cashews

For the dressing:

¹/₂ cup fresh orange juice

¹/₂ teaspoon Asian chile paste*

2 teaspoons Asian (toasted) sesame oil*

1 teaspoon fresh lemon juice

Kosher salt and freshly ground black pepper to taste

For the salad:

2 tablespoons vegetable oil

1 pound medium shrimp, peeled and deveined

1 garlic clove, minced

One 1-inch piece fresh ginger, peeled and minced

Kosher salt and freshly ground black pepper to taste

2 fresh Thai chiles, sliced into paper-thin rounds, or 1 serrano, stemmed, seeded, and sliced into thin rounds, or ¹/₄ teaspoon hot red pepper flakes

2 tablespoons shredded fresh mint leaves

2 large firm ripe Hass avocados, peeled, pitted, and thinly sliced

¹/₂ English cucumber, very thinly sliced

¹/₃ cup toasted salted cashews, coarsely chopped

2 scallions, white and green parts, trimmed and thinly sliced

*Available at Asian markets and many super-markets.

SERVES 4

Haven't you often wondered how they make the delicious citrus dressing that glorifies the Iceberg salads often served at sushi restaurants? The orange dressing in this recipe is my attempt at duplicating it, and I think I've come pretty close.

With the dressing in hand, I wondered just which ingredients—other than Iceberg lettuce—to dress. I came up with a refreshing combination of shrimp, avocado, and cucumbers. The chiles and mint also help to make this a lively first course. If you take a little time and style it beautifully on the plate—with alternating slices of avocado and cucumber and a nice mound of shrimp—your friends will be impressed.

To make the dressing, combine the orange juice, chile paste, sesame oil, and lemon juice in a small bowl. Whisk to blend and season with salt and pepper. You should have about ¹/₂ cup.

To prepare the salad, place the oil in a large skillet or wok. Heat over medium-high heat until almost smoking. Add the shrimp and cook, stirring often, until light pink, about 2 minutes. Add the garlic and ginger and season with salt and pepper. Cook for 1 minute longer. Toss the shrimp with three quarters of the dressing while warm. Stir in the chiles and the mint.

Arrange alternating slices of avocado and cucumber decoratively on 4 salad plates. Mound equal amounts of the shrimp in the center and sprinkle with the cashews and scallions. Drizzle the remaining dressing over the avocado and cucumber slices. Serve at room temperature.

avocados

I prefer the Hass avocado from California to any other I can buy at the supermarket. When I tell my Caribbean friends, they protest. They prefer the avocado they grew up with—which is similar to the Florida avocado and grows in their backyards. The Hass is smaller, darker, nubbly in texture, and higher in fat (which is probably why I love it). I am sure their avocado is delicious, too. You should do a taste test and decide which is your avocado of preference. Whichever you favor, this wonderful ingredient has the side benefit of offering more potassium than a banana.

Corn Cakes with Creole Shrimp

2 tablespoons all-purpose flour

$1/2$ cup cornmeal

1 tablespoon finely chopped
    scallion

$1/2$ teaspoon baking soda

$1/2$ teaspoon kosher salt

1 large egg, lightly beaten

2 cups fresh or thawed frozen
    corn kernels

6 tablespoons vegetable oil

$1/2$ to $3/4$ cup buttermilk

1 pound medium shrimp, peeled
    and deveined

1 medium onion, finely chopped

1 garlic clove, minced

1 pound plum tomatoes, seeded
    and chopped

1 small jalapeño, seeded and
    minced

1 tablespoon chopped fresh flat-
    leaf parsley, plus more for
    garnish if desired

Kosher salt and freshly ground
    black pepper to taste

2 tablespoons unsalted butter

SERVES 4 AS A MAIN
COURSE, 6 AS AN APPETIZER

Although you can enjoy these corn cakes all by themselves, it's also great to shrink them down and top them with salsa and sour cream or—even better—with smoked salmon and caviar. But when you add the shrimp Creole, you're talking about a dish substantial enough to double as an appetizer or a light lunch. In fact the Creole shrimp without the corn cakes can serve four as an entree. Serve with a green vegetable such as steamed sugar snap peas or roasted asparagus.

Stir the flour, cornmeal, scallion, baking soda, and salt together in a large bowl. Combine the egg, corn, and 2 tablespoons of the oil in a separate bowl. Add the corn mixture to the dry ingredients and stir well to blend. Pour in just enough of the buttermilk to make a thin cakelike batter. Set the batter aside while you prepare the shrimp sauce.

Cut the shrimp into $1/2$-inch pieces. Heat 2 tablespoons of the remaining oil in a large skillet over medium-high heat until almost smoking. Add the shrimp and cook, stirring, until pink, 1 to 2 minutes. Remove with a slotted spoon and drain on paper towels. Reduce the heat to medium and add the onion. Cook, stirring often, until softened, about 5 minutes. Add the garlic to the skillet and cook for 1 minute longer. Stir in the tomatoes and the jalapeño and cook, stirring often, until thickened, 5 to 10 minutes. Return the shrimp to the skillet, add the parsley, and season with salt and pepper. (The sauce can be made up to a day in advance. Reheat gently over low heat before serving.)

Preheat the oven to 200°F. Heat 1 tablespoon of the remaining oil and 1 tablespoon of the butter in a large nonstick skillet over medium heat. Working in batches, ladle about 2 tablespoons of the batter onto the skillet and spread out slightly with the back of a spoon to make individual cakes. Cook until browned and firm to the touch, about 3 minutes on the first side, 1 to 2 minutes on the second. Reduce the heat to low if the cakes brown too quickly. Repeat the process adding the remaining oil and butter as needed. The skillet should be hot before you add the batter. Keep the cakes warm in the oven while you prepare the remaining cakes.

Arrange the cakes on individual plates and spoon about $1/3$ cup of the shrimp sauce over each. Sprinkle with chopped parsley if desired and serve warm.

Three-Mushroom Tart

**1 recipe Basic Pie Pastry Dough
(page 351)**

1 ounce dried porcini

$^1/_2$ cup dry Madeira

3 tablespoons unsalted butter

1 large onion, finely chopped

**1 pound cultivated white
mushrooms, finely chopped**

**Kosher salt and freshly ground
black pepper to taste**

**$1^1/_2$ teaspoons chopped fresh
thyme or $^1/_2$ teaspoon dried**

$^1/_4$ pound cream cheese

$^1/_2$ cup whole milk

2 large eggs, lightly beaten

**One $3^1/_2$-ounce package enoki
mushrooms, ends removed**

**Fresh lemon juice for brushing
the mushrooms**

SERVES 6 AS A MAIN
COURSE, 8 AS AN APPETIZER

When I developed the original version of this recipe for a *Gourmet* column on mushrooms in the mid-eighties, porcini and enoki mushrooms were considered very exotic; the white button mushroom was still king. These days you see all sorts of once-exotic mushrooms in the supermarket—portobello, shiitake, chanterelle, etc.—and they don't cost nearly as much as they used to.

I am wild about mushrooms of all kinds and encourage you to substitute your favorites for the ones I've built into this recipe—although you might want to keep in the dried porcini. Dried porcini boast the most extraordinarily concentrated flavor, as does the juice in which you've resuscitated them. The enoki mushrooms are in the recipe mostly just for crunch and flair—they look so pretty baked on top of the tart—and the white button mushrooms play the role of mushroom helper, a cheap mushroom filler. Make your own pie crust or pick one up at the supermarket.

This tart makes a very nice vegetarian centerpiece for a Saturday lunch or brunch. Round it out with a salad of some kind.

Roll the dough into an $^1/_8$-inch-thick round on a lightly floured surface and fit it into a 10-inch tart pan with a removable bottom. Cut off excess dough from the edges and prick the bottom lightly with a fork. Chill for 1 hour.

Preheat the oven to 375°F. Line the tart shell with foil, fill with pie weights, dried beans, or rice, and bake in the lower third of the oven for 20 minutes. Carefully remove the weights and foil. Return the shell to the oven, and bake for 10 minutes more or until light golden. Cool in the pan on a wire rack..

Combine the porcini, Madeira, and $^1/_2$ cup cold water in a small saucepan. Bring to a simmer over medium-high heat, cover, and remove from the heat. Set aside until the porcini are softened, about 30 minutes. Drain, reserving the liquid. Strain the liquid through a fine-mesh strainer lined with a double thickness of rinsed and squeezed cheesecloth. Rinse the porcini to remove any grit and chop fine.

Melt the butter in a large skillet over medium heat. Add the onion and cook, stirring often, until softened, about 5 minutes. Add the cultivated mushrooms, season with salt and pepper, and cook, stirring, until the liquid the mushrooms give off has evaporated, about 15 minutes. Add the porcini, thyme, and strained liquid. Continue cooking over medium-high heat until all the liquid has evaporated. Stir in the cream cheese and season with salt and pepper. Pour into a large bowl and set aside to cool.

Turn down the oven to 350°F. Beat the milk and eggs in a small bowl until blended, then stir into the mushroom mixture. Pour into the tart shell and bake until slightly set in the center, about 20 minutes. (The filling will still be wobbly.) Arrange the enoki in a ring decoratively over the top of the filling and brush with lemon juice. Bake for 15 minutes longer or until firm and set in the center. Cool the tart on a wire rack for 10 minutes before serving.

Vegetables and Side Dishes

Borscht Beets

**2 pounds beets, scrubbed and all
but 1 inch of the tops
removed**

1¹/₂ teaspoons kosher salt

¹/₃ cup balsamic vinegar

1 teaspoon sugar

1 teaspoon caraway seeds

**¹/₂ small red onion, sliced paper-
thin**

1 cup sour cream or yogurt

1 tablespoon chopped fresh dill

**Additional kosher salt and freshly
ground black pepper to taste**

SERVES 4 TO 6

Although my husband loves beets—as a kid he drank cold borscht by the glass to refresh himself after ball games—I don't cook them for him very often because they tend to stain my delicate little fingers. If I were a truly dedicated wife, I would slip on surgical gloves and get to work, but the gloves make me feel like I'm trapped in a straitjacket.

Anyway, borscht was the inspiration for this recipe: all the elements of the classic eastern European beet soup—the acid, the sweetness, the sour cream and dill garnish—transformed into a side dish. If you have the time, it's better to roast your beets than to boil them. Roasting really seals in the flavor. Whether roasting or boiling, remember that small beets cook faster than big beets. You have to be vigilant and take out the little guys first.

Place the beets in a large saucepan and add enough cold water to cover. Add 1 teaspoon of the salt and bring to a boil over high heat. Reduce the heat to medium-high and simmer until tender, 45 to 50 minutes. (Alternatively, preheat the oven to 350°F, wrap the beets individually in foil, and roast for 1¹/₂ to 2¹/₂ hours or until tender.)

While the beets are cooking, combine the remaining ¹/₂ teaspoon salt, the vinegar, sugar, and caraway seeds with the onion in a small saucepan. Bring to a boil and remove from the heat.

Remove the beets from the water and set aside until cool enough to handle. Peel, slice thin, and toss with the onion mixture. Stir in the sour cream and dill and season with salt and pepper to taste. Serve at room temperature.

preparing beets

Use the old egg slicer to slice cooked beets. It is also a great tool for slicing cultivated mushrooms or an avocado (quarter the avocado first so it fits into the egg slicer).

handling beets

To keep your hands from getting stained while peeling beets (and if you hate those surgical gloves as much as I do), rub your hands with vegetable or olive oil before you start. It will keep your hands protected.

My husband Bill Adler, 2001

Mexican-Style Street Corn

4 ears corn, husks removed

$^1/_3$ cup mayonnaise

$^1/_4$ teaspoon paprika, preferably hot smoked paprika*

$^1/_2$ garlic clove, minced

$^1/_4$ pound very cold Cheddar cheese

*See Mail Order Sources.

SERVES 4

Grilled corn slathered with mayo and coated in grated cheese is a well-loved staple of Mexican street fare, for which *Gourmet* once ran a recipe using shredded *cotija*, a crumbly aged-curd Mexican cheese. It occurred to me that it might just be a hit at an American backyard barbecue if the cheese called for in the recipe was good old one-size-fits-all Cheddar. Sure enough, I tried it out on my kids, and they loved it.

The trick with grating the Cheddar—because it tends to gum up—is to make sure it is very cold. In fact, it's not a bad idea to sock it away in the freezer for 10 minutes. But feel free to experiment with the type of cheese you use and with the flavoring in the mayo—corn goes well with just about anything.

This recipe doubles as a substantial side dish or a great first course to keep the hordes happy while you're grilling the rest of the meal.

Prepare a charcoal grill and allow the coals to burn down to gray ash. (Alternatively, heat an oiled grill pan over medium-high heat until almost smoking.) Place the corn on the grill and cook, turning often, until tender and marked on all sides, about 10 minutes.

Meanwhile, mix the mayonnaise, paprika, and garlic together in a shallow dish or pie plate. Remove the cheese from the refrigerator and coarsely grate or chop in a food processor until it crumbles into small pieces. Place the cheese in another shallow dish or pie plate and return to the refrigerator to prevent the cheese from becoming too warm and clumpy.

Working with one cob at a time, spread the mayonnaise on the corn, then sprinkle on the cheese to coat on all sides. Serve immediately.

how do you pick the best ear of corn?

First of all, don't even look for corn on the cob out of season. Peas and corn share this in common: the moment you pick them, their sugar starts to turn to starch. So the best plan when you are getting ready to cook peas or corn is to have a garden in your backyard filled with these vegetables. You put a pot of water on to boil, rush out and pluck the corn or peas off the stalk, rush back to husk or shell them, and then cook and eat them immediately. Realistic, right? Especially when you live in the middle of a big city.

Some new varieties of corn are being grown in Florida that are called collectively "super sweet," because they retain their sugar for at least a week after they have been picked. They are available in the fall, when there is no locally grown summer corn, and they fill in a gap in the season. They are tasty and a good stopgap, but I prefer the summer local corn that tastes more like corn and less like sugar. Your best recourse is to buy your corn in season at a farmers' market or farm stand. It is not quite as good as having that field out back, but much more realistic. The best way to tell if corn is ripe and delicious is to feel on the outside of the husk all the way up to the tip. If it feels full and firm, you're in business. I once got chewed out (very pleasantly) by a farmer at the market when I was ferociously pulling down a strip of the husk to see if there were any worms or bugs. He said, calmly, "If you find a bug or worm, you should be happy—it means that I used few pesticides." He also enlightened me about this method of checking out the corn from the outside to see if it is fully formed.

Many cookbooks tell you to cook corn on the cob to death, which is probably a holdover from the days when we were eating mostly starchy field corn. Don't do it. These days, if you have purchased fresh corn, it barely needs a dip in the pan (30 seconds to 1 minute). And if you did manage to snatch it fresh out of the field or the farmer at the market swears he or she picked it just that day, try it raw. You will be in heaven.

Ruthie's Summer Camp Zucchini

3 medium zucchini, washed

1 cup fresh bread crumbs (page 347)

1/2 cup freshly grated Parmigiano-Reggiano

1 garlic clove, minced

1/2 teaspoon dried thyme

1/2 teaspoon dried oregano

1 cup all-purpose flour

1 teaspoon kosher salt

1/2 teaspoon freshly ground black pepper

2 large eggs, beaten with 1 teaspoon water

6 tablespoons or more extra virgin olive oil

Additional kosher salt and freshly ground black pepper to taste

SERVES 6

When my daughter Ruthie was six, she started attending "summer camp," which was actually extended day care based out of the home of a teacher she'd come to know and love. There were only four kids in the camp, and they did all sorts of fun things. Of course I was thrilled to learn that once or twice a week they had cooking classes. I had been trying to get Ruth into the kitchen from the age of two, but she hadn't shown much interest. (I figured that I could begin introducing her not only to the joys of cooking but to many other subjects as well—among them arithmetic, reading, history, and the cultures of other lands—*through* cooking.) Truthfully, at that age she preferred New York pizzeria pizza by the slice, McDonald's Chicken McNuggets, and macaroni and cheese out of the box to any of my lovingly prepared homemade versions of the same dishes.

Anyway, Ruthie was just crazy about this one dish she discovered at camp, which consisted of sautéed zucchini rounds that had been dipped in Parmigiano-Reggiano bread crumbs. The kids used serrated plastic knives to slice the zucchini and breaded the rounds themselves. Then their teacher panfried them. Ruthie and I started cooking it at home as a side dish, with store-bought bread crumbs— "Italian flavor, please, Mom." Over the years we've refined the original recipe by adding spices.

You could easily turn this into a vegetarian main dish. Arrange the zucchini in one layer in a baking pan, drizzle them with some garlicky tomato sauce, grate mozzarella over it all, and throw the pan into the oven to heat up and melt.

Trim off the ends of the zucchini and discard. Cut each zucchini lengthwise into $^1/_4$-inch-thick slices.

Combine the bread crumbs, cheese, garlic, thyme, and oregano in a large bowl and mix well.

Mix the flour with the salt and pepper on a large plate or in a pie plate. Place the beaten egg in a separate plate or bowl. Dredge the zucchini slices in the flour, making sure they are well coated, and shake off any excess. Dip the floured slices into the egg, let the excess drip off, and dip into the crumb mixture to coat. Transfer to a large baking sheet and keep uncovered in the refrigerator until ready to serve. (The slices can be prepared to this point up to 2 hours ahead.)

Just before serving, preheat the oven to 200°F and heat 2 table-spoons of the oil in a large nonstick skillet over medium-high heat. Add the zucchini to the skillet a few slices at a time. (Do not crowd the skillet, or the slices will not brown properly.) Cook, turning often, until browned, 2 to 3 minutes per side. Add olive oil as needed be-tween batches. Drain on paper towels and season with salt and pepper. Keep the zucchini in a warm oven while you cook the rest. Serve hot.

My daughter Ruthie, age 5, in 1991

Sautéed Shredded Zucchini with Lemon and Thyme

2 pounds zucchini

1¹/₂ teaspoons kosher salt

2 tablespoons olive oil

1 teaspoon fresh lemon juice

¹/₂ teaspoon finely grated lemon zest

1 teaspoon chopped fresh thyme

Additional kosher salt and freshly ground black pepper to taste

SERVES 6

I was never a big fan of zucchini. I always found it tasteless and watery. But ever since Ruthie was born we have spent our two weeks of summer vacation at the family farm—and there in the backyard is my uncle Steve's vegetable garden, complete with the usual overabundance of zucchini. After years of guiltily tossing these huge zeppelins onto the compost heap, I came up with a way to cook them that concentrated their flavor and produced some crunch.

Zucchini seems watery because it *is* watery. Lose the water and you discover the flavor. A preliminary grating, salting, and squeezing gets rid of the water. A quick trip to the pan creates a little crust. If you own a food processor with a grating disk, this process takes no time at all—and you can prep the whole thing ahead of time and then just cook it at the last minute.

Trim off and discard the ends of the zucchini. Coarsely grate the zucchini using the grating blade of a food processor or the large holes of a box grater. Toss the zucchini with the salt in a large colander. Drain for 15 minutes. Using your hands, gently but firmly squeeze out as much moisture as possible.

Heat the oil in a large skillet over high heat until hot. Add the zucchini and cook, stirring, for 2 minutes. Add the lemon juice, lemon zest, and thyme. Cook for 1 minute longer. Season with additional salt and pepper. Serve hot.

Provençal Tomatoes

Nothing beats fresh tomatoes in season. Usually I just slice them, salt them, drain them, and eat them straight up with avocado and basil and a drizzle of olive oil. (My sister-in-law Janis introduced me to this perfect lunch one summer vacation.)

But even perfection gets boring after a while, and so, in the interest of variety, here is a wonderful recipe to round out a late summer supper. It is very Provençal, meaning that it is rich with the signature produce of the south of France: tomatoes, garlic, basil, and olive oil. You can salt and drain the tomatoes and make the topping ahead and then just assemble and bake at the last minute.

Cut each tomato in half crosswise. Gently squeeze the tomato halves to remove the excess liquid and spoon out the seeds. Sprinkle the tops with the kosher salt, turn upside down on paper towels, and leave until much of the excess liquid has been drawn out, 30 to 60 minutes.

Preheat the oven to 375°F and lightly oil a baking dish large enough to hold the tomatoes in a flat layer. Heat 2 tablespoons of the oil in a small skillet over medium heat. Add the onion and cook, stirring often, until softened, about 5 minutes. Add the garlic and cook for 1 minute longer. Stir in the parsley, basil, thyme, and bread crumbs. Season with salt and pepper. Arrange the tomatoes cut side up on a sheet pan, divide the bread crumb mixture over the tomatoes, and spread out as evenly as possible. Sprinkle with cheese and drizzle with the remaining olive oil. Bake until browned and crisp on top, about 20 minutes.

3 large tomatoes

Approximately 1 teaspoon kosher salt

3 tablespoons extra virgin olive oil

1 small onion, finely chopped

2 garlic cloves, minced

1 tablespoon chopped fresh parsley

2 large basil leaves, finely chopped

1 teaspoon finely chopped fresh thyme leaves

1¼ cups fresh bread crumbs (page 347)

Additional kosher salt and freshly ground black pepper to taste

2 tablespoons freshly grated Parmigiano-Reggiano

SERVES 6

Mom's Brushed Eggplant

Oil for brushing the baking sheets

4 small eggplants, about ³/₄ pound each, stem ends trimmed off

¹/₃ cup vinaigrette, preferably homemade (page 344)

Kosher salt and freshly ground black pepper to taste

SERVES 4 TO 6

Growing up, we ate our fair share of frozen vegetables: corn, peas, French green beans with toasted almonds (fancy!), the dreaded limas, etc. But every so often my mom would boldly step out and experiment with fresh vegetables. She made a mean vinaigrette, and we always kept a jar of this homemade stuff in the fridge. She ended up inventing this very simple, very tasty eggplant side dish, which consists of nothing more complicated than sliced eggplant brushed with vinaigrette and baked. You can transform it into a fancy appetizer by rolling it around a meltable cheese of your choice, baking it, and topping it off with a garlicky tomato sauce.

Preheat the oven to 375°F and lightly oil 2 large baking sheets. Cut the eggplants crosswise into ¹/₄-inch-thick slices.

Lightly brush both sides of the slices with the vinaigrette. Arrange in a flat layer on the baking sheets and season with salt and pepper. Roast, turning often, until very soft, about 25 minutes. Serve hot or at room temperature.

how to pick an eggplant

Eggplant should be firm with a smooth skin, which is an indication of freshness. What makes eggplants bitter is they get too big with too many seeds (the more seeds, the more bitter they will be) and too old. Wrinkly skin and soft flesh are an indication of age. I got into a big argument with fellow Food Network host and chef Bobby Flay about male and female eggplants. He said it was the female egg-plants that had more seeds and were therefore bitter. I called the New York Botanical Society to verify if there was any such thing as sex in eggplants and they said no, they are actually hermaphrodites. (Who knew?) Eggplants don't like to be stored at too hot or too cold a temperature, so leave them on the kitchen counter and cook them within a day or two of purchase.

elizabeth moulton
sara's mother

Mother's Day 2000

Chinese Fried Eggplant with Pine Nuts

2/3 cup plus 2 teaspoons
  cornstarch

1/4 cup all-purpose flour

1 medium eggplant, about 1
  pound, peeled and cut into
  1-inch cubes

5 cups plus 1 tablespoon
  vegetable oil

1/2 cup pine nuts

Kosher salt and freshly ground
  black pepper to taste

2 teaspoons soy sauce

1 tablespoon sugar

2/3 cup chicken stock, preferably
  homemade (page 338)

One 2-inch piece fresh ginger,
  peeled and finely chopped

3 small scallions, white part only,
  finely chopped

2 garlic cloves, minced

1 teaspoon Asian chile sauce*

2 teaspoons Asian (toasted)
  sesame oil*

*Available at Asian markets and most super-
markets or see Mail Order Sources.

SERVES 6

This recipe was featured in a travel story on Taipei written by Fred Ferretti and published by *Gourmet* in January 1993. Served at a hotel called the Imperial Palace, this dish was tested and fine-tuned by Fred's wife, Eileen Yin-Fei Lo, one of my favorite cookbook authors and Chinese cooking experts. (She also happens to be shorter than me by at least an inch and is probably half my weight, but there is nothing small about her talent. She is masterful and I have learned a lot from her.)

This recipe should help you overcome your fear of frying. Something magical happens to the eggplant cubes after they are dusted in cornstarch and fried; they become crispy on the outside and meltingly tender on the inside. And they become positively ethereal when you add the sauce with the pine nuts. You will really delight your guests with this one. This would be a nice accompaniment to Indonesian-Style Chicken with Spicy Peanut Sauce (page 74).

Combine 2/3 cup cornstarch with the flour in a large paper or resealable plastic bag. Rinse the eggplant, drain, and add to the bag in batches. Shake until coated well and transfer to a large bowl.

Heat 1 cup of the oil in a wok or large deep saucepan over high heat until almost smoking. Add the pine nuts and cook, stirring, until golden, about 1 minute. Remove with a slotted spoon and drain on paper towels. Add 1 quart of the remaining oil to the oil in the wok and heat over high heat until a deep-fat thermometer reads 375°F. Add about a third of the eggplant to the hot oil and cook, stirring often, until golden brown, about 6 minutes. Drain on paper towels and season with salt and pepper. Repeat twice to cook the remaining eggplant. Discard the oil in the wok and wipe the wok clean with paper towels.

Combine the soy sauce, sugar, stock, and the remaining 2 teaspoons cornstarch in a small bowl. Stir until the cornstarch is dissolved.

Heat the remaining tablespoon of oil in the wok over high heat until almost smoking. Add the ginger, scallions, garlic, and chile sauce. Cook just until the mixture is fragrant, about 30 seconds. Stir the soy sauce mixture well and pour it into the scallion mixture. Bring to a boil, stirring, until thickened and smooth, 2 to 3 minutes. Stir in the sesame oil and pine nuts. Pile the eggplant in a large bowl and pour the sauce over it. Stir well and serve at once.

With Eileen Yin Fei Lo, 1994

frying at home

You need no special equipment to deep-fry at home, and if you follow a few simple rules it is very safe. You do need a deep saucepan (or wok, as Eileen uses here), a deep-fat thermometer (costs about $20), and vigilance. Use an oil that has a high smoke point such as peanut, soybean, canola, safflower, or a vegetable blend. I generally use Wesson oil. Add only enough oil to fill a third of the pan and make sure the oil reaches the right temperature before you begin frying. Dry your food very well before you fry it. Then fry it in batches, which will keep the temperature from dropping. If the oil gets too hot, 400°F or above, immediately turn off the flame or add a little cold oil.

Can you reuse the oil? You can if you like, but only if you didn't fry something that flavors it, like fish. I became sensitive to this question during the late seventies, when I was working behind the scenes with Julia Child on one of her TV series and had the chance to dine out with her occasionally. If the restaurant in question was using old fat, she'd smell it the instant we walked in the door. "They are frying in bad fat!" she'd say emphatically. Bottom line: Cooking oil breaks down after several uses and acquires an off taste. There is nothing worse than bad oil.

Sautéed Spinach with Garlic Chips

**Two 1-pound bunches fresh
spinach, large stems removed**

3 large garlic cloves, peeled

¼ cup olive oil

**Kosher salt and freshly ground
black pepper to taste**

SERVES 4

Sautéing spinach used to be an ordeal. I'd clean it, blanch it, shock it (throwing it into ice water after it was blanched to stop the cooking and set the bright green color), drain it, and squeeze out the water by hand. *Then* I would sauté it.

I must have been out of my mind. Somewhere along the way I learned an easier and much tastier method—just put the raw dried spinach into a large skillet with heated olive oil and cook it. The whole process is made even easier if you start by buying prewashed spinach. The only remaining problem is that with spinach—as with any leafy green— what looks like enough raw product to feed the whole neighborhood tends to wilt down to a precious little portion for two.

If you're a garlic fiend, like yours truly, be sure to add the garlic chips. First flavor the oil by placing the thinly sliced garlic in a cold pan with cold oil. (You get more flavor out of the garlic and into the oil when you start with cold oil.) Then turn the burner to low and gently cook the chips until they are pale gold. More color than that and they get bitter.

If the spinach wasn't prewashed, wash the leaves in several changes of cold water. Rinse well and drain in a colander. Spin dry.

Use a sharp thin-bladed paring knife or a truffle slicer to cut the garlic lengthwise into uniformly sized paper-thin slices. Place the slices in a large skillet and add the olive oil. Set the skillet over low heat and cook, stirring constantly, until the slices start to turn golden brown, about 5 minutes. Remove the chips with a slotted spoon and drain on paper towels.

Pile the spinach into the skillet and increase the heat to medium-high. Season with salt and pepper. Cook, stirring constantly, until wilted but not soft, 2 to 3 minutes. Season again if desired. Serve hot with the garlic chips sprinkled on top.

slicing garlic

Jackie Bobrow, my former second-in-command at *Gourmet,* has discovered the best way to slice garlic cloves: with a truffle slicer. A truffle slicer is a little tool resembling a cheese slicer that's used to slice raw fresh truffles over a finished dish. If you decide to buy one—and they're available at many kitchenware stores—make sure the blade is slightly serrated. Of course, if you don't just happen to have a truffle slicer kicking around in your cupboard, don't fret. A sharp knife will do just fine.

can you still use the garlic if it has a green shoot coming out of the top?

By the time a green shoot is coming out of the top of a garlic clove, that garlic clove is old and dried out and almost bitterly intense. You can use it; just use less. As for that shoot, I asked Jacques Pépin about it, and he said he knew people who actually grew garlic for the shoots, which were quite sweet and delicious.

Creamed Spinach with Crispy Shallots

For the shallots:

Vegetable oil for frying

2 large shallots, thinly sliced

1/2 cup all-purpose flour

Kosher salt and freshly ground
    black pepper to taste

For the spinach:

Three 1-pound bunches fresh
    spinach, large stems removed

3 tablespoons unsalted butter

3 tablespoons all-purpose flour

2¼ cups whole milk, heated

Pinch freshly grated nutmeg

Kosher salt and freshly ground
    black pepper to taste

SERVES 4 TO 6

Creamed spinach was one of those special-occasion side dishes my mom served us as kids. Although she usually worked with frozen spinach, which is fine, it's even better using fresh spinach. The richest and most luxurious way to make this recipe is with—surprise!—heavy cream. But because I like a *lot* of creamed spinach, and I don't like a lot of heavy cream, I prefer to make it using a béchamel sauce, which is milk thickened with a butter/flour mixture. I have prescribed whole milk for my béchamel, but you could get away with 2 percent or even 1 percent milk.

The crispy shallots provide a great contrasting garnish to the creamed spinach, but if you don't have the time or inclination to add them, the spinach is great all by itself.

To prepare the shallots, fill a deep saucepan with about 2 inches of vegetable oil. Heat over medium heat until a deep-fat thermometer reads 360°F. (Alternatively, use an electric deep-fat fryer.) Toss the shallots with the flour in a large bowl to coat. Transfer to a strainer and shake to remove the excess flour. Add the shallots to the hot oil and cook until golden brown, about 2 minutes. Remove the shallots with a slotted spoon, drain on paper towels, and sprinkle with salt and pepper.

Wash the spinach in several changes of cold water. Drain in a colander and pile into a large nonreactive pot. Place the pot over medium heat and cook, stirring, until just wilted, about 3 minutes. (The spinach will steam and cook in the water clinging to its leaves.) Drain and rinse under cold running water. Use your hands to squeeze out the water. Transfer to a work surface and chop coarse. Melt the butter in a small saucepan over medium heat. Add the flour and cook, stirring, for 2 minutes. Pour in the milk, whisking constantly, and increase the heat to medium-high. Bring to a simmer, stirring often, and cook until thick and smooth, 3 to 5 minutes. Season with nutmeg, salt, and pepper. Stir in the spinach just before serving and warm through over low heat, about 3 minutes.

Serve the spinach hot, garnished with the fried shallots.

removing excess moisture from spinach

When I was making creamed spinach on the show, a fellow named John from Brooklyn called in to tell me his favorite way to squeeze water out of blanched spinach: in a potato ricer! I tried it, and he is right.

Stir-Fried Spicy Carrots with Peanuts

¹/₄ cup unsalted peanuts

1 pound medium carrots

1 tablespoon vegetable oil,
    preferably peanut

2 tablespoons unsalted butter

¹/₄ teaspoon hot red pepper
    flakes or to taste

Kosher salt and freshly ground
    black pepper to taste

Squeeze of fresh lime juice

SERVES 4

When I was a kid, carrots seemed so *ordinary*. You ate them raw or, if you were lucky, they'd be boiled and glazed with a little butter and sugar.

But this recipe, so very quick and easy, is a real surprise and a guest dazzler. It has only a few ingredients, but it ends up remarkably tasty. If you have a food processor with one of those grating attachments, it will be ready in no time at all. If you don't, you can certainly use the coarse side of a box grater and allow yourself a little more time. (Of course, the quickest option of all would be to turf the job to the husband.) After that, it is a breeze—just throw everything in the pan and you are done. You could also pregrate the carrots and park them in the fridge until cooking time.

Everyone in my family likes this dish, even Sam, and he is generally pretty leery of cooked vegetables.

Preheat the oven to 350°F. Put the peanuts in a shallow pan and bake for 10 minutes. Let cool and chop coarse. Coarsely grate the carrots. Melt the oil with the butter in a large wok or skillet over high heat until hot but not smoking. Add the carrots and cook, stirring constantly, until cooked evenly, about 5 minutes. Stir in the peanuts and pepper flakes and season with salt and pepper. Finish with a squeeze of lime juice and serve hot.

Parsnip Puree

2 pounds medium parsnips, peeled and sliced $^1/_2$ inch thick

Kosher salt to taste

2 tablespoons unsalted butter

Freshly ground black pepper to taste

MAKES ABOUT 3 CUPS, SERVING 4

Everyone confuses parsnips with turnips, which resemble parsnips not at all other than they both end in *nip*. I love turnips, but they can be a tad funky. Parsnips are sweet, almost creamy, and with a nutty edge. I have served parsnip puree at dinner parties a zillion times, and my guests nearly always tell me that those are the most wonderful mashed potatoes they have ever eaten. I don't enlighten them until the meal is over.

It was Julia Child who taught me the best way to make this puree: rather than tossing out the cooking liquid, you reduce it and then puree it with the parsnips themselves. Try this recipe even if you think you don't like parsnips. You will become a believer.

Place the parsnips in a large saucepan and pour in cold water to cover. Bring to a boil over high heat and add a small amount of salt. Reduce the heat to medium-high and simmer until tender, 25 to 30 minutes. Drain and reserve the cooking liquid. Set the parsnips aside and return the liquid to the pan. Bring to a boil over high heat. Boil rapidly until reduced to $^3/_4$ cup. Return the parsnips to the pan and add the butter. Working in batches, empty the contents of the saucepan into the bowl of a food processor and puree until smooth. Season with salt and pepper. Serve anywhere you would have put mashed potatoes.

With Julia, 1996

Stewed Green Beans with Tomato and Mint

¹/4 cup extra virgin olive oil

1 small onion, finely chopped

3 garlic cloves, minced

1 pound green beans, trimmed

3 to 5 plum tomatoes, seeded and finely chopped (1¹/2 cups), or 1¹/2 cups chopped drained canned tomatoes

Kosher salt and freshly ground black pepper to taste

¹/4 cup shredded fresh mint leaves

SERVES 4

When we lived in Boston in the latter half of the seventies, my husband Bill and I used to frequent a Greek restaurant in Central Square in Cambridge. The menu was nothing out of the ordinary, but we liked this spot a lot because the food was very well prepared and inexpensive and the service was great. (Our favorite waiter was an exceptionally dapper, courtly, and mustachioed gent named Vasilis.) They offered a side dish of large green beans that we were crazy about. The beans themselves were long, broad, and flat, with a meatiness that recalled lima beans. They'd been stewed almost to a mush in a tomato sauce made fragrant with garlic and mint. Bill has been nagging me to make them at home ever since, and I think I've finally come up with a pretty good version.

You'll probably strike out in your search for those luscious Greek green beans—they're very hard to find—but not to worry. This recipe works very well using regular old green beans. Indeed, if the ones you start with are tough, the stewing process will tenderize them. By the way, I didn't cook them to a mush. I just couldn't do it. But I think this version still captures the spirit of the original. This recipe can be made a day ahead and reheated.

Heat the oil in a large skillet over medium heat. Add the onion and cook, stirring often, until softened, about 5 minutes. Add the garlic and cook for 2 minutes longer. Stir in the beans and tomatoes. Add just enough cold water to come slightly below the level of the beans. Increase the heat to high and bring to a boil. Reduce the heat to medium-low, season with salt and pepper, and cover. Cook, covered, stirring from time to time, until very tender, 20 to 25 minutes.

Use tongs to transfer the beans to a plate or platter. Place the skillet on top of the stove. Bring to a boil over high heat. Cook, stirring often, until the cooking liquid is reduced to about 1 cup. Return the beans to the skillet and season with salt and pepper. Reduce the heat to medium-low and cook until heated through, 3 to 5 minutes. Stir in the mint and serve.

Celery Root Rémoulade with Wasabi, Ginger, and Sesame

1 medium celery root, about 2 pounds

2 tablespoons fresh lemon juice

2¹/₂ teaspoons kosher salt

2¹/₂ teaspoons Dijon mustard

2¹/₂ teaspoons wasabi powder,* dissolved in 1 teaspoon cold water

1 garlic clove, minced

2 tablespoons plus 2 teaspoons rice vinegar

One 2-inch piece fresh ginger, peeled and thickly sliced

4 teaspoons Asian (toasted) sesame oil*

6 tablespoons mayonnaise

2 tablespoons toasted sesame seeds

2 tablespoons finely chopped fresh parsley

Additional kosher salt and freshly ground pepper to taste

*Available at Asian markets and some supermarkets or see Mail Order Sources.

MAKES ABOUT 5 CUPS, SERVING 4

Let's face it: Celery gets very little love in this world. Even when the stalks are cut up beautifully, arranged lovingly alongside a battery of carrot sticks, and fancifully dubbed *crudités*, there's no disguising the fact that they're basically bland, stringy, and watery. At best they're handy edible plates for some kind of dip or other.

Celery *root*, however, is a whole different story. Grown for its root, not its stalk, celery root is a round, hairy, knoblike thing, ugly as sin, that can be as small as an apple or as large as a cantaloupe. It has a milder, more delicate taste than stalk celery, and it cooks up with a potatolike creaminess. Readily available in America only for the last 20 years or so, celery root can be found in markets from fall through early spring.

The French, however, have been glorifying this homely vegetable for hundreds of years: They puree it and combine it with potatoes in a gratin, or they grate it raw and throw it into a mustard mayonnaise to make a rémoulade. I love the classic rémoulade, but I discovered that adding some toasted sesame and some wasabi (the blazing-hot Japanese relative of horseradish that always accompanies sushi) puts a nice new spin on it. Serve this salad as a first course or a refined substitute for coleslaw.

Peel the celery root and cut into thin julienne strips. You should have about 4 cups. Toss the lemon juice, salt, and celery root in a large bowl and set aside for 30 minutes, stirring often.

Meanwhile, make the dressing. Combine the mustard, wasabi, garlic, and vinegar in a large bowl. Pack a garlic press with pieces of the ginger and squeeze to extract the maximum amount of liquid. Add the liquid to the mustard mixture and whisk until blended. Add the sesame oil in droplets, whisking constantly. Add the mayonnaise and whisk until the dressing is blended.

Rinse the celery root under cold running water. Drain well and use a clean kitchen towel to gently squeeze out as much moisture as possible. Add to the bowl with the dressing and sprinkle on the sesame seeds and parsley. Toss the salad to coat the celery root thoroughly with dressing and to distribute the sesame seeds and parsley evenly. Season with salt and pepper. Mound on a large platter and serve at room temperature.

wasabi

Wasabi, as most of us know it, is that incendiary little green pile of hot stuff sitting on the side of the sushi plate that we are supposed to dip into at our own risk and eat with the bland little pieces of rice and fish. The ingredients are horseradish powder (dried and ground horseradish), mustard powder, cornstarch, and artificial color. It is nothing like the real stuff, which is made by finely grating a bright green rhizome (aboveground root—ginger is also a rhizome). The real McCoy is very hard to grow and very hard to find here. We have given you a source (see Mail Order Sources) for real wasabi, but for the purposes of this recipe we used the more readily available powdered stuff in the can.

Southern Braised Mustard Greens with Ham

2 pounds mustard greens

1 quart chicken stock, preferably homemade (page 338)

1 meaty ham hock, preferably split in half

¹/₂ teaspoon hot red pepper flakes

2 tablespoons red wine vinegar

¹/₂ teaspoon sugar

Kosher salt and freshly ground black pepper to taste

SERVES 4 TO 6

These are good old-fashioned mustard greens, cooked slow and low with a ham hock. It is a great make-ahead dish for a crowd, and it nicely rounds out a buffet. You can make the same recipe using kale or collard greens or mix up all three. Me, I prefer the strong bite of those mustard greens. I also like to substitute them for spinach in the recipe for Sautéed Spinach with Garlic Chips (page 232).

Remove the tough bottom stems from the greens and cut the leaves into wide strips. Pour the chicken stock into a large soup pot or kettle and bring to a boil over high heat. Add the greens and stir until wilted, about 2 minutes. Add the ham hock, reduce the heat to medium, and add the pepper flakes and the vinegar. Cook, partially covered, until the greens are very tender and the broth is full flavored, about 45 minutes. Season with the sugar, salt, and pepper.

Drain the greens, reserving the cooking liquid. Rinse out the pot and pour in the strained liquid (pot likker). Transfer the hock to a bowl and cool. When the hock has cooled, remove the skin, fat, and gristle. Cut the resulting lean ham into small pieces. Bring the liquid (about 2 cups) in the pot to a boil over high heat. Boil until reduced by half. Reduce the heat to medium and return the greens to the pot. Season with salt and pepper and stir until warmed through, about 3 minutes. Turn out into a warmed serving bowl and garnish with the pieces of ham. Serve hot.

Quick Sautéed Shredded Brussels Sprouts with Pancetta and Balsamic Vinegar

When I first started doing "Cooking Live" in 1996, Sue Fenniger and Mary Sue Milliken were co-hosting the Food Network's "Two Hot Tamales." I had been a fan of these talented chefs ever since I ate at one of their restaurants in the late eighties, so I was delighted when they made a guest appearance on my show. My favorite of the dishes they prepared that night was sautéed shredded Brussels sprouts with lime and brown butter. I'd never much cared for the little cabbage look-alikes, but the Tamales made me a believer. When you give the shredded sprouts a quick high-heat moment in a pan, they emerge fresh tasting and delicious. I have cooked them this way ever since.

Trim the Brussels sprouts and discard any damaged outside leaves. Fit a food processor with the slicing blade. Force the sprouts, a few at a time, through the chute with the blade in motion. You should have about 8 cups shredded sprouts.

Heat the vegetable oil in a large skillet over medium-high heat. Add the pancetta and cook, stirring often, until very lightly browned, 3 to 5 minutes. Add the sprouts and cook, stirring, until tender, about 5 minutes. Pour in the vinegar and increase the heat to high. Season with salt and pepper and stir until the vinegar has evaporated. Empty into a warmed serving bowl and top with the cheese.

1^1/$_2$ pounds Brussels sprouts

2 tablespoons vegetable oil

2 ounces pancetta* or bacon, finely chopped

^{1}/$_4$ cup balsamic vinegar

Kosher salt and freshly ground black pepper to taste

Several strips shaved Parmigiano-Reggiano

*Available at the deli counter of many supermarkets and at specialty food shops.

SERVES 4

Warm Cabbage with Bacon and Gorgonzola

6 thick slices bacon, about
   6 ounces

³/₄ cup dry white wine

1 small shallot, minced

1 tablespoon drained bottled
   green peppercorns

Kosher salt to taste

³/₄ cup heavy cream

1 small green cabbage, halved,
   cored, and sliced about ¹/₄
   inch thick (about 12 cups
   shredded cabbage)

Freshly ground black pepper
   to taste

3 ounces Gorgonzola cheese,
   crumbled (about ³/₄ cup)

1 tablespoon finely chopped
   fresh parsley

MAKES ABOUT 6 CUPS,
SERVING 6

This is a wonderful wintertime side dish and a great way
to glorify the humble cabbage. It would go well with lean
grilled sausages (lean because this is a relatively heavy side
dish), porkchops, or our Blasted Chicken (page 66).

Cook the bacon in a large skillet over medium-high heat until crisp.
Drain on paper towels and crumble. Reserve 3 tablespoons of the fat
in the skillet.

   Combine the wine, shallot, peppercorns, and a pinch of salt in a
small saucepan. Bring to a boil over high heat, reduce the heat to
medium-high, and simmer until reduced to about 2 tablespoons. Pour
in the cream and simmer until reduced by half.

   Heat half the reserved bacon fat in a large skillet over medium-
high heat. Add half the cabbage and season with salt and pepper.
Cook, stirring often, until it begins to wilt, about 5 minutes. Transfer
the cabbage to a bowl and cook the remaining cabbage in the same
manner. Return all the cabbage to the skillet and pour in the cream
mixture. Cook, stirring often, until the cabbage is tender yet still crisp,
5 to 7 minutes. Stir in the Gorgonzola and the parsley. Season with
salt and pepper and cook, stirring, until the cheese has melted. Sprinkle each portion with the crumbled bacon.

what makes cabbage smell and taste stinky?

In a nutshell the answer is overcooking. The sooner you get it out of
the pan, the better. Cook it just until it is tender, 5 to 7 minutes, and
it will keep its fresh sweet flavor.

Magda's Cauliflower

My housekeeper, Magda, who's worked with me for years, is also a wonderful cook. She's dubbed herself *"el jefe* to *el jefe"* and in that capacity she'll test out new recipes I've given her or serve us dishes from her own repertoire. This book boasts two of her specialties. When I asked about her cauliflower recipe, she said it was a typical dish from Guatemala, her homeland. Vegetables are often coated with egg batter and then cooked in tomato sauce. The good news is you can use your favorite store-bought tomato sauce. She also makes this recipe with green beans and chayote.

Bring a large pot of salted water to a boil over high heat. Cut off the outer leaves of the cauliflower, trim away the stem, and cut around the core to remove it. Break the cauliflower into large pieces, then use a paring knife to make florets that measure about 1¹/₂ inches long. Plunge the trimmed florets into the boiling water and bring back to a boil. Cook until tender but not mushy, 5 to 7 minutes. Drain and rinse under cold running water. Spread out on paper towels to drain thoroughly.

Combine the egg whites, salt, and 1 teaspoon water in an electric mixer. Beat until soft peaks form. Add the egg yolks and the flour and mix until incorporated, about 10 seconds.

Heat the oil in a large skillet until hot but not smoking. Dip the cauliflower florets, one at a time, into the batter and shake off the excess. Working in batches, add to the hot oil and cook, turning often, until browned, about 5 minutes. Drain on paper towels.

Heat the tomato sauce with the stock in the same skillet in which the cauliflower cooked. Add the cauliflower florets and stir over medium heat until warmed through, about 5 minutes. Season with salt and pepper and serve warm.

1 medium head cauliflower, about 2 pounds

2 large eggs, separated

¹/₄ teaspoon kosher salt

1 tablespoon all-purpose flour

3 tablespoons vegetable oil

2 cups Quick Tomato Sauce (page 342) or store-bought sauce

¹/₂ cup chicken stock, preferably homemade (page 338)

Additional kosher salt and freshly ground black pepper to taste

SERVES 4

Magda Alcayaga at work in my kitchen at home, 2001

Baked Acorn Squash with Mustard and Honey

3 acorn squash, about 1¹/₂ pounds each, stems cut off

6 tablespoons unsalted butter, softened

2 tablespoons Dijon mustard

6 tablespoons honey

Kosher salt and freshly ground black pepper to taste

SERVES 6

There are only 4 ingredients in this recipe (well, 6, if you count the salt and pepper), but it is a hit whenever I make it, an easy, tasty addition to a weeknight meal. Just remember to turn on the oven first thing when you get home.

And be very careful when you cut the squash. If you don't really steady it, it's going to start rolling around on the counter, and the next thing you know you'll have cut yourself.

Preheat the oven to 375°F. Set the squash on its side and, with a large knife, cut in half vertically. Trim a piece off the bottom of each squash half so they will lay flat in the pan. Scrape out the seeds and stringy membranes with a large spoon. Place cavity side up in a large roasting pan.

Mix the butter, mustard, and honey is a small bowl until blended. Fill each squash cavity with 2 tablespoons of the butter mixture. Season with salt and pepper. Bake until the squash is very tender, 1 to 1¹/₂ hours.

leftover squash

Sandra Colling from Rochester, New York, called in one night on the show when I was making a dish with winter squash. She pointed out that anytime you have leftover cooked squash you can freeze it for future use. She suggested freezing it in muffin tins for easy single portions. I suggest that you could also turn the cooked squash puree into a soup by adding vegetable or chicken stock to thin, then topping it off with some homemade rye, pita, or Parmesan croutons (pages 40, 56, and 62).

Mashed Potatoes

Everyone loves mashed potatoes, particularly if the meal includes ample gravy. My husband (admittedly an extremist on the subject) swears that he'd be content to make a whole meal out of nothing but mashed potatoes and gravy.

There are two main candidates for the preparation of mashed potatoes. The first choice, and the one we are all most familiar with, is the russet or baking potato. (The Idaho potato is the most famous of the russets.) It is high in starch and fluffs up nicely. Another good choice is the Yukon Gold, which is becoming increasingly available at the supermarket. A cross between a baking and a boiling potato, the Yukon Gold is naturally buttery. Whichever potatoes you choose, do *not* cut up them up into smaller pieces in an attempt to decrease the time it takes to boil them. That will only make them watery and dilute the flavor.

There are several good tools for mashing: the ricer (which looks like an enormous garlic press), the food mill, and the hand potato masher. Just don't mash them in the food processor unless you want an irretrievable gluey mess. Believe me, I know. I almost ruined our Thanksgiving one year by choosing the wrong tool.

If you like your potatoes fairly stiff, follow the recipe exactly. If you like them a little looser, just add more hot milk and more butter.

Quarter or halve the potatoes, depending on size. Place in a large saucepan and pour in enough cold water to cover by 1 inch. Add salt and bring to a boil over high heat. Reduce the heat to medium and

3 pounds Yukon Gold potatoes, peeled

Kosher salt to taste

$^1/_2$ to $^3/_4$ cup whole milk, heated

4 tablespoons ($^1/_2$ stick) unsalted butter, cut into tablespoons and softened

Freshly ground black pepper to taste

SERVES 4 TO 6

simmer until tender when pierced with the point of a sharp knife, 20 to 25 minutes. Drain the potatoes and return to the pan. Reduce the heat to low and stir to dry out for about 2 minutes. Transfer to a food mill fitted with the finest blade or to a ricer and puree. (Or just mash them with a handheld potato masher.) Stir in $1/2$ cup of the milk, the butter, and salt and pepper to taste. Thin with additional milk if you like a lighter texture. (I like my mashed potatoes pretty soft.) Serve right away or keep warm in a double boiler.

making mashed potatoes ahead

I get this question often from viewers of "Cooking Live": "Can I make mashed potatoes ahead and just reheat them?"

I say no—they come out tasting stale. My recommendation is something I learned from some restaurant chefs when we had an East versus West Coast mashed potato cookoff on "Good Morning America" several years ago. I asked them how they made mashed potatoes for service in their restaurants. I knew they didn't start from scratch every time someone placed an order. They said that they cooked and riced the potatoes and then kept them in resealable plastic bags. When it came time to finish the mashed potatoes, they would heat the riced potatoes in the microwave and then just stir in the hot milk and softened butter.

Mashed Potato Cakes

When I was kid, my mom devised this way of using the left-over mashed potatoes the next day. I actually prefer these to plain old mashed potatoes. She coats them in seasoned flour and then cooks them very slowly in lots of butter. You have to be patient with this recipe, because if you try to turn the cakes too soon you won't get the delicious buttery crust. Also, if you know you are going to recycle the leftovers into cakes, don't add any additional milk or butter to the mashed potatoes or your cakes will be too loose to form.

Divide the mashed potatoes into 8 equal portions. Use your hands to form $1/2$-inch-thick patties.

Heat the oil with the butter in a large nonstick skillet over medium-high heat until almost smoking. Mix the flour with the salt and pepper in a pie plate. Add the potato cakes and turn to coat thoroughly with the seasoned flour. Add the potato cakes to the pan and reduce the heat to medium-low. Cook until they have formed a golden crust, 15 to 20 minutes. (Peek underneath using a spatula before turning.) Turn and cook the other side until golden brown, about 15 minutes. Season with additional salt and pepper and serve hot.

2 cups chilled **Mashed Potatoes** (page 247)

2 tablespoons **vegetable oil**

2 tablespoons **unsalted butter**

$1/2$ cup **all-purpose flour for dredging**

$1 1/2$ teaspoons **kosher salt**

$1/4$ teaspoon **freshly ground black pepper**

Additional kosher salt and pepper to taste

SERVES 4

Perfect Hash Browns

2 large russet potatoes

2 tablespoons unsalted butter

1 medium onion, finely chopped

Kosher salt and freshly ground black pepper to taste

2 tablespoons vegetable oil

SERVES 4

Kinda boastful, right? How do I *know* these hash brown potatoes are perfect? Because I made zillions of them that *weren't* perfect. You want them crispy and brown on the outside and moist on the inside. I kept starting with waxy potatoes, and they just never turned out right. Then one night I baked too many russet potatoes. I tossed the extras into the fridge and forgot about them. The next day I started to peel them and noticed that their texture had changed. They had been mealy and light. Now they were dense and firm—ideal for cutting into little cubes for hash browns! I threw them into a large skillet with hot oil, resisted the temptation to turn them too soon (which ruins their chance to develop a crust), and out they came. Perfect. The kids went wild over them.

Baked potatoes are another staple—like rice (see Fried Rice, page 257), angel hair pasta (see Pasta Pizza, page 169), and mashed potatoes (see Mashed Potato Cakes, page 249)— of which you should cook twice as many as you need, especially during the workweek, when you don't have the time to make everything from scratch. Then you can recycle them into a second dish at another meal.

Preheat the oven to 400°F. Scrub the potatoes well and dry with paper towels. Poke several holes in them with a skewer to allow steam to escape. Place the potatoes on a small baking sheet and bake, uncovered, until tender, about 1 hour.

Allow the potatoes to cool to room temperature. Refrigerate in a plastic bag with a resealable closure overnight.

Peel the potatoes and cut into ¹/₃-inch dice. Melt the butter in a large skillet over medium heat and add the onion. Cook, stirring often, until softened, about 5 minutes. Season with salt and pepper. Use a slotted spoon to transfer the onion to a small bowl. Add the vegetable oil to the skillet and heat until almost smoking. Add the potatoes and leave to form a crisp crust. Do not disturb the potatoes until the crust is formed, about 5 minutes. Check to see if a crust has formed; if so, give a quick stir. If not, continue cooking for another minute or two, until the crust has formed. With a spatula, turn over large chunks of the crusted potatoes. Season with salt and pepper and continue cooking until golden brown. Stir in the onion, season again with salt and pepper, and stir until the hash is heated through, about 3 minutes. Serve hot.

Roasted Lemon Potatoes

**2 pounds white boiling potatoes,
peeled and cut into ³/₄-inch
cubes, or small red potatoes,
halved or quartered if large**

¹/₄ cup fresh lemon juice

**1 tablespoon chopped fresh
oregano**

**3 tablespoons chopped fresh
parsley**

¹/₄ cup extra virgin olive oil

**Kosher salt and freshly ground
black pepper to taste**

SERVES 4

Friday night is date night for Bill and me, a time for the two
of us, as husband and wife, to slow down and catch up with
each other at the end of another week gone by in a blur. We
take turns planning this evening, and I use my turn as an
opportunity to try new restaurants. One of the places we
discovered not long ago is a Greek seafood restaurant called
Avra in midtown Manhattan. You get to choose your own
whole fish from a large and beautiful display laid out on a
mound of ice next to the kitchen, after which they fillet and
grill your choice to perfection.

But equally as impressive as the fish in the middle of the
plate were the roasted lemon potatoes on the side. They
were a nice twist on plain old roasted potatoes and, as it
turns out, very easy to make.

Place the potatoes in a large pot. Pour in enough salted cold water to
cover by 2 inches. Bring to a boil over high heat. Boil until slightly
softened, about 5 minutes. Drain and transfer to a large bowl. Toss
with the lemon juice and let sit for 15 minutes.

Preheat the oven to 450°F. Add the oregano, parsley, olive oil, salt,
and pepper to the potatoes and toss. Transfer to a shallow baking
sheet and roast, stirring occasionally, until golden, about 35 minutes.
Serve hot.

Grilled Potato and Corn Salad with Chipotle Mayonnaise

The corn in this salad should be grilled, but what's the best way to do it? In the husk? With some of the husk removed? Stripped naked? My wholehearted vote is for the "naked," or fully husked, method, which creates an unbeatable toasted popcorn flavor.

The secret ingredients here are the chipotles in adobo. Chipotles are smoked jalapeños, and adobo is a tomato-based sauce. A little bit of these guys will perk up any dish.

This salad tastes best when the potatoes, corn, and red peppers are cooked on an outdoor grill, but you can do it all in a broiler, too. Serve with almost any barbecue dish or as part of a buffet for a large gathering.

Prepare a hot fire in a charcoal grill and let the coals burn down to a gray ash. (Alternatively, preheat the broiler and arrange the broiling pan about 5 inches from the heat.)

Rub the pepper with a small amount of the oil and place on the grill. Grill or broil 5 to 6 inches from the heat, turning frequently, until charred on all sides, about 10 minutes. Transfer the pepper to a bowl and cover the bowl with plastic wrap. When cool enough to handle, peel the pepper, remove the seeds, and chop fine. Let the fire cool to medium heat.

Toss the potatoes with a spoonful of the oil, add salt to taste, and arrange in one flat layer on the grill or under the broiler. Grill or broil, turning often, until browned and tender, about 15 minutes. Transfer the potatoes to a large bowl and toss with the vinegar while still hot.

Rub the corn with the remaining oil, season with salt, and grill or

1 large red bell pepper

2 to 2¹/₂ tablespoons olive oil as needed

1¹/₂ pounds large red potatoes, cut into ¹/₄-inch-thick slices

Kosher salt to taste

2 tablespoons white wine vinegar

3 medium ears corn, husks removed

¹/₄ cup plain yogurt

¹/₂ cup mayonnaise

2 small canned chipotle chiles in adobo sauce,* seeded and minced to a paste with ¹/₂ teaspoon of the adobo sauce

2 tablespoons finely chopped fresh cilantro

Freshly ground black pepper to taste

*Available in Latin markets and many supermarkets or see Mail Order Sources.

SERVES 6

broil, turning often, until light golden on all sides, about 10 minutes. Cut the corn off the cob and add to the bowl with the potatoes.

In a small bowl, whisk the yogurt, mayonnaise, chipotle, and salt to taste. Add the chipotle mayonnaise, red pepper, and cilantro to the potatoes and stir well. Season with salt and pepper.

what is the best kind of potato for potato salad?

Whether you are grilling, roasting, or boiling your potatoes for potato salad, the best kind of potato to use is a waxy or boiling potato as opposed to a baking potato (also known as the *russet potato*, the most famous of which is the Idaho variety). Waxy potatoes just hold their shape better. Waxy potatoes that might be familiar to you are the round red potatoes or the long white potatoes. Yukon Gold, the new potato on the block, can go both ways. It is not as mealy as a baking potato and not as waxy as a boiling potato and is a good candidate for any cooking method. In short, it would be fine in potato salad.

chipotles

Unless you are a crazy chile fiend, you probably won't go through a whole can of chipotles in adobo sauce before they begin to look a little sad around the edges. The solution is to freeze them. Spoon them with a little bit of the sauce individually onto a cookie sheet lined with parchment or wax paper. Put the cookie sheet into the freezer and freeze them until they are hard. Once they are hard, they will peel off the paper easily and you can transfer them to a resealable plastic bag for future recipes.

Couscous Tabbouleh

Here's a wonderfully refreshing summer salad that can take the place of potato salad or pasta salad at a backyard barbecue. The classic tabbouleh, a Middle Eastern salad, is made with bulgur (cracked wheat), not couscous. But I prefer this version, which is based on a recipe developed many years ago by Zanne Stewart, *Gourmet's* executive food editor. A staple of Middle Eastern cuisine, couscous is nothing more than tiny grains of semolina pasta. Although it can take hours to prepare in its native lands, most of the couscous sold in American supermarkets these days is of a very acceptable quick-cooking variety that steams up in 5 minutes.

The herbs are absolutely key to the recipe. Make sure you add them at the last moment and taste the salad for seasoning—additional salt and pepper—right before you serve it. (All salads tend to flatten out in flavor as they sit.)

1 cup chicken stock, preferably homemade (page 338)

$1/2$ cup fresh lemon juice

$1/3$ cup plus 2 tablespoons olive oil

$1 1/2$ cups couscous

8 plum tomatoes, seeded and cut into $1/4$-inch pieces

Kosher salt to taste

1 English cucumber, seeded and cut into $1/4$-inch pieces

2 to 3 scallions, finely chopped

1 garlic clove, minced

Freshly ground black pepper to taste

Several large lettuce leaves for garnish

2 cups firmly packed fresh parsley leaves, minced

1 cup firmly packed fresh mint leaves, minced

SERVES 6

Combine the stock, 1 cup water, half of the lemon juice, and 2 tablespoons oil in a small saucepan. Bring to a boil over high heat and stir in the couscous. Remove from the heat, cover the pan, and let stand for 5 minutes. Fluff the couscous with a fork and cool in the pan.

Sprinkle the tomatoes with salt and drain in a large strainer for 10 to 15 minutes. Combine the cucumber, tomato, scallions, and garlic with the remaining lemon juice and oil in a large bowl. Season with salt and pepper to taste. Let stand for 15 minutes. Stir in the couscous. Mix well, season again with salt and pepper, cover, and refrigerate for 1 hour. Line a large platter with lettuce leaves. Stir the parsley and mint into the couscous. Mound the tabbouleh in the center of the platter and serve cold.

Rice for the Rice Impaired

Kosher salt to taste

1 cup long-grain rice

Unsalted butter to taste

**Freshly ground black pepper
to taste**

SERVES 4 TO 6

I can't tell you how many of my guests, particularly those from the Far East, have come onto the show and tried to teach me how to make rice. I just can't seem to get the ratio and timing right, and I always forget when you are supposed to leave it alone and when you are supposed to stir it. I know that in many countries where rice takes center stage the natives own electric rice steamers. But I don't eat enough white rice to warrant purchasing yet another piece of equipment that will clutter up my kitchen counter.

So I always go back to a little trick I learned at La Tulipe, the restaurant where I worked in the early eighties. There we simply boiled the rice in a big pot of salted water, much as we would pasta. No ratio of rice to water to remember, no worry. If you are going to eat your rice right away, you just drain it and toss it with a little butter.

If you are going to cook it ahead of time, you drain it, then rinse it to get rid of the excess starch. You can park it in the fridge in a resealable plastic bag and simply reheat it in a strainer set over a pot of boiling water, covered with a lid, when it is time for dinner. It is a great thing for those nights when you get home from work and need to round out the meal with a fast and easy starch. And if you make more than you need, you can take what's left over and turn it into Fried Rice for dinner the next night (page 257).

Bring a large pot of salted water to a boil over high heat. Gradually pour in the rice and bring back to a boil. Boil rapidly until the rice is tender, about 17 minutes. Drain well and return to the pot. Add butter and season with salt and pepper. Serve at once.

Fried Rice

This is not at all a traditional recipe for fried rice. I just made it up one night after opening the fridge and spying a leftover carton of take-out Chinese rice. The kids loved it, especially since I made a point of sautéing the rice until it was crispy.

Consider this recipe a blueprint for leftovers. In fact, whenever you boil rice, make a double recipe to guarantee leftovers. That way you have an exciting side dish or the base for dinner a few nights later. This recipe calls for peppers, bacon, eggs, and peas. You could substitute broccoli, ham, and Cheddar cheese—whatever you have kicking around in the fridge. Almost anything tastes good cooked in fried rice.

Cook the bacon in a large skillet over medium heat, turning often, until browned and crisp. Drain on paper towels. Crumble into small pieces.

Pour off all but 2 tablespoons of the fat from the skillet and add 1 tablespoon of the olive oil. Add the onion and peppers. Cook, stirring often, over medium heat until softened, about 5 minutes. Remove from the skillet with a slotted spoon and reserve.

Add the remaining tablespoon olive oil to the skillet. Add the rice to the skillet, turn up the heat to medium-high, and stir until lightly browned, about 5 minutes.

Reduce the heat to medium-low and stir in the eggs, onion mixture, bacon, and peas. Cook, stirring, until the eggs are cooked, 3 to 5 minutes. Season with soy sauce, salt, and pepper. Turn out into a warmed serving bowl and garnish with the sliced scallions.

6 thin slices bacon

2 tablespoons olive oil

1 medium onion, finely chopped

1/2 red bell pepper, finely chopped

1/2 yellow bell pepper, finely chopped

2 cups cooked rice

2 large eggs, lightly beaten

1/2 cup frozen peas, thawed

2 teaspoons soy sauce or to taste

Kosher salt and freshly ground black pepper to taste

Thinly sliced scallions for garnish

SERVES 4

Magda's Sofrito Rice

1 small onion, coarsely chopped

¹/₂ red bell pepper, coarsely
   chopped

4 garlic cloves, coarsely chopped

1 small tomato, coarsely
   chopped

¹/₂ cup packed fresh cilantro
   leaves

2 cups long-grain rice

2 tablespoons vegetable oil

1 teaspoon kosher salt

¹/₄ teaspoon cayenne pepper

SERVES 6 TO 8

Sofrito is a sautéed vegetable and sometimes spice mixture—different Latin cultures make it differently—that is used as a flavor base in Spain and throughout Latin America. Magda, our Guatemalan housekeeper, was taught how to make it by some Puerto Rican friends, improved it according to the dictates of her own taste, and now uses it to glorify her rice (a weekly favorite at our house), among other dishes. She always makes a big batch of sofrito and then freezes it in ice cube trays for use in future recipes. It would be a great addition to almost any soup or stew. (See Sofrito Clams or Mussels with Prosciutto, page 151.)

Combine the onion, bell pepper, garlic, tomato, and cilantro in a blender or food processor. Add 2 tablespoons cold water and process or blend until smooth. You should have about 1 cup sofrito. (This recipe needs only ¹/₄ cup, but it is difficult to make less than this amount. The remaining sofrito can be refrigerated for up to 3 days and frozen for up to a month. Freeze in ¹/₄-cup portions.)

Rinse and drain the rice. Heat the oil in a large saucepan over medium-high heat. Stir in ¹/₄ cup of the sofrito and cook, stirring, until fragrant, about 1 minute. Stir in the salt and cayenne. Pour in 1 quart water, increase the heat to high, and bring to a boil. Stir in the rice and bring back to a boil. Boil, uncovered, until the water has been absorbed and holes appear on the surface, about 10 minutes. Reduce the heat to low and cover the saucepan. Cook until fluffy and tender, about 10 minutes. Fluff the rice with a fork, cover, and let sit for 5 minutes. Serve hot.

Herbed Spaetzle

I was working in the test kitchen at *Gourmet,* on the hunt for an alternative to the usual starches, when I cooked spaetzle for the first time. It struck me right away that this homemade, irregularly shaped German pasta was so delicious and easy to make that I should add it to my home recipe repertoire. Sure enough, spaetzle was a hit at home and quickly became one of Sammy's all-time favorite foods, the one dish—along with matzo ball soup—that he invariably requests whenever I'm making a special holiday meal for the four of us at home. (If you have the right gadget—see Mail Order Sources—you can have a fragrant, steaming batch of spaetzle about 10 minutes after you put on a pot of water to boil.)

But, as with any kind of pasta, spaetzle really requires some gravy or sauce—or some butter at the least—to complete it. So if I'm serving it as a side dish, I make sure we have a saucy meat or chicken as the main dish. You can boil it, drain it, toss it with butter and herbs, and serve it. Or you can make it ahead of time, even by as much as a day or two. Just boil and drain it, rinse it, and put it in a resealable plastic bag. When it's time to sit down to dinner, sauté it in a hot pan until it's crispy, season it, and serve. (Sam *loves* his spaetzle crispy.)

Combine the flour, salt, and nutmeg in a large bowl and stir well. Whisk together the eggs and ²/₃ cup water and add to the flour mixture, beating until just smooth. The texture should be the consistency

2 cups sifted all-purpose flour

1 teaspoon kosher salt

Pinch freshly grated nutmeg

2 large eggs, lightly beaten

2 tablespoons unsalted butter

2 tablespoons vegetable oil

2 tablespoons snipped fresh chives

Additional kosher salt and freshly ground black pepper to taste

SERVES 4 TO 6

of thick pancake batter. If too thick, whisk in 2 to 3 tablespoons more water.

Drop the mixture through a spaetzle maker into a large pot of salted boiling water. Simmer until tender, 3 to 4 minutes. Drain and rinse under cold running water. (Spaetzle may be made a day in advance. Keep covered and chilled.)

Heat the butter and oil in a large skillet over high heat until hot. Add the spaetzle and cook, stirring often, until lightly browned and heated through, about 5 minutes. Add the chives and season with salt and pepper.

Desserts

Summary Blueberry Pudding

3 cups fresh blueberries, preferably wild

²/₃ cup sugar

2 teaspoons fresh lemon juice

2 tablespoons unsalted butter, softened

6 slices homemade-style white bread, about ³/₄ pound, crusts removed

Ground cinnamon for sprinkling

Vanilla ice cream or whipped cream as an accompaniment

SERVES 6

Wild blueberry bushes line two sides of a large field at my parents' farm in northern Massachusetts. In a good year these bushes are so productive that we just can't keep up with them. Every able-bodied human on the premises, young or old, blood relation or guest, is enlisted in the campaign to pick, pick, pick. My technologically inclined uncle Steve—a great blueberry lover before his death in September 2001—even designed and engineered his own blueberry holding unit. He tied a string around the top of an empty tennis can and hung the can around his neck. This deceptively simple device freed up both his hands, allowing for simultaneous nonstop two-handed picking. (Patent pending.)

All this bounty produces at least two happy results: Aunt Alice's Blueberry Muffins (page 304) and my mom's blueberry pudding. Mom's recipe is actually just a variation on an English summer pudding, a kind of uncooked bread pudding. You have to set it up the night before, but then you don't have to worry about it when dinner rolls around the next day. This is a flavorful seasonal dessert, easy to make, and, doubled or tripled, great for a crowd.

Pick over the blueberries and remove the stems. Rinse well, place in a heavy large saucepan, and stir in ¹/₄ cup water and the sugar. Bring to a boil and cook, uncovered, until the berries are slightly softened and the juices are released, about 10 minutes. Stir gently from time to time. Remove from the heat, cool slightly, and stir in the lemon juice.

Spread the butter on the bread slices and sprinkle on the cinnamon. Line the bottom of an 8¹/₂ x 4¹/₂ x 2¹/₂-inch loaf pan with some of the bread slices, trimming to form a tight fit. Spread half the berries and juice evenly over the bread. Top with another layer of bread and the rest of the berries and juice.

Refrigerate for 6 to 8 hours. Spoon onto plates and serve with vanilla ice cream or whipped cream.

Uncle Steve, May 2000

Andrea's Blackberry Crumble

¹/₃ cup sugar

1 cup all-purpose flour

¹/₂ teaspoon table salt

5 tablespoons unsalted butter, chilled

6 cups blackberries, preferably wild, picked over and rinsed, or frozen

1 recipe Vanilla Sauce (page 355)

SERVES 6 TO 8

This delicious dessert was contributed by Andrea Hagan, my backup recipe tester. A native Seattleite, Andrea was 11 years old when she and the 44 other members of the Northwest Girl's Choir toured England in 1981. When the tour hit Shrewsbury, the choir split up to bunk at the home of local citizens. Andrea's host served her raspberry crumble with a boiled custard sauce for dessert. "It was the greatest dessert that I had ever tasted and the first fruit dessert that I ever liked," she recalls. "I loved it so much that I asked my host for the recipe—the first time I'd ever done such a thing—and she ended up making it for me twice in the three nights I stayed with her."

Back home in Seattle, Andrea wanted to make the recipe for herself and decided to substitute blackberries for raspberries. "Blackberries grow wild all over my neck of the woods," she says. "I love them, and I can walk out my back door and pick as many as I want off a bush not 20 feet away."

She also tinkered with the custard sauce. "In England, boiled custard is so popular that you can buy it as a powder in the store," she says, but back in America she used a recipe from *The Joy of Cooking*. This version of the crumble should be served with our Vanilla Sauce. Andrea notes, by the way, that "boiled custard" is a misnomer: "If you do boil it as you cook it, the eggs will scramble."

"Everybody I've ever made this for loves it," Andrea says. "It's uncanny how good these flavors are together—and it's so easy to make."

This recipe works equally well using blueberries or raspberries.

Preheat the oven to 400°F.

Combine the sugar, flour, and salt in a large bowl. With your fingertips or a pastry blender, mix the butter into the flour until it resembles coarse meal.

Place the berries in a buttered shallow 2-quart baking dish. Grab some of the crumble topping in your hand and squeeze together. Gently crumble all the topping evenly over the berries.

Bake until the berries are bubbling and the top is golden, 30 to 40 minutes. Serve hot with vanilla sauce.

Strawberry-Rhubarb Cobbler
with Gingered Biscuit Topping

For the cobbler:

2 pints strawberries, rinsed and quartered

1 pound rhubarb, 4 to 5 large stalks, peeled and cut into 1-inch-thick slices

1/2 cup plus 2 tablespoons sugar

2 tablespoons all-purpose flour

2 teaspoons finely grated lemon zest

1/8 teaspoon table salt

1 tablespoon unsalted butter, cut into slivers

For the topping:

1 cup all-purpose flour

1 tablespoon sugar, plus more for sprinkling

1 teaspoon baking powder

1/4 teaspoon baking soda

1/4 teaspoon table salt

1/4 cup very finely chopped crystallized ginger

4 tablespoons (1/2 stick) unsalted butter, cut into small pieces

1/2 cup buttermilk, plus more for brushing

SERVES 6

Technically a vegetable, rhubarb is so darn tart that it's usually paired with a sweeter buddy, like the strawberry, in an effort to temper its tang. Try to find field-grown rhubarb. Darker in color, it has a much shorter season than the hothouse variety (late winter to early summer) but is more flavorful. In England rhubarb is often paired with ginger, so I added some to the biscuit topping for a surprise crunch.

To prepare the cobbler, place the strawberries and rhubarb in a large, heavy saucepan. Add 2 tablespoons sugar. Stir over high heat until the sugar has started to dissolve, 1 to 2 minutes. Reduce the heat to medium and cook, stirring often, until the fruit has exuded some of its liquid, about 5 minutes.

In a large bowl, combine the fruit and all liquid with the remaining 1/2 cup sugar, the flour, lemon zest, and salt. Cool slightly, pour into a lightly buttered 2-quart baking dish, and dot with the slivers of butter.

To make the topping, preheat the oven to 400°F. Combine the flour, sugar, baking powder, baking soda, and salt in a large bowl. Use a pastry blender or your fingertips to mix in the ginger and to cut in the butter until the mixture resembles the texture of small peas. Quickly stir in the buttermilk to form a soft dough. Turn out onto a well-floured work surface, knead into a ball, and roll out to a thickness of about 1/2 inch. Use a 3-inch cookie cutter (or a wide-mouth jar or glass) to cut out 4 biscuits. Gather the trimmings and roll out again. Cut out 2 more biscuits.

Arrange the biscuits snugly over the fruit. Brush lightly with additional buttermilk, sprinkle with sugar, and bake until the cobbler is bubbly and the biscuits are golden brown, 25 to 30 minutes. Serve hot.

Homemade Applesauce

**5 to 6 medium to large apples,
about 3 pounds**
$^1/_4$ to $^1/_2$ cup sugar
$^1/_4$ teaspoon table salt
Fresh lemon juice to taste

MAKES ABOUT 4 CUPS

I learned how to make this no-muss, no-fuss applesauce in the mid-eighties, when I had to teach it as part of the curriculum at Peter Kump's New York Cooking School, now redubbed the Institute of Culinary Education. Brilliantly simple, this recipe requires no peeling and no coring. All you do is wash and quarter the apples, throw them into a pot with a little bit of water and sugar, and simmer them until they fall apart. Remove the apples from the pot, run them through the food mill, and there you have it—fresh, delicious applesauce with more pectin and more body than the kind made with apples that were peeled and cored . . . and with more color, too.

Since then I've learned that unless you are an absolute nut for McIntosh or Granny Smith or any other particular variety of apple, you want your applesauce to be made from a mix of apples. They all add something unique to the flavor and texture of the finished product. (I would never make an apple pie from just one kind of apple either.)

This applesauce is great all by itself or with blintzes (page 306) or homemade sausages (page 323).

Wash the apples well and cut into quarters. Place in a large soup pot or kettle and pour in $^1/_2$ cup water. Add $^1/_4$ cup of the sugar and the salt and bring to a boil over high heat. Reduce the heat to medium and cook, covered, stirring often, until the apples are very tender and falling apart, 25 to 30 minutes. Transfer to a food mill fitted with the coarse blade and puree. Add the remaining sugar, if desired, and the lemon juice if the applesauce seems flat.

With Peter Kump and Julia, 1996

Vermont Apple Crisp with Maple Sauce

For the topping:

1 cup old-fashioned rolled oats (not quick cooking)

$1/3$ cup all-purpose flour

$1/3$ cup firmly packed dark brown sugar

3 tablespoons granulated sugar

$1/4$ teaspoon table salt

1 teaspoon ground cinnamon

6 tablespoons ($3/4$ stick) unsalted butter, cut into small cubes and chilled

For the filling:

4 to 5 medium apples such as Granny Smith, Golden Delicious, Stayman, or McIntosh

$1/2$ cup maple syrup, preferably Vermont Grade B*

$1/2$ teaspoon ground cinnamon

$1/4$ teaspoon freshly grated nutmeg

1 tablespoon fresh lemon juice

$1/2$ cup chopped dried apricots, preferably California

For the sauce:

1 cup maple syrup, preferably Vermont Grade B*

1 teaspoon vanilla extract

$1/2$ cup firmly packed premium vanilla ice cream

*See Mail Order Sources.

SERVES 6

I developed this recipe for a spot on "Good Morning America." The key to its deliciousness is Grade B maple syrup, which is more intense than the readily available Grade A. It can be found in specialty food stores or ordered directly from a producer (see Mail Order Sources). The topping can be made a day or two in advance and kept covered in the refrigerator until you're ready to assemble the crisp.

Preheat the oven to 375°F and butter a shallow 2-quart baking dish.

To make the topping, combine the oats, flour, brown sugar, granulated sugar, salt, and cinnamon in a large bowl. Add the butter and, using your fingertips or a pastry blender, mix until well combined. Keep refrigerated until you're ready to bake the crisp. (The topping can be made up to 2 days in advance.)

To prepare the filling, peel and core the apples. Thickly slice and place in a large bowl. Add the maple syrup, cinnamon, nutmeg, lemon juice, and apricots. Stir well and spoon into the baking dish.

Sprinkle the topping over the apples and bake until the apples are tender and the top is nicely browned, 45 to 50 minutes.

Meanwhile prepare the sauce. Combine the syrup, vanilla, and ice cream in a small saucepan. Whisk over medium heat until the mixture is smooth and heated through, about 5 minutes. Remove from the heat and cool slightly. Serve with the crisp while still warm.

what makes grade b maple syrup so special?

Years ago when I was in the test kitchen at *Gourmet,* I was trying to develop a dessert recipe that had a strong maple flavor. Although I was using the real stuff, Grade A maple syrup, I just couldn't get enough of a maple essence without adding maple extract. Someone suggested trying to find Grade B; I didn't even know it existed. But I found it and used it in the recipe and, wow, what a difference in flavor. The Grade A pales by comparison.

The maple syrup harvest starts in February, March, or April, depending on the climate; the sap begins to flow when the temperatures during the day rise above freezing and the nights are still freezing. The harvest usually lasts for 10 days, although the sap can be collected for 6 to 10 weeks. Maple syrup grading is based on the color of the sap. The earlier in the season, the lighter the sap and the more delicate the flavor. Grade B is the last of the harvest and the strongest in flavor. I don't use it just for cooking; I put it on pancakes.

Dried Apple and Cheddar Strudel

³/₄ **pound dried apples***

3 cups apple cider

1¹/₂ cups loosely packed grated Cheddar cheese, about 6 ounces

¹/₄ cup dried cranberries

¹/₄ cup sugar

2¹/₂ teaspoons ground cinnamon

¹/₄ teaspoon ground allspice

3 tablespoons fresh bread crumbs (page 347)

Six 18 x 14-inch sheets phyllo

5 tablespoons unsalted butter, melted

*Available at natural foods stores and most supermarkets.

SERVES 6 TO 8

My grandmother Ruth Moulton was a fabulous old New England cook. She attended the Garland School of Home Economics in Boston, a competitor of the original Fanny Farmer's cooking school. Roast beef and Yorkshire pudding, fish chowder, Johnny cakes, and other regional fare—these were her signature dishes. When I was about five years old, it was Granny who gave me my first cookbook—*Mud Pies and Other Recipes*. Even though it was a pretend cookbook, it somehow persuaded me that real cooking must be fun. Bottom line, it was Granny Moulton who hooked me on what has become my lifelong vocation.

This recipe is a variation on the old New England custom of serving a slice of warm apple pie with a wedge of sharp Cheddar, a custom duly followed by Granny. The starkness and strength of the flavors—sweet apple and sharp cheese—make this combination a perennial winner. It works very well for a crowd, and because dried apples are wonderful year-round, you can make it anytime. Of course, if you think it's weird to mix together apples and Cheddar cheese, just leave out the cheese. The strudel is great without it.

Combine the apples with the cider in a large saucepan. Simmer over medium-high heat until softened but not mushy, about 15 minutes. Drain well, discard the liquid, and let the apples cool completely. Toss the apples with the cheese, cranberries, 3 tablespoons of the sugar, ¹/₂ teaspoon of the cinnamon, and the allspice. (The filling can be made up to 1 day in advance. Keep covered in the refrigerator.)

Stir the bread crumbs with 1 teaspoon of the remaining cinnamon in a small bowl and reserve. Stir the remaining tablespoon of sugar with the remaining cinnamon and reserve.

Preheat the oven to 425°F. Stack the phyllo between 2 pieces of parchment paper or plastic wrap and cover with a dampened kitchen towel. Arrange another clean kitchen towel on a work surface with the long side facing you. Put a sheet of phyllo on the towel with the long side facing you. Brush the phyllo with some of the butter and sprinkle it with about 2 teaspoons of the reserved bread crumb mixture. On this layer, brush and sprinkle 4 more sheets of phyllo in the same manner and lay the sixth sheet of phyllo on top.

Spread on the filling in a 3-inch-wide strip, mounding it on the phyllo 4 inches above the near long side, leaving a 2-inch border at each end. Using the kitchen towel as a guide, lift the bottom 4 inches of the pastry over the filling, fold in the ends, and tightly roll up the strudel. Carefully transfer the strudel, seam side down, to a lightly buttered baking sheet. Brush with the remaining butter. Arrange 1-inch-wide strips of wax or parchment paper 1 inch apart diagonally across the strudel. Transfer the reserved cinnamon sugar to a small strainer, shake it evenly over the strudel, and carefully remove the wax paper strips. Bake the strudel in the lower third of the oven for 20 to 25 minutes or until golden brown. Cool on the baking sheet set on a wire rack. (The strudel may be made up to 1 day in advance. Keep covered in the refrigerator. Reheat in a preheated 400°F oven for 20 minutes.) Use a serrated knife to cut into 1-inch slices. Serve warm.

My grandmother Ruth Moulton on her 10th birthday, November 1902

Almond-Stuffed Pears in Pastry

For the almond stuffing:

1 cup whole blanched almonds, about 3 ounces

6 tablespoons sugar

6 tablespoons unsalted butter, cut into small pieces and chilled

1 large egg

1 tablespoon all-purpose flour

For poaching the pears:

4 firm but ripe Anjou pears with stems, 2^1/$_2$ pounds

2 cups sugar

2^1/$_2$ cups dry white wine

Two 1-inch-wide strips lemon zest

1 vanilla bean,* halved lengthwise

For baking the pears:

1 recipe sweetened pastry (page 351)

1 large egg, beaten with 1 teaspoon cold water

For serving the pears:

1 cup Quick Raspberry Sauce (page 352) or Best Raspberry Sauce in the World (page 353)

*Available at specialty food shops or see Mail Order Sources.

SERVES 4

This is definitely a dessert for a dinner party. It takes a little bit of work, but it will wow your guests.

The pears are poached first, hollowed out a little to make room for some almond stuffing, then wrapped in pastry dough decorated with dough cutouts in the shape of leaves. You can make the dough and poach and stuff the pears a day ahead of time. Wrap the pears in the pastry a few hours before your guests arrive. Finally, pop them into the oven just 25 minutes before you want to serve dessert. Baked, they look so great on the plate—like a pastry version of a pear.

You might also want to try this recipe in the fall, when those wonderful little Seckel pears are in season. Each of your lucky guests would be served two or three of these tiny delights.

To prepare the almond stuffing, grind the almonds with the sugar to a very fine powder in a food processor. Add the butter and process just enough to blend, about 5 seconds. Add the egg and flour and process until the mixture gathers into a ball. You should have about 1^1/$_2$ cups. (This makes more than you'll need for this recipe, but it is difficult to prepare less. The almond stuffing can be made 2 to 3 days in advance and kept refrigerated. It also freezes beautifully.)

Peel the pears for poaching. (Keep the stem intact if possible.) Use a melon baller to scoop out the bottom of each pear. With a very small spoon, continue to remove the core, leaving a cavity large enough to hold 2 tablespoons of filling. Combine the sugar, wine, and lemon zest in a large saucepan. Scrape the seeds from the vanilla bean into the pan and add the bean to the pan as well. Pour in 2^1/$_2$ cups cold water. Bring to a boil over high heat, stirring just until the sugar has dissolved. Reduce the heat to medium-low, add the pears, and cover. Simmer gently until the pears are tender but not mushy, about 20 minutes. Carefully transfer to a plate and cool to room temperature. Discard the poaching liquid or reserve for another use.

When ready to bake the pears, cut the dough into 4 equal pieces. Working with one quarter at a time, roll out $1/8$ inch thick into an 8-inch circle. (An 8-inch round cake pan is a good guide.) Reserve all trimmings. Keep the circles refrigerated while you continue with the remaining quarters of the pastry.

Pat the poached pears dry with paper towels. Fill each cavity with 1 to 2 tablespoons of almond stuffing. Stand 1 pear upright on a work surface and brush with some of the beaten egg. Cut out a wedge that measures about a third of the dough, starting from the center of the circle. (Add the cutout wedge to the other pastry trimmings.) With the center of the circle at the stem, drape the dough around the pear as if you were making a cone and let the stem stick out. Press the overlapping seam against the dough beneath and gently tuck in the extra pastry. Continue with the remaining pears.

Gather the pastry scraps into a ball and roll out $1/8$ inch thick. Make decorative leaves by cutting them out of the dough freeform with a paring knife. Brush the pastry with beaten egg and place the leaves around the stem. Brush the leaves with more beaten egg. Chill the pears for 30 minutes.

Preheat the oven to 425°F. Place the pears on a buttered baking pan and bake for 25 minutes or until the pastry is golden brown. Cool slightly and serve warm with raspberry sauce spooned around the pear.

Michael Green says:
just desserts

Still one of the stepchildren of the wine world, dessert wines are underappreciated and ignored. It is a shame, because these wines, so often decadent and luscious, offer a brilliant finale to most any meal. Dessert wines can be served as dessert or with dessert, and the best versions strike a balance of sweetness, alcohol, and acidity.

When serving a dessert wine with dessert, choose desserts that are not overly sweet. Serving a sweet dessert wine with a sweeter dessert will make the wine taste thin and dry. While there are countless versions of wines produced from a variety of regions and grapes, look for wines produced from Muscat and Riesling, as well as the famed sweet wines of the Bordeaux region of Sauternes. A little goes a long way—figure on half a glass of wine ($2^1/_2$ ounces) per guest. One bottle will yield 10 servings.

Jiggly Orange Wedges

2 navel oranges

2 juice oranges

1 envelope (1 tablespoon) unflavored gelatin

1½ ounces vodka (optional)

SERVES 4

I saw these orange wedges many years ago in Australian *Vogue*, a magazine that I tried to look at as often as possible because it had a consistently interesting food section. Although it was well past the heyday of my Jell-O years, I thought this recipe was clever, particularly as a snack for kids. Asked years later to come up with some recipes for a little booklet for *Gourmet* advertisers entitled "Healthy Home Cooking," I remembered these orange wedges and adapted them for the book.

Essentially, we're talking about fresh orange juice gelled with unflavored gelatin. Big deal, right? But when you pour the orange juice back into the orange half, let it set, and then cut it into wedges, it gets everyone's attention. A plateful of these crayon-colored snacks set out on a warm summer's day makes everyone happy. And grown-ups who add a little vodka to the recipe end up with a killer gelled screwdriver.

Cut the oranges in half crosswise and squeeze out the juice. Strain and measure. You should have about 1¾ cups juice. Add more juice if you have less than this amount and remove juice if you have more.

Carefully scrape out and discard the pulp from the 2 navel oranges to form half shells. Combine ¼ cup of the juice and the gelatin in a small saucepan. Set aside for 5 minutes to dissolve the gelatin. Heat the mixture slowly over low heat and stir constantly until smooth, 3 to 4 minutes. Whisk in the remaining juice and the vodka, if desired. Arrange the orange shells cut side up in muffin tins or ramekins. Divide the mixture among the 4 shells and cover each with plastic wrap. Chill until firm, at least 4 hours and preferably overnight. Cut each half into 3 wedges before serving.

Snow Pudding

1 envelope (1 tablespoon) unflavored gelatin

1 cup sugar

$1/4$ teaspoon table salt

$1/4$ cup fresh lemon juice

1 teaspoon freshly grated lemon zest

3 large egg whites* at room temperature

1 cup fresh blueberries, raspberries, or blackberries

Vanilla Sauce (page 355) or Quick Raspberry Sauce (page 352) for serving

*If you are concerned about salmonella, use pasteurized egg whites or powdered egg whites.

MAKES ABOUT 6 CUPS, SERVING 6

This is another of those wonderful recipes Granny used to make for us when we were kids that is now treasured by the whole Moulton clan as a family heirloom. Although it sounds like something scooped out of a blizzard, snow pudding is nothing more than foamy gelled lemon juice. Of course, it may be more useful (or at least more elegant) to imagine a lemon meringue pie in which the meringue itself has been charged with lemony tartness and the gluey filling jettisoned. Indeed, the good news is that this recipe has no fat. It is quite light and refreshing, and it can be dressed up with fresh berries, raspberry sauce, and/or vanilla sauce.

Snow Pudding may well take you by surprise. My cousin Abby tried some in the testing stage, thoughtfully pronounced it "very close to the original," and proceeded to kill two portions back to back. Ruthie's friend Harley likewise downed 2 servings the first time she tasted it and has since bugged me to make it again. It is one of those old recipes (I think my grandmother adapted it from Fanny Farmer) that tastes not just new again but modern.

Pour $1/4$ cup cold water into a small saucepan. Sprinkle on the gelatin and set aside for 5 minutes to dissolve. Add the sugar, salt, and $1 1/4$ cups cold water. Set over medium-high heat and cook, stirring constantly, until the sugar and gelatin have dissolved, about 2 minutes. Remove from the heat and stir in the lemon juice and zest. Pour into a large bowl and refrigerate until almost set, about 2 hours.

Use an electric mixer to beat the gelled mixture until light and airy, 3 to 5 minutes. Add the egg whites and continue beating until the mixture increases in volume and begins to form gentle, soft peaks, about 5 minutes.

Place a few berries in the bottom of decorative glasses or dishes (a wine goblet, parfait glass, or martini glass, for example). Spoon in the pudding, cover with plastic wrap, and chill until firm, at least 3 hours and preferably overnight. Serve in the glass with the vanilla or raspberry sauce.

separating eggs

When you are separating eggs, it is best to do it when they are cold. You want to keep the yolks out of the whites or the whites won't beat up properly. The yolks have a tendency to break easily when they are warm. You can separate the eggs many different ways, the most popular being to pass the yolk back and forth between the broken shells while letting the white drip into a bowl beneath. Use just one bowl to separate over and then transfer each clean white to another bowl. Perhaps you've had the experience, as I have, of separating eleven eggs perfectly, only to have the twelfth yolk break, fall into the whites, and render all 12 useless for beating. If you should happen to drop an egg shell fragment into the whites, the best way to fish it out is with another shell. The broken bit will snuggle right into the larger piece of shell, and you'll be able to lift it out easily.

Another way to separate eggs, my preferred way, is to use your impeccably clean hands. The egg white falls cleanly and completely through your fingers. Try it, but make sure your hands are well washed first.

Three-Citrus Flan

1 lemon

1 lime

1 orange

¹/₂ cup plus ¹/₃ cup plus
   1 tablespoon sugar

1 cup whole milk

1 cup heavy cream

1 vanilla bean*, halved
   lengthwise

2 large eggs

2 large egg yolks

Pinch table salt

*Available at specialty food shops or see
Mail Order Sources.

SERVES 4

I learned this recipe from my pal Sandy Gluck when I was her sous chef at the Café New Amsterdam in New York's West Village in the early eighties. We'd met in 1977, both of us fresh out of cooking school, both of us winners of a scholarship from Les Dames d'Escoffier, a national culinary association dedicated to the advancement of women in the field. The scholarship was supposed to send us on a gastronomic cruise to Italy. The plans changed, and we ended up on the maiden voyage of a jazz cruise to Cuba that featured much better music than food. We sailed with Dizzy Gillespie, Stan Getz, and Earl "Fatha" Hines and their bands and attended a great jazz concert in Havana during which the American musicians paired up with their Cuban counterparts and made beautiful music together. It was also in Havana that I ate some of the best roast suckling pig I will probably ever encounter.

Sandy and I became fast friends on board that ship. I spent the next four years working in restaurants in Boston, and when I returned to New York in 1981, jobless, Sandy took me in. The Café New Amsterdam was a small restaurant on West Fourth Street where Sandy, as chef, was making beautiful food based on fresh local ingredients. Her citrus flan was one of my favorite desserts.

Remove the rinds from the lemon, lime, and orange and cut away the bitter white pith. (Reserve the flesh for another use.) Combine the zest with 1 tablespoon sugar in a food processor. Process until finely ground, 20 to 30 seconds.

Pour the milk and cream into a large saucepan. Add the ground zest and the vanilla bean. Place the saucepan over medium heat and cook until bubbles form around the edges. Remove the saucepan from the heat, cover, and let steep for 30 minutes.

Meanwhile, make a caramel syrup by spreading $1/2$ cup sugar in the bottom of a heavy skillet. Cook over medium heat until the sugar starts to melt, 5 to 7 minutes. Stir gently so that the sugar melts evenly. Cook, watching carefully to prevent burning, until the sugar turns dark, 7 to 10 minutes. Remove from the heat and carefully pour into four 1-cup custard cups or ramekins. Immediately turn to coat the base and sides evenly with the hot caramel. Set aside.

Strain the cream and milk mixture into a large bowl. Discard the zest and scrape the seeds from the vanilla beans into the strained milk and cream. (Rinse and dry the scraped beans and reserve for another use.)

Preheat the oven to 350°F. Line the bottom of a baking pan large enough to hold the ramekins snugly with a clean kitchen towel and bring a large saucepan of water to a boil. (The towel will prevent the ramekins from hitting the pan as they bake.) Beat the eggs and yolks with the salt in a large bowl until blended. Whisk in the remaining $1/3$ cup sugar. Stir in the milk and cream. Stir briefly to mix and pour into the caramel-lined cups. Arrange the filled ramekins on the towel in the pan. Place the pan on the middle rack of the oven and carefully pour in enough of the boiling water to come halfway up the sides of the pan. Bake until the custard is just set in the center, 35 to 40 minutes.

Remove from the oven and cool to room temperature. Cover with plastic wrap and refrigerate until well chilled, at least 6 hours or overnight. Just before serving, run a knife around the edge of the custard and unmold onto individual plates. The caramel will have made a sauce for the flan.

With my friend and colleague Sandy Gluck, 1993

Pumpkin Flan

1 cup sugar

$^1/_2$ cup whole milk

One 5-ounce can evaporated milk

2 cinnamon sticks, broken into small pieces

3 large eggs

$^1/_4$ teaspoon table salt

1 cup cooked or canned pureed pumpkin

2 tablespoons dark rum

$^1/_2$ teaspoon ground ginger

$^1/_4$ teaspoon freshly grated nutmeg

$^1/_2$ cup heavy cream

1 teaspoon sugar

2 tablespoons minced crystallized ginger

SERVES 6

One of our favorite neighborhood restaurants is La Taza de Oro, a great little Puerto Rican spot on Eighth Avenue in Chelsea. The menu always features five or six entrees, accompanied by your choice of yellow or white rice and several different kinds of beans. (When Ruthie was three and four years old, she was such a nut for La Taza's black beans that the counter guy there dubbed her Black Bean and set her up with a little dish of them as soon as we entered the restaurant.) The portions are ample, the service is friendly, the prices are modest, and the food is soulful, all the way down to the *café con leche*.

For years we had takeout La Taza for dinner on Friday nights. Our big sinful treat was dessert: *café con leche* and flan. The texture of the flan was so creamy that I had to find out the secret. It turned out to be the same ingredient that makes their *café con leche* so special: evaporated milk.

This pumpkin flan is the ultimate comfort dessert. The ginger whipped cream dresses it up, but it's real good all by itself.

Make a caramel syrup by spreading half of the sugar in the bottom of a heavy skillet. Cook over medium heat until the sugar starts to melt, 5 to 7 minutes. Stir gently so that the sugar melts evenly. Cook, watching carefully to prevent burning, until the sugar turns dark, 7 to 10 minutes. Remove from the heat and carefully pour into six 1-cup custard cups or ramekins. Immediately turn to coat the base and sides evenly with the hot caramel. Set aside.

Combine the milk and evaporated milk in a small saucepan. Warm over medium-high heat until bubbles appear around the edges. Add the cinnamon sticks and cover. Remove from the heat and set aside to infuse for 15 minutes.

Preheat the oven to 350°F. Line the bottom of a baking pan large enough to hold the ramekins snugly with a clean kitchen towel and bring a large saucepan of water to a boil. (The towel will prevent the ramekins from hitting the pan as they bake.)

Beat the eggs with the remaining sugar and the salt in a large bowl until light and lemon colored. Beat in the pumpkin, rum, ginger, and nutmeg. Pour the milk mixture through a fine-mesh strainer into the bowl and discard the cinnamon. Stir the mixture until smooth and ladle equal amounts into the ramekins.

Arrange the filled ramekins on the towel in the pan. Place the pan on the middle rack of the oven and carefully pour in enough of the boiling water to reach about halfway up the sides of the dishes. Bake until a knife inserted into the center comes out clean, about 30 minutes. Remove the ramekins from the water bath and cool on wire racks. Cover with plastic wrap and refrigerate until very well chilled, at least 6 hours.

To unmold, run a knife around the flan to loosen. Hold a dessert plate or individual serving bowl with a flat bottom over the ramekin and invert quickly. Caramel will pour out and surround the flan.

Whip the cream with an electric mixer until it forms soft peaks. Add 1 teaspoon sugar and whip until it holds soft peaks. Serve the flans with a dollop of whipped cream and a sprinkling of crystallized ginger.

canned or fresh pumpkin—which is better?

Fresh pumpkin flesh can be delicious from those little pumpkins (see headnote, page 42) or the slightly larger sugar pumpkins. But once pumpkins get much bigger than that, their flesh tends to be watery and not very flavorful. From a flavor point of view, canned pumpkin is a fine alternative to fresh, as long as it is cooked with a bunch of other ingredients such as in pumpkin pie. Canned and fresh are both a good source of beta-carotene, vitamin C, and potassium. But canned pumpkin has a better nutritional profile than fresh because it is so concentrated.

Karen's Mango Streusel Tea Cake

For the batter:

12 tablespoons (1½ sticks) unsalted butter, softened

1 cup sugar

4 large eggs

1¾ cups all-purpose flour

¼ cup cornstarch

2 teaspoons baking powder

¼ teaspoon table salt

1 cup buttermilk

1 tablespoon vanilla extract

2 large ripe mangoes, about 1 pound each, peeled, pitted, and thinly sliced

For the streusel:

4 tablespoons (½ stick) unsalted butter, cut into small pieces and chilled

½ teaspoon freshly grated nutmeg

¼ cup firmly packed light brown sugar

1 cup all-purpose flour

SERVES 12

I was working at La Tulipe when I met Karen Pickus, who would become one of my best and oldest friends. One morning in 1982 she knocked on the door to apply for a job, and I happened to be the one who answered. I don't know why, but it made such an impression on me when Karen stuck out her hand and introduced herself, as if I were the one in charge. Maybe it was because, like me, she is sort of a midget, and it just seemed funny, the two of us standing there acting so formal.

Karen was hired, and we became friends instantly. I think we would have ended up friends no matter how or where we met, but working in a restaurant is sort of like fighting a war; you are in the trenches and you go through a lot together. After I left La Tulipe, Karen and I kept in touch and occasionally worked together. Today she is the executive chef at "Good Morning America," and when I do my little spots there, I know I am in good hands. She always preps and styles my food beautifully.

Karen is a fabulous intuitive cook at home, and we're always delighted when we get invited to dinner at her place. But her real forte is pastry, so it is two of her desserts that we feature here: Mango Streusel Tea Cake and Mango Ice.

Preheat the oven to 350°F. Butter and flour a 10-inch springform pan.

To prepare the batter, beat the butter and sugar together with an electric mixer on high until pale yellow and creamy, about 2 minutes. Add the eggs one at a time, beating well after each addition. Stop and scrape down the sides of the bowl often.

Sift the flour, cornstarch, baking powder, and salt together onto a sheet of parchment paper. Lift up the parchment paper and add the flour mixture to the egg mixture all at once. Mix at low speed for 10 seconds and scrape down the sides. Slowly add the buttermilk and vanilla, continuing to mix at low speed until the batter is smooth, 1 to 2 minutes.

Pour the batter into the prepared pan, smoothing the top with a rubber spatula. Arrange the mango slices decoratively around the top surface of the batter in a circular pattern, with a few slices placed in the center.

For the streusel, combine the butter, nutmeg, sugar, and flour in a large bowl. Mix with your fingertips until well combined and crumbly. Sprinkle over the batter and mangoes.

Bake in the center of the oven for 1 hour or until the center is firm. Check the center with a toothpick; if it does not come out clean, bake for 10 minutes longer. Cool completely on a wire rack before serving.

working with parchment paper

I learned a wonderful trick about adding dry ingredients to wet ingredients from Elizabeth Alston, the former food editor of *Woman's Day* and author of several excellent cookbooks (especially in the baking category). I used to sift my dry ingredients into a bowl and then add them to the wet ingredients. This is not an easy task to do, and quite a bit of the flour from the bowl ends up on the counter. Then I saw Elizabeth sift her dry ingredients right onto a piece of parchment. After that it was very easy to pick up the parchment at both ends and just slide the sifted flour mixture into the wet ingredients bowl. Now I reach for the parchment paper every time. I also use it when I am measuring dry ingredients, especially spices. I mound the item in the measuring cup or spoon and level the top by running the dull edge of a knife over it. Then it is easy to put the excess back in that tiny spice bottle by just lifting up the parchment and pouring it back in.

Mango Ice

**2 large ripe mangoes, about
  1 pound each**

**¹/₂ cup Simple Sugar Syrup (page
  356), chilled**

**1 teaspoon ground cardamom
  (optional)**

MAKES ABOUT 2¹/₂ CUPS
PACKED, SERVING 4 TO 6

Karen Pickus developed this recipe to go with her Mango
Streusel Tea Cake (page 282), but it stands up very nicely
on its own, too. What we call ice the Italians call *granita* and
the French call *granité*. A kind of sorbet with ice crystals,
granita is ridiculously simple to make and requires no
special equipment. Everyone will go for this dessert, which
is low in fat but high in flavor.

Peel the mangoes and cut away the flesh from the pit. Cut the flesh
into 1-inch pieces. You should have about 3 cups.

Combine the flesh and the syrup in a blender or food processor
and blend at high speed until completely pureed. Blend in the cardamom if desired.

Pour the mixture into a 9 X 13-inch glass dish. Transfer to the
freezer and freeze, stirring with a fork every hour, until crystals form
throughout, 4 to 5 hours.

**With my friend and colleague
Karen Pickus, 1999**

Butterscotch Bread Pudding with Coffee Sauce

When I was a kid, one of my all-time favorite desserts was coffee ice cream and hot butterscotch sauce. I'm not sure if I loved it for the slightly bitter coffee taste counterbalanced by the sweet buttery sauce or for the canned whipped cream and Day-Glo red cherries on top.

I flatter myself that my tastes have matured as I've grown up, but sometimes I'm not so sure. Although I have indeed kissed off canned whipped cream and dyed cherries, this recipe still boasts that swell butterscotch-and-coffee combo. (Light brown sugar cooked to a caramel state provides the butterscotch taste, and the coffee is in the custard.) If you don't want to make the sauce, coffee ice cream would be a great stand-in.

12 slices homemade-style white bread, about $3/4$ pound, crusts removed

6 tablespoons ($3/4$ stick) unsalted butter

$1^1/2$ cups firmly packed light brown sugar

3 cups half-and-half

$1/2$ teaspoon table salt

2 large eggs

2 large egg yolks

2 teaspoons vanilla extract

1 recipe Vanilla Sauce (page 355)

1 tablespoon instant espresso powder

SERVES 6

Preheat the oven to 350°F and butter six $1^1/4$-cup ramekins or a shallow 2-quart ceramic or glass baking dish. Line the bottom of a baking pan large enough to snugly hold the ramekins or baking dish with a clean kitchen towel and bring a large saucepan of water to a boil. (The towel will prevent the ramekins from hitting the pan as they bake.)

Spread the bread out in a single layer on a baking sheet and place in the oven until slightly dried out, about 7 minutes. Let cool. Cut the bread into $1/2$-inch cubes and divide evenly among the ramekins.

Combine the butter, sugar, and 2 tablespoons water in a large saucepan. Stir over low heat until smooth and bubbling at the edges, about 10 minutes. Add 2 cups of the half-and-half and the salt. Increase the heat to medium-high and bring almost to a boil.

Whisk the eggs and egg yolks with the remaining cup of half-and-half and the vanilla in a large bowl until well blended. Slowly pour in the hot half-and-half mixture, whisking constantly. Ladle the mixture evenly into the ramekins or baking dish.

Arrange the filled ramekins or baking dish on the towel in the pan. Place the pan on the middle rack of the oven and carefully pour in enough of the boiling water to reach about halfway up the sides of the dishes. Cook until golden and set in the middle, 35 to 40 minutes for ramekins, 40 to 45 minutes for the 2-quart dish. Transfer to wire racks to cool.

Prepare the vanilla sauce as directed. Stir the espresso powder into the sauce while warm. Cool and chill before serving with the pudding.

what do you do if your brown sugar has gotten hard in the box?

There are several tricks to remoisten it. The quickest way is in a microwave, and there are instructions right on the side of the brown sugar box that tell you how to do it. If you don't own a microwave, just stick an apple wedge or a piece of bread inside the plastic liner in the box, close it up, and let the brown sugar chill overnight in the fridge. The next day, take out and discard the apple or bread, and the sugar will be soft and moist again. You can prevent your sugar from ever hardening if you put it in the fridge after you open it.

By the way, if you've ever wondered what brown sugar is, it is a combination of white sugar and molasses. Dark brown sugar has more molasses than light.

Dulce de Leche Rice Pudding with Toasted Almonds

2 1/4 cups whole milk
1/3 cup long-grain white rice
1 cinnamon stick
3 large egg yolks
1/2 cup dulce de leche*
1 teaspoon vanilla extract
1/4 cup slivered almonds, toasted

*Available at many supermarkets or see Mail Order Sources.

SERVES 4

When Häagen-Dazs introduced its *dulce de leche* ice cream several years ago, the company hoped it would sell well to American Latinos, but I don't think it had any idea that *everyone* would quickly end up loving it. Hey, what's not to love? Long popular throughout South America, where it is known by many names, *dulce de leche* is condensed milk, heated in the can and caramelized, which gives it a toasty flavor. Rafael Palomino, in his cookbook *Bistro Latino*, applauds the versatility of this sweet, which works as "dessert on its own or as an ingredient in cookies, cakes, muffins, and ice cream." Today, thanks to our growing Latino population, concentrated *dulce de leche* is available at most American supermarkets. (I use it in this recipe.) We also have a source for it in the back of the book.

Rice pudding flavored with *dulce de leche* makes delicious sense. They are both comfort foods. The toasted almonds add a nice crunchy counterpoint.

Mix together 2 cups of the milk, the rice, and the cinnamon stick in a medium saucepan. Bring to a boil and simmer over medium-low heat until the rice is tender, 40 to 45 minutes. Discard the cinnamon stick and set the pan aside.

Whisk the remaining 1/4 cup milk with the egg yolks in a large bowl. Add a little of the rice mixture at a time, whisking constantly. When all the rice has been added, return the pudding to the pan and cook over low heat, stirring, until the temperature of the pudding reaches 160°F, 3 to 5 minutes. Remove from the heat and stir in the *dulce de leche* and vanilla. Stir until incorporated. Pour the pudding into a bowl, cover, and refrigerate until cold, at least 4 hours or overnight. Serve cold, sprinkled with almonds.

Janis's Coconut Almond Pseudo-Strudel

1 cup all-purpose flour

$^1/_2$ teaspoon table salt

8 tablespoons (1 stick) unsalted butter, cut into tablespoons

$^1/_2$ cup sour cream

1 cup apricot jam or one 12-ounce jar

1$^1/_2$ cups slivered almonds, about 6 ounces

1 cup lightly packed sweetened flaked coconut, about 3$^1/_2$ ounces

1 cup golden raisins

Confectioners' sugar for dusting

Vanilla ice cream or whipped cream as an accompaniment

MAKES 2 STRUDELS, SERVING 10 TO 12

Every year Bill's sister Janis bakes two of these luscious foot-long pastries and mails them to him in time for his birthday in December. He savors them one rich slice at a time, which usually means that he doesn't polish off the last slice until deep into January. (It helps that they freeze beautifully.)

A part-time lawyer and full-time mother of two, Janis claims to have come to her love of baking by default. "From the time I was nine years old, Mom always told me, 'I'm not a baker, so *you* be the baker,'" she says. In that way this recipe was quickly passed from Shirley Ward to Esther Adler to Janis Adler. Shirley and Esther were lifelong friends and neighbors in Detroit, even though Shirl was a wonderful baker and Esther was not.

We've dubbed this *pseudo-strudel* because it's made with regular pastry dough instead of typical strudel dough. "I like working with dough, and this dough is really satisfying because you can roll it paper-thin and it doesn't fall apart on you," says Jan. "It's foolproof."

Combine the flour, salt, butter, and sour cream in a large bowl. Use a pastry cutter or 2 forks to blend just until the mixture forms a stiff dough. Turn out onto a floured work surface and pat into a flat disk. Wrap in plastic wrap and chill overnight.

Preheat the oven to 350°F. Place the jam in a small saucepan and stir over low heat until melted. Remove from the heat, cover, and keep warm. Place the almonds in a food processor and process until finely ground.

Divide the chilled dough in half. Working with one half at a time, roll out on a lightly floured work surface into a 12-inch square. (The dough will be very thin.) Brush the surface of the dough with half the jam. Sprinkle on half the ground almonds, half the coconut, and half the raisins, leaving a $^1/_2$-inch-wide border on all sides. Fold in the sides about 1 inch and roll up to enclose the filling. Repeat with the remaining dough and the remaining jam, almonds, coconut, and raisins. Score the top of each strudel with a diagonal cut about 12 times. (The strudels may be prepared up to this point and kept frozen, tightly wrapped, until ready to bake.) Transfer both strudels to a sheet pan lined with parchment paper. Bake in the middle of the oven until golden brown, 35 to 40 minutes. (If cooking from the frozen state, give them an additional 5 minutes.) Sprinkle with confectioners' sugar and serve with ice cream or whipped cream.

My sister-in-law Janis Adler with her daughter Eileen, 1998

New Wave Zabaglione

6 large egg yolks

6 tablespoons sugar

1 cup dessert wine, preferably Moscato d'Asti

SERVES 4

I was still a schoolgirl dreaming of one day going to cooking school when Nicola Paone—owner of the great old-school Italian restaurant on East 34th Street in Manhattan that still bears his name—took me into his kitchen and taught me how to make authentic zabaglione.

Born in Pennsylvania and raised in Sicily, Nicola was a pop singer in his earlier years, reaching the Hot 100 in 1959 with a ditty called "Blah Blah Blah." When he got into the restaurant business, his pop flair was key to his success. These days, of course, everyone understands that running a restaurant is just another way of saying that you're in show-biz. But when we were kids we were deeply impressed by Paone's flamboyant decor—his album covers were framed and mounted on the wall—and by the panache evident even in the titles of his recipes, "The Nightgown" and "Boom Boom" among them, which tasted even better than they sounded. Paone's was for special occasions only.

Zabaglione is a hot custard made with wine, usually marsala. What is "new wave" about this recipe is the replacement of marsala with any of today's great dessert wines. You can eat it all by itself or serve it spooned over fresh berries.

Beat the yolks with the sugar in an electric mixer on high speed, scraping the sides of the bowl as necessary, until light and fluffy, about 5 minutes. Beat in the wine and transfer the mixture to a metal bowl set over a pan of simmering water. Whisk until light and fluffy and an instant-read thermometer registers 160°F. Divide among 4 red wine goblets or decorative small bowls and serve warm or chill.

testing the temperature of eggs and sugar

Sugar and eggs will become thick and foamy if you simply beat them together. You might think your zabaglione is done when you have barely cooked the mixture. So it is important to make sure the egg mixture in the bowl gets quite hot. If you have an instant-read thermometer (a worthwhile investment and very affordable), you are looking for a temperature of 160°F. If you don't have one, just take a little of the custard out and put it on your wrist. If it feels almost hot (about 160°F on a thermometer), it is done.

Michael Green says:
wine for zabaglione

Marsala is the classic wine used in a traditional zabaglione recipe. Produced in the western part of Sicily, this fortified wine (a wine with the addition of distilled spirits) adds rich and assertive flavors to the zabaglione. In this new-wave version, where a low-alcohol, slightly sparkling Moscato is substituted for the marsala, the result is lighter and more floral. In cooler months, consider substituting other fortified wines such as ruby port or Pedro Ximenez sherry. Whichever wine you elect to use for the recipe, serve the same wine alongside this delicious dessert.

Paone on record, early '60s

Ruth Moulton's Spice Balls

**12 tablespoons (1¹/₂ sticks)
  unsalted butter, softened**

1¹/₄ cups sugar

1 large egg

¹/₄ cup molasses

2 cups all-purpose flour

2 teaspoons baking soda

1 teaspoon ground cinnamon

1 teaspoon ground cloves

**¹/₂ teaspoon freshly grated
  nutmeg**

¹/₂ teaspoon ground ginger

¹/₂ teaspoon table salt

MAKES ABOUT 48 SMALL
COOKIES

My sister Anne is the baker in our family. Even now, as a doctor at a busy hospital, the mother of two kids, the wife of a doctor husband, and the owner of a generally hectic life, she'll take time out every so often to make that delicious Fanny Farmer pound cake or whip up a batch of wonderfully crisp Toll House cookies. (Her trick? Cut back on the flour and flatten out the cookies by banging the sheet pan on the oven shelf when they are halfway done. Flattened out, the cookies have more surface area and bake up nice and crispy.)

Like me, Anne was introduced to baking as a kid by our grandmother Ruth. Together we made bread from scratch, zillions of cookies, and all kinds of pies. (It was Granny who turned us on to the joys of pie for breakfast!) A generation later Anne has passed on these skills to her kids, Peter and Katie.

This recipe is one of Anne's favorites. To begin with, the dough freezes very well. Unfreeze it and bake your cookies whenever you like. Like chewy gingerbread without all the ginger, they are a special treat at holiday time and comfort food anytime.

Please note: Even though these are called spice "balls" they end up flat after baking.

Combine the butter and 1 cup of the sugar in the bowl of an electric mixer. Beat until light and fluffy, 3 to 5 minutes. Beat in the egg and molasses.

Sift the flour, soda, cinnamon, cloves, nutmeg, ginger, and salt together onto a piece of parchment. Add to the butter mixture in

2 batches, beating just until combined. Cover with plastic wrap and chill for 2 to 3 hours.

Preheat the oven to 350°F. Place the remaining $1/4$ cup sugar in a pie plate. Shape the dough into walnut-size balls and roll in the sugar to coat. Arrange 2 inches apart on greased baking sheets and bake until cracked and dry but still soft, about 10 minutes. Cool on the baking sheets for 5 minutes, then transfer to cool on wire racks.

spraying measuring cups

Anytime you are measuring something sticky like peanut butter or molasses, spray the measuring cup first with nonstick vegetable oil spray. The peanut butter will slip right out.

My sister Anne Moulton with her daughter Katie, 1989

Fresh Ginger Gingerbread

18 tablespoons (2¹/₄ sticks) unsalted butter, slightly softened

2 cups sugar

3 large eggs

1 cup molasses

²/₃ cup minced fresh ginger

2 tablespoons freshly grated orange zest

1 teaspoon ground cinnamon

¹/₂ teaspoon freshly grated nutmeg

¹/₄ teaspoon ground cloves

¹/₄ teaspoon table salt

1 teaspoon baking soda

1 tablespoon cider vinegar

3¹/₄ cups sifted all-purpose flour

1 cup whole milk

Whipped cream or vanilla ice cream as an accompaniment

MAKES 16 SERVINGS

When I was six or seven months pregnant with Sam, my boss at *Gourmet* volunteered me to cook a dish at a fundraising event for 300 to 400 people. I was not thrilled. Even when I'm at the top of my game, that kind of large-scale cooking is not my forte. But being pregnant really increased my dread. To top it off, the organizers of this gala charged me with making dessert. Of course! Of the dozen chefs working on this event, only two were women, so naturally at least one of us was assigned to pastries, where women predominate. Unfortunately, dessert is not my forte either.

I was rescued by my good friend and mentor Jean Anderson, who put me on to her recipe for gingerbread made with fresh ginger. It is simple to make, very tasty, and easy to transport and serve. It was also a smash hit on the night in question. The whole evening the other participating chefs—including a number of New York's biggest culinary stars—spent more time buzzing around my booth than they did anyone else's. The gingerbread was just that good. I think the fresh ginger is what makes the difference.

Preheat the oven to 375°F. Butter and flour a 13 X 9-inch baking pan, preferably nonstick.

Beat the butter in an electric mixer until smooth. Gradually add the sugar and continue beating until light and fluffy. Add the eggs one at a time, beating well after each addition. Add the molasses and beat until well blended. Add the ginger, orange zest, cinnamon, nutmeg, cloves, and salt. Mix the soda with the vinegar in a small bowl and add to the batter. Transfer to a large bowl.

Add the flour by hand, alternating with the milk, beginning and ending with flour. After each addition, stir only enough to combine.

Spread the batter evenly in the prepared pan and bake until a cake tester inserted in the center comes out clean, 55 to 60 minutes. Cool the gingerbread in the pan on a wire rack. Cut into squares and serve with whipped cream or vanilla ice cream.

Giant Chocolate Turnovers with Orange Custard Sauce

2 tablespoons orange liqueur or to taste

1/2 recipe Vanilla Sauce (page 355)

2 ounces bittersweet chocolate, finely chopped

2 ounces almond paste, chopped

1 puff pastry sheet (from a 17 1/4-ounce package)

1 large egg, lightly beaten

2 tablespoons sugar

SERVES 4

Good frozen puff pastry is readily available throughout the country these days. I find that the key to success with puff pastry (homemade or store-bought) is the proper amount of cooking. If there are any signs of white, undercooked layers of dough after the prescribed time called for here, continue cooking until the pastry is golden brown and the layers are indeed puffed and crispy. Garnish with sections of fresh orange if desired.

Stir the orange liqueur into the vanilla sauce and chill for several hours or overnight. You should have about 1 1/4 cups.

To prepare the turnovers, preheat the oven to 425°F. Combine the chocolate and almond paste in a small bowl. Trim any uneven edges from the pastry sheet and cut into 4 equal squares that measure 5 inches on each side. Brush the edges of the squares with a small amount of the beaten egg. Place equal amounts of the chocolate-almond mixture on the center of each square and fold in half diagonally to form triangles. Decoratively crimp the edges to seal.

Brush the tops of the turnovers with a small amount of the beaten egg and sprinkle with sugar. Cut a small steam vent in the top of each and arrange 2 inches apart on a large baking sheet. Cook in the middle of the oven until golden brown, 15 to 18 minutes. Cool slightly on wire racks.

Pour some of the custard sauce on the bottom of 4 dessert plates. Place a turnover on top and serve. Pass the remaining sauce on the side.

Chocolate Bits Pudding

6 ounces semisweet chocolate chips

1 cup whole milk

1 tablespoon sugar

1 teaspoon vanilla extract

Pinch table salt

3 large eggs

Whipped cream or vanilla ice cream for garnish

SERVES 4

On a shelf in the kitchen at my parents' old farmhouse in northern Massachusetts are metal file boxes filled with recipes written by my grandmother Ruth Moulton. I plucked this gem from one of those boxes (as well as the recipes for the Cheese Sandwich Soufflé, page 312, and Southwestern Egg Bake, page 322). Using regular old chocolate chips, Ruth somehow concocted a very dense essence-of-chocolate pudding. Kids of all ages will love it, but I recommend serving it with whipped cream or vanilla ice cream as a counterpoint to all that chocolate intensity.

Set a metal bowl over a pan of simmering, not boiling, water. Combine the chocolate and milk in the bowl and heat until the chocolate is melted. Whisk in the sugar, vanilla, and salt. Add the eggs one at a time, whisking well after each addition. Regulate the heat so that the water stays at a constant slow simmer. Cook the pudding, stirring often, until thick and an instant-read thermometer reaches 160°F, 5 to 10 minutes. Pour into four $^1/_2$-cup ramekins and cool to room temperature. Cover with plastic wrap and refrigerate until well chilled, at least 3 hours. The pudding can be made up to 2 days in advance. Top with a dollop of whipped cream just before serving.

My grandmother Ruth Moulton with young Steve Moulton

Chocolate Caramel Peanut Truffles

1 cup sugar

2/3 cup heavy cream

9 ounces bittersweet chocolate, finely chopped

2 tablespoons creamy peanut butter

1/4 teaspoon table salt

1 teaspoon vanilla extract

1/2 cup finely chopped peanuts for coating

MAKES ABOUT 40 TRUFFLES

Here is everything you want in one candy—chocolate, caramel, and nuts—and these truffles couldn't be simpler to prepare. Make a big batch, box them attractively, and you have the perfect holiday gift.

Place the sugar in a heavy saucepan. Cook over medium-high heat, stirring just until the sugar has melted. Continue cooking, swirling the pan often, until the sugar is a dark golden caramel. Remove the pan from the heat and carefully pour in the cream. Return the pan to the heat and simmer, stirring, until the caramel has dissolved.

Remove the pan from the heat and, while hot, stir in the chocolate, peanut butter, salt, and vanilla. Let stand for about 5 minutes or until the chocolate and peanut butter have dissolved. Transfer to a bowl and cool to room temperature. Cover the bowl with plastic wrap and chill until firm, about 2 hours.

Use a small spoon to scoop out the truffles and form into 1-inch balls. Roll the truffles in the peanuts and transfer to a tray covered with wax paper. Chill until firm, about 1 hour. Store in an airtight container for up to 2 weeks.

Mocha Cookies "The Bakery"

These are my all-time favorite essence-of-chocolate cookies. The original recipe, which first ran in *Gourmet* several years ago, comes from a restaurant in Los Angeles called The Bakery. I have adapted it slightly by adding chunks of bittersweet chocolate in place of the chips and chilling the dough overnight so that the dough is easier to scoop and bake. You have to plan ahead for these cookies, but it is so worthwhile. Make sure you take them out of the oven in time, while the center is still quite soft.

These freeze nicely, so make a double batch.

Combine the unsweetened chocolate, half the bittersweet chocolate, and the butter in a large bowl. Place the bowl over a large saucepan of simmering but not boiling water and melt, stirring often, until smooth.

Sift together the flour, baking powder, and salt.

Using an electric beater, beat the eggs and sugar in a large bowl until thick and pale, about 10 minutes. Beat in the espresso powder and the vanilla.

Carefully fold the melted chocolate mixture into the egg mixture. Fold in the flour mixture, then stir in the remaining bittersweet chocolate. Refrigerate the batter overnight.

Preheat the oven to 350°F. Drop the batter by heaping tablespoons, leaving at least $1^{1}/_{2}$ inches between cookies, onto buttered baking sheets or baking sheets lined with parchment. Bake for 8 to 10 minutes, until slightly undercooked. They should be puffed, shiny, and beginning to crack on top. Let the cookies cool on the baking sheets, then transfer to cool completely on wire racks. They will keep for 5 days at room temperature, wrapped tightly, or for 1 month frozen.

4 ounces unsweetened chocolate, finely chopped

8 ounces bittersweet chocolate, coarsely chopped

8 tablespoons (1 stick) unsalted butter, cut into small pieces

$^{1}/_{2}$ cup all-purpose flour

$^{1}/_{2}$ teaspoon baking powder

$^{1}/_{2}$ teaspoon table salt

4 large eggs, at room temperature

$1^{1}/_{2}$ cups sugar

$1^{1}/_{2}$ tablespoons instant espresso powder

2 teaspoons vanilla extract

MAKES ABOUT 36 COOKIES

Sam's Chocolate Chip Pizza

¹/₂ teaspoon sugar

²/₃ cup warm water (110° to 115°F)

1 envelope (2¹/₂ teaspoons) active dry yeast

2 cups all-purpose flour

¹/₂ teaspoon salt

Vegetable oil

6 ounces semisweet or bittersweet chocolate, broken into large chunks

MAKES TWO SMALL PIZZAS, SERVING 8 TO 10

Sam was seven years old when he dreamt up this recipe and asked me to help him make it real. I know he envisioned a regular pizza, complete with sauce and cheese, topped off by chocolate chips. For his own good, I purposely misunderstood him (I am his mother, after all), reinterpreting the recipe as plain pizza dough topped with chocolate chips. At that point Sam's dream dish wasn't much more outlandish than the dark chocolate sandwich on French bread that serves as an afternoon snack for French schoolkids. Check it out for yourself. Sam's pizza is really very tasty. Grown-ups will like it, too. It's great with a cup of coffee in the afternoon.

Combine the sugar and water in a large bowl. Stir until the sugar has dissolved. Sprinkle on the yeast and let stand until foamy, about 5 minutes. Stir in the flour and salt and blend until the mixture forms a dough. Add warm water by the tablespoon if necessary to reach the right consistency. Add more flour by the tablespoon to the kneading surface if the dough appears to be too wet. The dough should be soft and pliable. Transfer to a floured surface and knead until smooth and elastic, about 5 minutes.

Place the dough in a deep oiled bowl and turn gently to coat. Cover with plastic wrap and leave in a warm place for 1 hour or until doubled in bulk. Punch down the dough and cut into 2 equal pieces.

Preheat the oven to 400°F. Lightly oil 2 cookie sheets. Working with one half of the dough at a time, roll each into a ¹/₃-inch-thick round. Transfer to the cookie sheets and arrange the chocolate chunks over the surface. Bake on the bottom shelf of the oven for 15 minutes. Let cool slightly before serving.

My son Sam Adler, age 9, 1999

Breakfast and Brunch

Apricot Scones

2 cups all-purpose flour

1 tablespoon baking powder

3 tablespoons sugar, plus more
for sprinkling

$1/2$ teaspoon table salt

$1/2$ cup chopped dried apricots,
preferably from California

$1^{1}/_{2}$ cups plus 2 tablespoons
heavy cream

MAKES 12 SCONES

Back in the days when I worked in *Gourmet*'s test kitchen, I was assigned an article on biscuits. I proceeded as if it were a science experiment. Starting with no preconceptions, I worked with all kinds of ingredients in all kinds of combinations in my quest to produce the most tender, delicious end product. I tried buttermilk, cream, milk, butter, and shortening in various combinations and settled on just cream, which did double duty as the best provider of both liquid and fat.

This would not have come as news to James Beard, whose cream biscuits had long been famous, but I had to find out for myself. My test kitchen colleagues agreed with me, and the biscuits became the starting point for many other recipes, including these apricot scones.

Always a smash in the *Gourmet* dining room, these scones are so easy to make that we bake them to order and serve them hot. I recommend you do the same.

By the way, try to get California apricots. They have a much brighter, sunnier taste than the more widely available Turkish variety.

Preheat the oven to 425°F. Sift the flour with the baking powder, sugar, and salt into a large bowl. Stir in the apricots. Pour in $1^{1}/_{4}$ to $1^{1}/_{2}$ cups cream or enough to just form a dough. On a lightly floured surface, knead the dough gently 3 times and pat it out into a $^{1}/_{2}$-inch-thick circle. (Handle the dough as lightly as possible to avoid tough scones.) Cut the circle into 12 wedges. Transfer the wedges to a large ungreased baking sheet. Brush the tops with the remaining 2 tablespoons cream and sprinkle liberally with sugar. Bake for about 15 minutes or until pale golden. Serve hot.

Biscuit Sticky Buns

This is another great recipe based on cream biscuits.

Normally, sticky buns are made with yeast dough, which scares off lots of folks. These are blessedly yeast-free. But you don't have to tell your brunch guests. Let them assume that you got up at the crack of dawn to give the dough time to rise.

To prepare the glaze, combine the sugar, honey, and butter in a small saucepan and stir over medium heat until melted and smooth. Pour into a nonstick 9-inch round cake pan and sprinkle on the pecans.

To make the buns, place the currants in a small bowl and add the rum. Pour in $1/4$ cup hot water and set aside until the currants are softened, about 20 minutes. Drain well.

Preheat the oven to 425°F. Sift the flour, granulated sugar, baking powder, and salt into a large bowl. Pour in $1^1/4$ to $1^1/2$ cups cream or just enough to form a dough. On a lightly floured surface, knead the dough gently 3 times and roll into a rectangle that measures 18 inches long and 10 inches wide. Place the brown sugar in a small strainer and tap lightly to spread over evenly. Sprinkle on the cinnamon and the drained currants.

Beginning with a long side, roll up the dough tightly, jelly roll fashion, and use a sharp knife to cut 1-inch-thick slices. Fit the slices, cut side up, into the pan with the glaze and gently press down. Bake for 20 minutes or until a cake tester or toothpick inserted into the dough comes out clean.

Invert the buns onto a large plate and set aside for 5 minutes. Carefully reinvert onto a serving platter, plain side up, and brush with the heated honey. Cool completely before serving.

For the glaze:

$1/4$ cup packed light brown sugar

$1/4$ cup honey

4 tablespoons ($1/2$ stick) unsalted butter

$1/2$ cup finely chopped lightly toasted pecans

For the buns:

$1/2$ cup dried currants

2 tablespoons rum or brandy

2 cups all-purpose flour

3 tablespoons granulated sugar

1 tablespoon baking powder

$1/2$ teaspoon table salt

$1^1/4$ to $1^1/2$ cups heavy cream

$1/2$ cup packed light brown sugar

2 teaspoons ground cinnamon

$1/4$ cup honey, heated

MAKES 18 SMALL BUNS

Aunt Alice's Blueberry Muffins

4 tablespoons (¹/₂ stick) unsalted
   butter, softened

1 cup sugar

³/₄ cup whole milk

1 large egg

1³/₄ cups plus 1 tablespoon
   all-purpose flour

2¹/₂ teaspoons baking powder

¹/₂ teaspoon table salt

1 cup fresh blueberries,
   preferably wild

MAKES 15 MUFFINS

One bite of these muffins and I'm transported back in time to my childhood visits with Aunt Alice and Uncle Pat and my cousins at their summer place in Kittery Point, Maine. On those evenings when Alice herself wasn't cooking up something wonderful, the whole rowdy bunch of us would trek down the road to the Chauncey Creek Lobster Pier.

A dock with picnic tables, Chauncey Creek features almost none of the amenities that might qualify it as a restaurant. There are, however, large tanks full of the day's catch of succulent local lobsters. You squint into a tank and point a finger at a likely-looking suspect, grab a few bags of potato chips and an ice-cold bottled drink, and then park yourself at one of the picnic tables while the proprietors boil up your nominee and melt down a sinful amount of butter. We'd round out our feast with some of the delicious muffins Aunt Alice had brought from home. Each one boasted an enormous amount of blueberries and—thanks to the high sugar content—a flat and crispy top. We loved them.

Preheat the oven to 400°F and butter fifteen 2¹/₂ x 1¹/₄-inch muffin cups. Beat the butter with the sugar in a large bowl until well blended. Pour in the milk, add the egg, and beat until smooth.

Sift the 1³/₄ cups flour with the baking powder and salt onto a piece of parchment. Add the dry ingredients to the wet mixture and mix until just moistened. Toss the blueberries with the remaining tablespoon of flour in a large bowl and fold into the batter. Fill the muffin tins halfway with the batter. Bake for 15 minutes or until lightly browned on top. Cool in the pan for 5 minutes, then run a thin knife blade around each muffin. Lift slightly on one side and tilt gently to remove from the tin. Cool briefly on a wire rack. Serve warm.

cultivated vs. wild blueberries?

Cultivated blueberries are more readily available than the wild and for a longer time of the year. They are bigger and paler in color and flavor. The wild are small, firm, tart, and intense. I recommend you pick them up whenever you can, and if you can't use them right away, freeze them. Here's how: Pick through the berries and remove any stems. Wash and dry them gently by patting them between paper towels and arrange them in one layer on a pan that will fit in the freezer. Freeze until they are hard and then transfer them to a resealable plastic bag. When you are ready to use them, don't defrost them; use them frozen.

My aunt Alice Moulton

Cheese Blintzes

1 1/2 cups whole-milk cottage cheese

1 vanilla bean, halved lengthwise

1 tablespoon sugar

1 large egg

1/2 teaspoon ground cinnamon

1/4 teaspoon table salt

8 crepes (page 349)

4 tablespoons (1/2 stick) unsalted butter

Sour cream and applesauce (page 267) for serving

MAKES 8 BLINTZES,
SERVING 4

Growing up in Manhattan in the sixties, I used to read a column in *New York* magazine called "The Underground Gourmet." Co-authored by Milton Glaser and Jerome Snyder, it was based on the belief that great food isn't necessarily French and expensive. This was a fairly radical notion at the time but one that was very attractive to a junior high school girl trying to expand her culinary horizons on an allowance of $7.50 a week. It was "The Underground Gourmet" that pointed me in the direction of Ratner's Delicatessen, the landmark Jewish dairy restaurant on the Lower East Side.

The blintzes at Ratner's reminded me of cheese Danish, one of my favorite breakfast foods as a kid. Blintzes are supposed to be made with farmer's or pot cheese—both are soft fresh cheeses—but neither is reliably available at the supermarket, so I have substituted cottage cheese. You really should use whole-milk cottage cheese to get the full flavor. If you don't want to make crepes, you can pick some up at many supermarkets.

Blintzes are traditionally garnished with sour cream or applesauce, but I also love them with fresh blueberries. You can also sprinkle them with a little confectioners' sugar right before serving. This is a lovely dish for brunch.

Line a large colander with a double thickness of rinsed cheesecloth. Add the cottage cheese and cover with plastic wrap. Refrigerate and drain for at least 12 hours or overnight.

Force the drained cottage cheese through a fine-mesh strainer into a large bowl. Scrape the seeds from the vanilla bean into the bowl. Add the sugar, egg, cinnamon, and salt. Stir until well blended. You should have about 1 cup of filling.

Place about 2 tablespoons of the filling into the center of each crepe. Fold over all 4 sides to shape like an envelope. (The blintzes can be covered and chilled in the refrigerator for up to 3 hours.) Just before serving, melt the butter in a large skillet over medium heat. Working in batches if necessary, add the blintzes, seam side down. Cook, turning often, until well browned on all sides, about 5 minutes. Serve hot topped with sour cream and applesauce.

Ruthie's Chocolate French Toast with Raspberry Sauce

6 large eggs

2 cups whole milk

1 teaspoon vanilla extract

1 tablespoon sugar

1/2 teaspoon table salt

3 tablespoons unsalted butter

Eight 1/2 -inch-thick slices brioche or egg bread

4 ounces bittersweet or semisweet chocolate, broken into large chunks and finely chopped

1 cup Quick Raspberry Sauce (page 352)

1/2 cup fresh raspberries

Several fresh mint sprigs for garnish

SERVES 4

My daughter Ruthie loves French toast. Most Sundays she gets up and cooks her own using thick slices of French bread. She dips it in a quick batter made of 2 eggs, about 2/3 cup milk, and some vanilla extract and sautés it in some butter in a nonstick pan until golden. (I buy one baguette a week, slice it for French toast and melted cheese sandwiches, wrap it tightly, and freeze it. That way we always have some on hand.)

I developed this fancy-shmancy French toast years ago for an article in New York's *Daily News* entitled "Mother's Day Mystery: What do you do for Mom if she's a chef every other day of the year?" At the time Ruthie was five and Sam a whopping one. Neither of them was actually ready to cook this recipe or anything else besides pizza dough, but it was definitely the sort of recipe Ruth liked.

In fact she turned out to be a chocolate lover and a sweetaholic in general, and she loves this recipe. So do I. It lives here in the breakfast chapter, but I think it would also be great served as a dessert at an elegant dinner. And when Valentine's Day rolls around, just cut out the bread slices with a heart-shaped cutter and go from there.

Beat the eggs with the milk, vanilla, sugar, and salt in a large shallow dish. Working in 2 batches, melt half of the butter in a large nonstick skillet over medium-high heat or heat a griddle to medium hot. Dip half the bread slices quickly in the egg mixture until lightly soaked. Transfer to the skillet and sprinkle each slice with one-fourth of the chocolate. Dip the remaining bread in the egg mixture and place on top of the chocolate. Press gently but firmly with a spatula so the slices adhere. Turn down the heat to medium and cook, turning once, until well browned and cooked through, 5 minutes per side. Cut in half on the diagonal and serve on warmed plates. Spoon a small amount of the raspberry sauce around the toast and garnish with whole raspberries and a sprig of mint. Serve the remaining sauce on the side.

Ruthie again, age 3, 1989

Breakfast Strata

3 tablespoons olive oil

1 medium onion, thinly sliced

15 to 18 medium shiitake mushrooms, about 10 ounces, stems removed and caps thinly sliced

1 large red bell pepper, thinly sliced

1 large green bell pepper, thinly sliced

3 to 4 large scallions, white and 1 inch of the green parts, finely chopped

Kosher salt and freshly ground black pepper to taste

6 large eggs

3 cups whole milk

2 tablespoons Dijon mustard

One 1- to 1½-pound loaf French or Italian country bread, crusts removed

1½ cups coarsely grated extra-sharp Cheddar cheese

¾ cup grated Parmigiano-Reggiano

Several fresh basil leaves, shredded, for garnish

SERVES 6 TO 8

Dreaming up a brunch for friends and family is a lot of fun, but when it gets down to the morning of the grand event and you're chained to the stove cooking up scrambled eggs and omelets to order, it often boils down to an awful lot of work. This dish will solve your brunch problems. You set it up the night before and then just bake it 60 minutes before it is time to eat. Breakfast strata is nothing more than a savory bread pudding with layers (*strata* in Latin) of bread cubes, vegetables, and cheese, all bound by eggs and milk. It is crusty on top and creamy in the center, my favorite combo.

This strata is as versatile and accommodating as an omelet. Once you feel comfortable with this version, you can make up your own: change the cheese, change the vegetables; add some ham, sausage, or bacon. It is a great vehicle for using up leftovers (and your guests will never know). And once you've decided that this is the way to go, you can kick back and read the Sunday paper before they arrive.

Heat the oil in a large skillet over medium heat. Add the onion and cook, stirring often, until softened, about 5 minutes. Stir in the mushrooms, peppers, and scallions. Season with salt and pepper. Cook, stirring often, until softened, 10 to 15 minutes. Cool completely. (The recipe can be done up to a day in advance to this point. Keep tightly covered in the refrigerator until ready to assemble the strata.)

Whisk the eggs with the milk in a large bowl until blended. Whisk in the mustard and season with salt and pepper.

Cut the bread into 1-inch cubes. You should have about 8 cups of cubed bread. Butter a 2-quart shallow baking dish and spread half the bread over the bottom. Season with salt and pepper and scatter half the mushroom and pepper mixture over the bread. Sprinkle on half the Cheddar cheese and half the Parmigiano-Reggiano. Pour in half the egg mixture. Repeat the layering with the remaining bread, vegetable mixture, and cheeses. Slowly pour in as much of the remaining egg mixture as possible. (Place the dish on a baking dish to catch any spillovers.) Cover and refrigerate overnight.

Preheat the oven to 350°F. Bake the strata, uncovered, until lightly browned on top and set in the center, about 1 hour. Serve warm, garnished with basil leaves.

storing eggs

You know those happy little open-air plastic egg containers that live on the door of the fridge? Throw them out or use them for one of your kids' art projects. Eggs are porous; they absorb air and aromas through their shells. They need to be protected. Keep them in their closed cartons in the back of the fridge. The door is the warmest part of the fridge, the perfect place for items that don't spoil easily, like jams and pickles.

Michael Green says:
on wine with brunch

Some are content with juice and coffee in the morning, but on weekends and special occasions a glass of wine can add a fantastic element to the start of a romantic or leisurely day. Look for wines that are modest in alcohol, fresh, and lively. From the Loire Valley of France, try a Sancerre with the Southwestern Egg Bake (page 322) or a German Riesling with Cheese Blintzes (page 306). One of my favorite brunch wines is the slightly sparkling, aromatically intoxicating Moscato d'Asti from the Piedmont region of Italy. Low in alcohol and wonderfully floral, the wine is a vibrant morning pick-me-up.

Cheese Sandwich Soufflé

8 slices homemade-style white bread, 3 to 4 inches square, crusts removed

$1/4$ pound thinly sliced cheese (Muenster, provolone, fontina, or Gruyère)

2 ounces prosciutto or boiled ham, thinly sliced (optional)

3 large eggs

2 cups whole milk

$1/2$ teaspoon kosher salt

SERVES 4

This is a recipe from my grandmother Ruth that I love for its simplicity. It is nothing more than a ham and cheese sandwich over which you pour some beaten eggs and milk, let soak, and then bake. (I confess that I dressed it up a little by adding the ham ... and that my son Sam insists I should have added even more.) Any flavorful sliced melting cheese and any flavorful pork product—cooked bacon, pancetta, prosciutto, or good old-fashioned country ham—would work here. This dish can serve as a great light lunch or supper for two or—because it requires so little prep—as the main attraction at a brunch for a bunch of friends.

Lightly butter an 8-inch square baking dish and arrange 4 slices of the bread flat on the bottom. Cover each with equal amounts of cheese and the ham if desired. Top with the remaining bread.

Beat the eggs lightly in a small bowl and pour in the milk. Season with the salt and blend well. Pour over the sandwiches, cover, and refrigerate for 1 hour.

Preheat the oven to 350°F. Bake the sandwiches, uncovered, until lightly browned around the edges and set in the center, 40 to 45 minutes. Serve hot.

Johnnycakes

1 cup Kenyon's johnnycake
   cornmeal*

1 teaspoon sugar

1/2 teaspoon kosher salt

3 tablespoons vegetable oil

*See Mail Order Sources.

MAKES ABOUT 20 SMALL
CAKES

In Rhode Island, johnnycakes, to be called johnnycakes, must be made from meal ground from Rhode Island White-cap flint corn. The corn is stone-ground, and the germ is not removed, which means that this cornmeal has more flavor than the commercially produced stuff. It also means that you should keep it in a plastic bag in the fridge, because it has a higher oil content and will turn rancid faster than regular store-bought cornmeal.

Bring 2 cups of water to a boil.

Mix together the cornmeal, sugar, and salt in a large bowl. Pour in the boiling water. Mix well.

Heat 1 tablespoon of oil per batch in a frying pan or griddle over medium heat. Working in batches, drop tablespoonfuls of the corn-meal mixture onto the heated pan or griddle. Leave the cakes for 6 minutes, then flip over. Cook for an additional 6 minutes. Transfer to a pan and keep in a warm oven until ready to serve. Serve warm with Creamed Finnan Haddie (page 314).

Creamed Finnan Haddie

½ pound finnan haddie (smoked haddock)*

1½ cups heavy cream

3 cups whole milk

1 small onion, thinly sliced

1 bay leaf, preferably Turkish

3 tablespoons unsalted butter

3 tablespoons all-purpose flour

Kosher salt and freshly ground black pepper to taste

1 tablespoon Dijon mustard

2 teaspoons chopped fresh dill

2 teaspoons fresh lemon juice

Johnnycakes (page 313) for serving

*See Mail Order Sources.

SERVES 4

The smoked haddock known as *finnan haddie* is a Scottish thing and therefore a New England thing. My dad grew up loving it for breakfast—almost always prepared in the creamed version detailed here—as a kid in Milton, Massachusetts.

I added the johnnycakes to the recipe. Corncakes made from stone-ground flint corn, johnnycakes are another New England family tradition. There is a raging controversy about whether johnnycakes should be thick and fluffy or thin and crispy (my preference) and another about whether to serve them with butter (my preference) or maple syrup.

There's nothing controversial about suggesting that it's a shame that johnnycakes tend to be confined to the breakfast ghetto; they happen to be a great base for any topping. My pal Jasper White used to serve them topped with caviar and sour cream at his restaurant in Boston, and it was an ethereal match.

Cut the fish into 6 pieces. Combine the cream, half of the milk, the onion, and the bay leaf in a large saucepan. Bring to a boil over medium-high heat. Reduce the heat to medium and add the fish. Simmer until the fish is softened and flaky, about 10 minutes. Transfer the fish to a bowl and cool.

Melt the butter in a small saucepan over medium-high heat. Stir in the flour and cook, stirring often, about 2 minutes. Heat the remaining 1½ cups milk. Whisk in the milk and increase the heat to high. Bring to a boil, whisking constantly. Reduce the heat to medium and season with salt and pepper. Simmer gently, stirring often, for 5 minutes. Remove from the heat and stir in the mustard, dill, and lemon juice. Thin to a pourable consistency with additional milk if desired.

When the fish is cool enough to handle, remove and discard any skin and bones. Break the fish into small flakes and add to the saucepan with the sauce. Stir well to blend and taste again for seasoning. Add more salt and pepper if desired. Cook over low heat just to warm through, about 3 minutes. Serve warm with johnnycakes.

finnan haddie

My friend and fellow chef Jasper White says in his book *Jasper White's Cooking from New England* that finnan haddie, smoked dried haddock, is produced from haddock caught off the north coast of Scotland. It was discovered by accident in a little town called Findon near Aberdeen, Scotland. "A fire swept the town and smoked tons of fish which had been left to dry."

With my dad on Labor Day, 2001

Eggs Baked in Red Wine

4 slices homemade-style white bread, crusts removed

2 garlic cloves, one halved and one minced

6 strips bacon

2 shallots, minced

2 cups dry red wine

1 1/2 cups chicken stock, preferably homemade (page 338)

2 tablespoons unsalted butter

1 tablespoon all-purpose flour

Kosher salt and freshly ground black pepper to taste

8 large eggs

2 tablespoons chopped fresh herbs, such as chives, parsley, tarragon, lemon thyme

SERVES 4

At first glance this recipe may seem a little odd—eggs and red wine?—but it is based on a French classic called *oeufs en meurette,* and who am I to argue with the French? In truth, it is my favorite kind of dish because the yolk and the sauce beg to be mopped up with some crusty bread. It lives here in the breakfast chapter because it is essentially eggs and bacon, but it would also make a great light lunch or weeknight dinner.

You can set it up ahead of time by making the sauce a few hours—or a few days—in advance. Then, about 30 minutes before the meal, just heat the sauce, pour it into the ramekins, and proceed with the recipe. Everyone is always delighted with his or her own elegant little ramekin of bacon and eggs. (And if you invest in the ramekins, you can use them for other individual dishes, like fruit crisps or custards.)

Cut each slice of bread into 2 triangles and toast lightly. Rub with the halved clove of garlic while warm.

Preheat the oven to 350°F. Cook the bacon in a large skillet over medium heat until browned and crisp. Drain on paper towels. Crumble when cooled and set aside. Pour off all but 1 tablespoon of the bacon fat from the skillet and add the minced garlic and the shallots. Cook over low heat, stirring often, until softened, 2 to 3 minutes. Pour in the wine and increase the heat to high. Bring to a boil and cook, stirring to scrape the browned bits from the bottom of the skillet, until reduced to 1/2 cup. Pour in the chicken stock and bring back to a boil.

Use a fork to blend the butter and flour into a smooth paste in a small heatproof bowl. Whisk about $^1/_4$ cup of the boiling liquid into the bowl and blend until smooth. Empty the bowl into the skillet and boil, whisking constantly, until slightly thickened, about 2 minutes. Season with salt and pepper.

Arrange 2 bread triangles in the bottom of 4 individual 1-cup casserole dishes or ramekins. Pour a quarter of the red wine sauce over the bread and carefully break 2 eggs on top. Arrange the dishes on a sheet pan and bake in the middle of the oven until the eggs are just set, 18 to 20 minutes. Sprinkle with fresh herbs and the crumbled bacon. Serve hot.

"Onion Soup" Omelets

For the onion filling:

2 tablespoons unsalted butter

4 to 5 medium onions, about
    2 pounds, halved crosswise
    and very thinly sliced

1 teaspoon finely chopped fresh
    thyme leaves

1½ cups chicken stock,
    preferably homemade brown
    (page 339)

¼ cup red wine

Kosher salt and freshly ground
    black pepper to taste

1 teaspoon Dijon mustard

For the croutons:

3 slices ⅓-inch-thick country
    bread, crusts removed

1 to 2 tablespoons olive oil

For the individual omelets:

3 large eggs

Kosher salt and freshly ground
    black pepper to taste

1 tablespoon unsalted butter

A heaping ¼ cup grated Gruyère
    cheese

MAKES SIX 3-EGG OMELETS

Two years ago on "Cooking Live" we devoted a week of shows to the culinary challenges faced by newlyweds. We chose a representative couple and planned on setting them up with all the right equipment and a few basic recipes and launching them into their brave new life together. As usual, however, the learning went both ways. Britta Larsen, the bride-to-be, turned me on to a great recipe from her mother.

The concept was a winner. Instead of pouring all the delicious components of classic onion soup—slow-cooked onions, Gruyère cheese, and croutons—into a broth, you tuck them into an egg casing. What could be better? Served with a vegetable on the side and a salad, this omelet is hearty enough to be dinner. Alone, it is perfect for a weekend brunch or lunch. The onions can be cooked ahead and kept in the fridge. And if you don't feel like making homemade croutons, go ahead and toss in your favorite store-bought brand.

By the way, this is where your nonstick pan comes in handy. A good nonstick pan is essential not only for omelets but also for potato pancakes, fish fillets, crepes, and all those other dishes that break your heart when they stick to the pan.

To prepare the filling, melt the butter in a large heavy skillet over medium-high heat. Add the onions and thyme and reduce the heat to medium-low. Cover and cook, stirring often, until the onions are very soft, about 20 minutes. Uncover and increase the heat to medium-high. Cook, stirring often, until the onions are light brown, about 20 minutes. Add the stock and wine. Season with salt and pepper. Simmer until the mixture is thick and pulpy, 10 to 15 minutes. Stir in the mustard and taste and season with additional salt and pepper if desired. You should have about $1^{1}/_{2}$ cups filling.

For the croutons, preheat the oven to 400°F and cut the bread into $^{1}/_{3}$-inch dice. Toss the cubes with the olive oil until well coated and place on a baking sheet. Bake until golden brown, 8 to 10 minutes. Let cool.

For each omelet, break the eggs into a small bowl and add 2 teaspoons water and a pinch of salt and pepper. Beat with a fork until the whites and yolks are well blended. Heat 1 tablespoon butter in a small omelet pan or nonstick skillet over high heat until foaming and just starting to brown. Have a warmed plate ready to receive the omelet. Add the eggs and stir quickly with the flat part of a fork until they begin to thicken, about 10 seconds. Push the egg that begins to set on the sides into the center of the pan and tilt the pan to pour the uncooked egg to the sides. Cook until the omelet is slightly firm, 15 to 20 seconds longer.

Stop stirring and let the omelet brown slightly on the bottom. Sprinkle a heaping $^{1}/_{4}$ cup cheese over the surface. Spread about $^{1}/_{4}$ cup of the onion mixture on the cheese and add $^{1}/_{4}$ cup croutons. Fold the sides of the omelet over the filling and tilt the pan to half roll, half slide it onto the plate, seam side down. Serve at once.

Michael Green says: mimosa variations

The Mimosa is a classic breakfast drink and a fine way to greet the day. While the mixture of Champagne or sparkling wine mixed with orange juice remains a classic, consider other fruit variations such as cranberry, mango, and even pureed cantaloupe. The flavors and colors are wonderful. The proportions of two-thirds Champagne to one-third fruit juice can be adjusted to your taste. And remember, when mixed in a drink, it is not necessary to use true and expensive French Champagne. Look for excellent and affordable sparkling wines from other regions of the world such as California, Spain, Italy, and France's Loire Valley.

Serrano Ham and Manchego Cheese Roulade

For the roulade:

4 tablespoons (¹/₂ stick) unsalted butter

6 tablespoons all-purpose flour, plus more for dusting the pan

1¹/₄ cups whole milk, heated

4 large eggs, separated

¹/₂ teaspoon kosher salt

Freshly ground black pepper to taste

For the filling:

2 cups coarsely grated Manchego or Parmigiano-Reggiano

3 ounces thinly sliced serrano ham or prosciutto

1 large roasted red bell pepper, seeded, peeled, and cut into thin strips (optional)

¹/₄ cup finely chopped fresh parsley

SERVES 6 TO 8

An egg roulade is sort of like an enormous spongy omelet. It is a big rolled-up container for just about any tasty ingredients. From an entertaining point of view, the beauty of an egg roulade is that you can make it the day ahead, chill it overnight, and then fill it up just before your guests arrive. Fifteen minutes before you want to eat, pop it in the oven. Great for brunch, egg roulade, stuffed with your savory leftovers, also makes a great weeknight dinner.

I fell in love with Spain and Spanish ingredients years ago when I joined a press junket to Spain to learn about the country's olive oil. At the time serrano ham, a delicious aged ham similar to the Italian prosciutto, was not allowed into America. Today it is available here, as are many of the wonderful Spanish cheeses that used to be kept out. If you can find them, you will fall in love with them, too. If you can't, by all means substitute other good ingredients. Use prosciutto or thinly sliced ham and the sharp tasty cheese of your choice.

Preheat the oven to 350°F. Line a buttered 15 X 10 X 1-inch jelly roll pan with parchment paper. Butter the paper, dust with flour, and tap out the excess. Melt the butter in a small saucepan over medium-high heat. Add the flour and cook, stirring, for 3 minutes. Increase the heat to high, whisk in the milk, and bring to a boil. Reduce the heat to medium and simmer for 5 minutes. Transfer to a large bowl and whisk in the egg yolks one at a time. Season with the salt and pepper. Beat the egg whites until soft peaks form. Stir one third of the whites into the yolk mixture and fold in the rest. Pour the batter into the bottom of the prepared pan and smooth gently with a metal spatula. Transfer to the oven and cook until golden and firm to the touch, about 15 minutes.

Increase the oven heat to 375°F. Cover the egg sponge with a buttered piece of parchment paper, buttered side down. Cover with a damp kitchen towel and invert onto a work surface. Peel off the paper from the top.

Sprinkle the cheese over the sponge, leaving a $1/2$-inch border on all sides. Arrange the ham and pepper strips on top and sprinkle on the parsley. Place a flat baking sheet next to the sponge. Starting with one of the longer sides, use the towel to help roll the sponge up jelly roll fashion. Carefully roll onto the baking sheet. Return the roulade to the upper third of the oven and bake until the cheese has melted, 8 to 10 minutes. Use a serrated knife to cut crosswise into $1/2$-inch-thick slices.

grating cheese

When you are grating cheese, place a piece of parchment or wax paper underneath. That way when you are done grating, all you have to do is pick up the paper to transport the cheese to its destination.

Southwestern Egg Bake

One 8-ounce can mild green
chiles, drained and stemmed

1 pound Monterey Jack cheese,
coarsely grated

12 large eggs, lightly beaten

2 cups sour cream

Kosher salt and freshly ground
black pepper to taste

Salsa, additional sour cream, and
guacamole for serving
(optional)

SERVES 6 TO 8

This is another of the recipes I found in the treasure trove that is my grandmother Ruth's recipe box. How my New England grandmother learned about southwestern cuisine is a mystery to me. I certainly don't remember ever eating a dish spiced with chile at her house. But this recipe looked so simple and tasty I had to give it a try. Sure enough, it was delicious and the sort of dish you can throw together at the last minute for guests as long as you keep that can of chiles in the cupboard. It makes a great weeknight supper, too, if you don't mind having eggs for supper occasionally. I don't.

Preheat the oven to 350°F. Cut the chiles in half lengthwise and remove the seeds. Arrange in one layer on the bottom of a buttered 13 X 9-inch baking dish. Cover with the cheese. Whisk the eggs with the sour cream in a large bowl until blended. Season with salt and pepper. Pour the eggs over the cheese, smooth the top, and bake in the middle of the oven until golden, about 45 minutes. Serve with salsa, sour cream, and guacamole on the side if desired.

quick guacamole

Coarsely mash 1 peeled, pitted ripe avocado, preferably Hass. Add some fresh lime juice, chopped cilantro, chopped cherry tomatoes, 1 small minced garlic clove, $1/2$ serrano or jalapeño, minced, and kosher salt to taste.

Breakfast Sausage

My husband took one bite of this recipe while I was still
testing it and wondered why I would even attempt to
compete with the great product Jimmy Dean's been hawk-
ing for decades on TV. I reminded him, rather crisply, that
I have always liked making my own homemade versions of
those store-bought favorites. My ingredients will be fresher,
cheaper, and have fewer chemical additives, and the finished
dish will be at least as good as store-bought.

I was inspired in this belief by one of my most treasured
cookbooks, *Better Than Store-Bought,* by Elizabeth Schneider
Colchie and Helen Witty. *Better Than Store-Bought* boasts
homemade versions of everything from tortilla chips to tarragon mustard. Unfortunately, it is out of print. Then again,
that's why we brake for yard sales.

One note about this recipe: It's not easy to find fresh
pork fat these days. You'll have to make friends with your
butcher and ask him or her to put some aside for you.
Otherwise you'll need to start saving up the fat that you
trim off your pork roasts/chops and stowing it away in a
resealable plastic bag in the freezer in anticipation of your
very own assault on store-bought. (These days my husband
swears that the only time he even *thinks* of Jimmy Dean is
when the radio plays "Big Bad John.")

Process half of the fat in a food processor until finely chopped. Add
half of the pork and pulse until medium-finely ground. (Do not over-
mix. The texture should be chunky and chopped, not pureed.) Transfer to a bowl. Repeat with the remaining fat and pork. Stir in the salt,

**¹/₂ pound fresh pork fat, cut into
¹/₂-inch cubes**

**1 pound lean trimmed pork loin
or tenderloin, cut into 1-inch
cubes**

2 teaspoons kosher salt

**1 teaspoon freshly ground black
pepper**

1 teaspoon rubbed sage

1 teaspoon dried thyme

**Applesauce (page 267) as an
accompaniment**

MAKES ABOUT 12 PATTIES,
SERVING 4

pepper, sage, and thyme. Make a small meatball about the size of an olive and fry in a small saucepan until browned and cooked through. Taste for seasoning and correct as necessary. Using wet hands, form the mixture into $2^1/_2$-inch patties that measure about $^1/_2$ inch thick. Keep covered in the refrigerator until ready to cook.

Just before serving, heat a large skillet over medium heat. Add the patties and cook until well browned on the bottom, about 5 minutes. Pour off the accumulated fat and turn to the other side. Cook until browned and cooked through, about 5 minutes longer. Serve hot with applesauce.

Cheese Grits

My tireless mentor, Jean Anderson, a native of Raleigh, North Carolina, has introduced me to all foods southern— starting with grits. Cooked grits turn into cornmeal mush, a breakfast staple across the South. I like mine with cheese. Charles Pierce, the recipe tester on this book and a good southern boy himself, had no trouble coming up with this recipe for me.

Preheat the oven to 350°F and butter a 1¹/₂-quart baking dish. Bring the stock to a boil over high heat. Stir in the grits and reduce the heat to medium-high. Simmer, uncovered, stirring often, until very thick, about 5 minutes. Pour into a large bowl and add the butter, cheese, and garlic. Stir until the butter has melted. Cool slightly, stir in the egg yolks, and season with salt and pepper.

Beat the egg whites until they hold soft peaks. Fold into the grits and turn out into the baking dish. Smooth the top with a knife and sprinkle on the Parmigiano-Reggiano. Bake until golden brown on top and set in the center, about 45 minutes.

3 cups chicken stock, preferably homemade (page 338), or water

1 cup grits, preferably stone-ground*

8 tablespoons (1 stick) unsalted butter

1 cup grated sharp Cheddar cheese

2 garlic cloves, minced

2 large eggs, separated

Kosher salt and freshly ground black pepper to taste

2 tablespoons freshly grated Parmigiano-Reggiano

*See Mail Order Sources.

SERVES 4 TO 6

grits, cornmeal, polenta— what's the difference?

All three come in different grades of coarseness:

Grits—a meal made from ground dried hominy. Hominy is white field corn, soaked in an alkali, husked, degermed, and then frozen, canned, or dried.

Cornmeal—a meal made from ground dried white or yellow corn kernels whose outer husk and germ have usually been removed. (Whole-grain cornmeal, meaning cornmeal with the germ still in, is not only more flavorful but more nutritious and can be found at health food stores. It turns rancid quicker, so keep it in the fridge.)

Polenta is the same as yellow cornmeal.

Instant polenta and instant grits have been precooked.

Beverages

Fresh Lemonade

³/₄ cup fresh lemon juice

¹/₂ cup Simple Sugar Syrup (page 356) or 6 tablespoons granulated sugar

MAKES 1 QUART

Is there another drink as refreshing as lemonade in the summer? Drink it plain or add strawberries, blueberries, or watermelon ice cubes (page 330). Or crush some fresh mint into the glass with the side of a spoon and then pour in the lemonade. You can't go wrong.

Combine the lemon juice with the syrup in a large pitcher. Stir in 3 cups cold water. Stir well and serve over ice cubes.

variation: Combine ²/₃ cup cleaned fresh strawberries or blueberries, the lemon juice, and syrup in a blender and pour in 3 cups cold water. Blend until uniform in color, 10 to 15 seconds. Strain into a large pitcher and serve over ice cubes.

lemonade

My friend and mentor Jean Anderson likes to infuse her lemonade with fresh lemon herbs. She adds one of the following to her hot sugar syrup and lets it steep: two 3- to 4-inch stalks of lemongrass, which she has smashed lightly with the side of a knife, or a fistful of lemon verbena leaves, which she has crushed with her hands, or two 4- to 5-inch sprigs of lemon geranium. Chill infused sugar syrup for 30 minutes, strain, and add to the recipe. If you are not making sugar syrup, you could crush these herbs with the granulated sugar and add them to the lemonade. Chill for 30 minutes and strain. Any one of these herbs would be wonderful in iced tea as well.

lemon

How do you get the most juice out of a lemon or lime?
   Before you cut it in half to juice it:

1. Roll it on the counter, pressing down firmly on it 5 or 6 times, *or*
2. Nuke it in the microwave for 20 seconds, *or*
3. Bake it in a preheated 300°F oven for 10 minutes.

Watermelon Screwdrivers

1 pound cubed watermelon flesh, about 5 cups

1 quart orange juice, preferably fresh

¾ cup vodka or to taste

SERVES 4 TO 6

It's summertime, the sun is blazing, and, if you're lucky, you're sitting on the beach or by the pool. But wherever you are, city or country, there's one thing you want more than anything else: an ice-cold drink.

This one fits the bill, especially if you take the trouble to squeeze or buy fresh orange juice. What puts it over the top? The watermelon ice cubes. They melt slowly in your drink as you sip it down, flavoring and coloring your drink ever more intensely as you get to the bottom of the glass. How good is it? So good that you don't even have to add the vodka.

Remove all the seeds from the watermelon and place in a blender. Blend the melon until liquid. Pour into an ice cube tray. Freeze until solid, at least 4 hours.

In a pitcher, combine the orange juice and vodka. Place 3 frozen watermelon cubes in each glass, pour in the orange juice mixture, and serve immediately.

how do you pick a watermelon?

If you are having the neighborhood over and buying a whole one, look for a yellow oval patch on the top or bottom of it—that means it stayed longer on the vine (that side of the watermelon saw no sun) and is riper. If you are buying a cut piece or chunks, look for dark rich color and moist flesh. Watermelons dry out after they are cut, so keep them well wrapped in the fridge and eat them quickly. Or make them into ice cubes!

summer drinks tip

Summer drinks like fresh lemonade or watermelon screwdrivers are so much more come-hither when served in a frosted glass. Play around with different clear glasses, big red wine goblets, martini glasses, etc. Just throw them in the freezer at least 30 minutes before you put the drink in the glass. Dress up the drink with a splashy garnish. A small triangular slice of watermelon with some of the rind left on and a sprig of mint will do nicely here.

Frozen Café au Lait

**3 cups strong brewed coffee,
cooled**

1 cup whole milk

**3 tablespoons sugar or more to
taste**

SERVES 4

This is my homemade version of the frozen coffee drinks
that have become hugely popular at the gourmet coffee
franchises in the last few years. As lip-smackingly good as
the commercial concoctions, mine is also much lower in
calories because it doesn't use cream or half-and-half and it
isn't loaded with sugar.

This recipe gets its depth of flavor from coffee ice
cubes. So from now on, anytime you have leftover coffee,
don't throw it out; make cubes. They are great in good
old-fashioned iced coffee, too.

Pour the coffee into 2 ice cube trays. Freeze until solid, at least 4
hours. Working in 2 batches, blend the ice cubes, milk, and sugar in a
food processor or blender until the consistency is smooth and even,
about 1 minute. Pour into chilled glasses and serve at once.

Michelle's Trinidadian Tonic

2 cinnamon sticks

2 whole cloves

One 3-inch piece fresh ginger, peeled and grated

Honey to taste (optional)

MAKES ABOUT 1 QUART

Years before the Food Network's Michelle Beckles turned me on to her ginger tonic, I'd long since been convinced of the healing powers of ginger tea. Running a restaurant in Boston in the late seventies, I came down with a vicious cold that just kept getting worse. I should have taken to my bed and pulled the covers up over my head, but the show had to go on, so I kept working and getting sicker and sicker. One of my line cooks took pity on me, brewed up a bottomless pot of ginger tea—essentially just chopped fresh ginger boiled in water—and insisted that I drink it around the clock. I got better in one day.

The assistant producer on "Cooking Live," Michelle believes as strongly in her ginger tonic—her mom taught her how to make it when she was growing up in Trinidad— as I do my ginger tea. She brews it anytime one of our colleagues begins to look a little under the weather. In fact she's converted me. Her ginger tonic, which is flavored with spices, tastes better than my plain old ginger tea. But don't wait until you are sick to enjoy it.

Pour 5 cups water into a large saucepan. Add the cinnamon sticks and the cloves. Bring to a boil over high heat. Remove from the heat and add the ginger and the honey if desired. Let steep for 10 minutes. Strain well, discarding the solids. Serve at once or chill and drink on ice.

Deep Hot Chocolate

1 quart whole milk

10 ounces bittersweet chocolate, finely chopped

Marshmallows (page 357) or whipped cream (optional)

MAKES 1 QUART

The most extraordinarily delicious hot chocolate I have ever drunk was served at a teahouse called Angelina's near the Louvre in Paris. Dubbed *chocolat africain,* it was so rich you could nearly stand up a spoon in it. I am not quite sure how they make it, but I suspect, from the density of the drink, that the dairy element is heavy cream and, from the impossibly deep flavor, that the chocolate is top-quality bittersweet.

Here is my version, with milk replacing the cream. You could serve it on a cold winter's day as an afternoon pick-me-up or after dinner, spiked with a little liqueur. If you're feeling ambitious, you can top it off with whipped cream or homemade marshmallows.

Pour the milk into a small saucepan and bring it just to a simmer over medium-high heat. Remove from the heat, stir in the chocolate, and whisk until smooth. Serve hot with marshmallows or whipped cream if desired.

Michael Green says:
hot chocolate: note to adults!

Similar to adding various liqueurs to coffee for flavor and strength, adding a dessert liqueur to this cocoa recipe can give the beverage complexity. Simply add liqueur to taste—$1/2$ to $1^1/2$ ounces—after the cocoa is prepared. Experiment with the following liqueurs in your next chocolaty mug: Drambuie, a scotch-based liqueur; Grand Marnier, an orange-based liqueur; Kahlúa, a coffee-based liqueur; Pernod, an anise-flavored liqueur; Bailey's Irish Cream, a chocolate- and whiskey-flavored liqueur.

Easy Eggnog

2 pints premium-quality vanilla ice cream

¹/₂ cup rum, cognac, or bourbon or more to taste

Pinch freshly grated nutmeg

SERVES 4 TO 6

Traditional eggnog calls for raw eggs, and a lot fewer people are messing with raw eggs today, thanks to a minuscule but real risk of salmonella. Accordingly, revelers serving those in high-risk groups should heat eggnog's basic ingredients—eggs, cream, and sugar—to 160°F and do it *carefully*, or the eggs will curdle. That is a lot of work for a happy little holiday libation.

But some anonymous genius has finessed this sorry situation. Given that eggnog and ice cream are made from the same ingredients, and that eggs are already safely built into ice cream, start your eggnog with premium vanilla ice cream. Just pull it out of the freezer, put it in the fridge, and let it melt. Add rum or brandy and a little grating of fresh nutmeg, and there you have it—homemade-tasting eggnog. Brilliant!

Place the ice cream in a large covered glass or stainless-steel bowl in the refrigerator to thaw. Stir in the rum or desired flavoring and nutmeg. Blend well. Serve cold.

Pantry

Chicken Stock

5 pounds chicken wings, rinsed and patted dry

2 medium onions, quartered

2 small carrots, halved

2 celery ribs, halved

2 small parsnips, halved

1 bay leaf, preferably Turkish

1 teaspoon whole black peppercorns

8 fresh parsley stems

2 fresh thyme sprigs or 1 teaspoon dried

MAKES ABOUT 2 QUARTS

Whenever I have homemade chicken stock in the freezer, I feel happy. I like starting with a base of nothing but chicken wings, which have the perfect ratio of meat to bone and which respectively contribute flavor and body to the stock. And give yourself some time to do it right. If you make the stock one day and chill it overnight, the fat will rise to the top and solidify, making it very easy to scoop off. (You'll then want to freeze the fat, which has great flavor, for special occasions, like making matzo balls.) After scooping off the fat, you will need to boil down the stock to concentrate its flavor. When it has cooled down, you can divide it into several resealable plastic bags and freeze it.

By the way, I think I've finally figured out what makes Jewish chicken soup so special (aside from the fact that it is made by Jewish mothers and grandmothers). Watching my mother-in-law make her soup one day, I saw her add a parsnip. I have been doing the same ever since.

Place the chicken wings in a large stockpot and pour in enough cold water to cover by 2 inches. Bring to a boil over medium-high heat, skimming the scum that rises to the surface. Reduce the heat to medium-low and simmer, skimming often, for 20 minutes. Add the remaining ingredients. Simmer for $2^1/_2$ hours.

Strain the stock, cool slightly, and skim off the fat that rises to the top. (Alternatively, chill in the refrigerator overnight. Remove the fat that accumulates on the surface.) Return the stock to the stockpot and bring to a strong simmer over medium-high heat. Simmer until the liquid has reduced by one third to concentrate the flavor.

Brown Chicken Stock

One of the very first classes I took at cooking school was "Soup, Stock and Vegetable Kitchen," during which it was pounded into us that homemade stock is the irreplaceable base of any great soup or sauce. Today a new generation of innovative chefs has demonstrated that you don't necessarily need a stock to make a great soup or sauce—consider, for example, the exquisite carrot juice ginger sauce created by New York's Jean-Georges Vongerichten.

Still, a great meat-based stock remains a staple of good cooking. The problem today is that very few of us can invest 8 hours in the making of a classic veal stock. On the other hand, such snappy mid-20th-century solutions as bouillon cubes and canned stocks from the supermarket just don't cut it tastewise. This brown chicken stock recipe is a happy compromise, a good-tasting and relatively easy-to-make replacement for veal stock and beef stock.

Brown chicken stock is nothing more than white chicken stock with all the parts browned first. Because we're browning wings, which have such a high ratio of bone to meat, the end product is nicely gelatinous, very much like a veal stock. Because the wings are so meaty, the stock is very flavorful.

If you make a batch of this stock and then boil it down until it is so thick it can coat the back of a spoon (the French call this a *glace*), you can keep it in the fridge for weeks and just scoop out a couple tablespoons and dilute it with a little water whenever you want to make a quick pan sauce. In effect, you will have created a stock nearly as

5 pounds chicken wings, rinsed and patted dry

2 medium onions, coarsely chopped

1 large carrot, coarsely chopped

2 cups dry red or white wine

1 celery rib, coarsely chopped

1 cup chopped fresh or canned tomato

10 garlic cloves (optional)

6 to **8** fresh parsley stems

1 fresh thyme sprig or **1** teaspoon dried

1 bay leaf, preferably Turkish

1 teaspoon whole black peppercorns

MAKES ABOUT 2 QUARTS

instant as those old bouillon cubes and infinitely more flavorful. And, like bouillon cubes, this stock will keep for weeks because you've boiled out most of the liquid. My regard for this recipe is so high that my husband teases me by referring to it as "liquid gold," but I do indeed feel very wealthy when I have it in the house.

Preheat the oven to 450°F. In 2 shallow roasting pans, arrange the wings in one layer and roast for 20 minutes. Turn the wings over and roast for 15 minutes longer. Add the onions and carrots. Roast until golden, 20 to 25 minutes. Transfer the wings and vegetables to a stockpot. Discard the fat from the roasting pans. Place the pans over medium heat on top of the stove and carefully pour 1 cup of wine into each. Cook, scraping to pick up the browned bits on the bottom, until the liquid comes to a simmer. Pour the liquid into the stockpot.

Add the remaining ingredients to the pot. Pour in enough cold water to cover by 1 inch. Bring to a boil over high heat, skimming off the scum that rises to the surface. Reduce the heat to medium and cook, adding water if necessary to keep the bones covered at all times, for $2^{1}/_{2}$ hours. Strain the stock. Let cool and, if possible, chill overnight. Remove the fat that accumulates at the top. (If chilled overnight, the fat will solidify, making it easy to remove.)

Place the stock in a large saucepan and bring to a boil over high heat. Reduce the heat to medium-high and simmer until reduced by one third. To make a glaze, continue simmering until the liquid has reduced by three fourths or until it has the consistency of thick honey.

chicken fat

When I was making chicken stock on the show, Elaine from Springfield, Massachusetts, called in with this tip. Save the chicken fat that you scoop off from the top of the stock and cook it with an equal amount of flour to make a roux. Then you can freeze the roux in small portions (pull out those good old ice cube trays) and use it to thicken and flavor sauces. Chicken fat has a ton of flavor.

Vegetable Stock

Most vegetable stocks have all the robust flavor of warm water. Obviously, I was determined to do something better. The long roasting process in this recipe delivers the goods. This is a full-bodied stock that will serve as a sturdy base for any vegetarian soup or stew.

Preheat the oven to 400°F. Combine the onions, carrots, parsnips, leeks, and mushrooms in 2 shallow roasting pans and toss with the vegetable oil. Roast, stirring every 15 minutes, until the vegetables are golden brown, $1^1/4$ to $1^1/2$ hours. Transfer to a stockpot. Place the roasting pans on top of the stove and pour 1 cup cold water into each. Bring to a boil over high heat, stirring to pick up any brown pieces on the bottom. Pour the liquid into the stockpot and add the remaining ingredients. Pour in enough cold water to cover the ingredients by $1/2$ inch. Bring to a boil over high heat, skimming to remove any scum that rises to the top. Reduce the heat to medium and simmer for 45 minutes. Strain the stock and discard the solids. Return the liquid to the pot and boil until reduced to 6 cups.

3 large onions, coarsely chopped

6 medium carrots, coarsely chopped

4 parsnips, coarsely chopped

2 leeks, white and 2 inches of the green parts, coarsely chopped

8 cultivated white mushrooms, trimmed and quartered

3 tablespoons vegetable oil

6 celery ribs, coarsely chopped

1 head garlic, halved

4 plum tomatoes, coarsely chopped

3 fresh thyme sprigs

3 fresh parsley sprigs

8 whole black peppercorns

1 bay leaf, preferably Turkish

MAKES 6 CUPS

Quick Tomato Sauce

2 tablespoons extra virgin olive
  oil

1 small onion, finely chopped

2 garlic cloves, minced

One 28-ounce can Italian plum
  tomatoes, including juice

Kosher salt and freshly ground
  black pepper to taste

1/4 cup shredded fresh basil
  leaves

1 teaspoon hot red pepper
  flakes

MAKES ABOUT 2 CUPS

It wasn't until after "Cooking Live" had booked a week's worth of Italian-American home cooks and I'd judged a spaghetti sauce competition in New Jersey that I began to understand that one of the culinary world's touchiest subjects is How to Make a Proper Tomato Sauce. Apparently, tomato sauce is just too basic to Italian cuisine and its methods of preparation too varied. Italians tend to get really passionate about questions like: How long do you cook the sauce? What kind of tomatoes do you use? Do you or don't you add that little pinch of sugar? Think I'm going to step into the middle of that kind of controversy and present you with my happy little idea of the ultimate tomato sauce? Fuggedaboutit!

Accordingly, I make no claims for this tomato sauce other than that it is quick and simple and flavorful—ready to go in just 25 minutes. If you start with high-quality canned plum tomatoes—many Italians swear by the San Marzano brand—you will end up with something quite satisfactory.

There are, of course, a few good prepared tomato sauces available, but most of them put in way too much sugar for my taste. If you insist on going that route, you must read the label.

Heat the oil in a small saucepan over medium heat. Add the onion and garlic. Cook, stirring often, until softened, about 5 minutes. Empty the canned tomatoes into a large bowl and use your hands or a fork to crush. Add the crushed tomatoes and juices to the saucepan. Increase the heat to high and bring to a boil. Season with salt and pepper, and simmer, stirring often, until thickened, about 20 minutes. Stir in the basil and pepper flakes.

Rick's Barbecue Sauce

Once again, my cousin-in-law Rick Bzdafka—of Roast
Turkey with Sauerkraut (page 84) fame—strikes gold. The
soul of affability, Mr. Rick always whips up two separate
batches of his barbecue sauce: mild and very spicy. (Note
the variations.) Whatever your preference, you'll find that
this versatile sauce is equally delicious on grilled chicken or
ribs. (See Slow-Roasted Spiced Baby Back Ribs, page 96.)
It'll keep for a month in the fridge and for several months
in the freezer.

Heat the oil in a large saucepan over medium heat. Add the onions
and cook, stirring, until softened, about 5 minutes. Add the garlic,
jalapeño, and pepper flakes. Stir until fragrant, about 1 minute. Add
the Worcestershire sauce, mustard, brown sugar, and granulated sugar.
Reduce the heat to medium-low and cook until slightly thickened,
about 10 minutes. Stir often to prevent scorching. Pour in the
ketchup, add 2 cups cold water, and cook, uncovered, stirring often,
until thick, pulpy, and dark red, about 40 minutes. Season with salt
and pepper.

variations: Add 1 seeded, deveined, and finely diced habanero pepper
to the sauce as it is cooling. Substitute maple syrup for one of the
sugars. Finish with chopped fresh rosemary, sage, or thyme.

2 tablespoons vegetable oil

2 to 3 onions, to taste, finely
chopped

3 garlic cloves, minced

1 jalapeño, stemmed, seeded,
and minced

$1/2$ teaspoon hot red pepper
flakes

$1/4$ cup Worcestershire sauce

$1/2$ teaspoon dry mustard

$1/4$ cup packed dark brown sugar

$1/4$ cup granulated sugar

3 cups ketchup

Kosher salt and freshly ground
black pepper to taste

MAKES ABOUT 1 QUART

Once-a-Week Vinaigrette

¹/₂ teaspoon kosher salt

1 teaspoon Dijon mustard

¹/₄ cup white wine, red wine, or sherry vinegar

³/₄ cup extra virgin olive oil

MAKES 1 CUP

My husband is the kind of caveman who still thinks it's terribly funny to refer to salad as rabbit food. Every once in a while I can get him to buy in by adding "salad helper" to the greens (blue cheese, say, or avocado and cherry tomatoes), but usually it's no sale. My daughter Ruthie and I, however, believe that a meal without salad is like a day without sunshine—which means we need to keep a big supply of dressing on hand if we don't want to make it from scratch every night.

In cooking school they taught us that the basic ratio for a vinaigrette dressing is three parts oil to one part vinegar. I generally stick to it, but it is a matter of preference. Julia Child likes almost five-to-one oil to vinegar, and my old boss at La Tulipe liked even more oil than that. Whatever your pleasure, if you're mixing up any, you might as well make a week's worth. It'll keep just fine sitting out on the counter, covered.

My mom, by the way, makes the best vinaigrette, and she never measures a thing. I don't know how she does it. She just pours it all into a bowl and whisks it up, and it turns out perfectly balanced. That doesn't work for me; if I don't measure, it ends up too oily or too vinegary. On the other hand, if I do measure, it still isn't as good as my mom's. Humble in the face of this mystery, I pull out all the ingredients whenever she visits and beg her to whip up a triple batch.

Combine the salt, mustard, and vinegar in a 1-cup glass measuring cup and whisk with a fork until the salt is dissolved. Slowly add the oil in a stream, whisking. The vinaigrette keeps, covered, at room temperature for 1 week or in the fridge for a month.

Pickled Jalapeños

Pickled jalapeños combine two of my favorite things in one recipe: hot chiles and pickles. You can buy pickled jalapeños in a jar at the supermarket, but they're easy to make at home and much tastier that way, so why not do it yourself?

Admittedly, even fresh jalapeños these days seem to lack the heat I love. Time and again I add jalapeños to my salsa or sauce, figuring I am adding excitement, only to discover that the peppers in question are DOA. Amazingly, as soon as you pickle a jalapeño, its heat blazes up again. I always keep a jar of pickled peppers in the fridge in case the fresh ones fall flat.

Wash and rinse the jalapeños. Combine the vinegar, garlic, bay leaves, salt, and peppercorns in a large nonreactive saucepan. Bring to a boil over high heat. Add the jalapeños and reduce the heat to medium-low. Simmer gently until softened, about 5 minutes. Remove from the heat, cover, and cool to room temperature. Remove and discard the bay leaves.

Pack the jalapeños in a clean 1-quart glass jar. Pour on the liquid and seal. Refrigerate until ready to use. Keeps for about 1 month in the refrigerator.

1¹/₂ pounds jalapeños, stems removed

1 quart distilled white vinegar

12 garlic cloves, peeled and halved

2 fresh bay leaves

2 tablespoons kosher salt

10 to 12 black peppercorns, to taste

MAKES 4 CUPS

Pickled Red Onions

2 medium red onions, sliced
¹/₄ inch thick

1¹/₂ cups cider vinegar

2 garlic cloves, peeled and
halved

3 tablespoons sugar

1 tablespoon pickling spice

1¹/₂ teaspoons kosher salt

MAKES ABOUT 2 CUPS

These pickled onions, which take maybe 10 minutes to make, last for a week in the fridge and perk up any dish in need of a little acid and crunch. Try them with the Smoked Salmon and Salmon Roe on Crispy Potato Pancakes (page 24), Grilled Southwestern Pizza (page 204), or with virtually any sandwich or stewed dish. They also happen to look beautiful, like little jewels.

Combine the onions, vinegar, garlic, sugar, pickling spice, and salt in a small saucepan. Bring to a boil over high heat. Reduce the heat to medium and simmer for 2 minutes. Remove from heat and cool to room temperature before serving. Chop fine.

Homemade Bread Crumbs

**6 slices homemade-style
white bread**

MAKES ABOUT 2 1/2 CUPS

You can buy bread crumbs at the supermarket, but it's so easy to make your own that it's ridiculous not to. Whir the bread in a food processor or blender for a few seconds and you're done. You can use them right away or freeze them. If you freeze them, you need to dry them out in a 350°F oven for about 5 minutes before using to remove excess moisture.

I use fresh bread crumbs when I am trying to add bulk or moisture to a recipe. I use dry bread crumbs when I am trying to remove moisture from, or add crust to, a recipe. You can make dry bread crumbs by toasting your bread lightly in a 350°F oven for 10 to 15 minutes, letting it cool, and then grinding it up in the blender.

Homemade-style bread is the bread of choice for crumbs.

Cut off and discard the crusts from the bread and tear into large pieces. Place in a food processor or blender and process until very fine.

Creole Spice Mix

1 tablespoon plus 1 teaspoon hot paprika

1 tablespoon kosher salt

1 tablespoon garlic powder

1 1/2 teaspoons freshly ground black pepper

1 1/2 teaspoons onion powder

1 1/2 teaspoons cayenne pepper

1 1/2 teaspoons dried oregano

1 1/2 teaspoons dried thyme

MAKES ABOUT 1/2 CUP

These days every great New Orleans chef has a spice mix bearing his or her name. But the first time I wanted to reproduce Paul Prudhomme's blackened fish at home, the recipe's secret ingredient—Paul's spice mix—wasn't commercially available. So I made up my own. Essentially it is just a mix of black, white, and cayenne pepper with garlic and onion flavoring. Today Paul's spice mix is for sale at your local specialty food store, and it's great. But if you need a stand-in in a pinch, this homemade mix will do. Use it in the Blackened Fish (page 136) and the Turkey Burgers (page 86) or in any dish that needs a little perking up.

Mix all ingredients together in a small bowl. Store in an airtight container.

Basic Crepe Recipe

In France, the birthplace of the crepe, the right tool for making crepes is a metal crepe pan. Through constant use the pan becomes perfectly seasoned, meaning that it stays well oiled and doesn't stick. Here in America, where we are not so crepe-crazy, it is unlikely that you would use the pan so often that it would stay seasoned. That's why I recommend purchasing a good old 6-inch nonstick skillet instead, which can double as an omelet pan and which—as good as its name—keeps your crepes from sticking to the pan. You might want to keep crepes in your freezer for the same reason you'd want homemade pastry or pasta dough in there—because they can be used as a wrapper for both sweet and savory recipes. (See Cheese Blintzes, page 306, and Roasted Ratatouille Crepes with Goat Cheese, page 196.) With these edible envelopes at the ready, you can make a filling on the spot when that unexpected guest walks in the door.

Place the milk, flour, eggs, butter, and salt in a blender or food processor. Blend briefly to mix, about 5 seconds. Turn off the motor, scrape down the sides with a rubber spatula, and blend for 20 seconds. Strain the batter through a strainer set over a large bowl and let stand, covered, at room temperature for 1 hour.

Lightly brush a 6- to 7-inch nonstick skillet with vegetable oil. Heat over medium heat until hot. Stir the batter and thin with additional milk if necessary to reach the consistency of heavy cream. Fill a $1/4$-cup measure halfway and pour the batter over the bottom of the skillet. Tilt and rotate the skillet quickly to cover the bottom with a thin layer of batter. Return any excess to the bowl. Place the skillet

$1^1/_4$ cups whole milk, plus more as needed

1 cup all-purpose flour

3 large eggs

3 tablespoons unsalted butter, melted and cooled

$^1/_4$ teaspoon table salt

Vegetable oil as needed

MAKES ABOUT 16 SMALL CREPES

over the heat and cook until the crepe is set in the center and slightly browned around the edges, 1 to $1^1/_2$ minutes. Loosen the edge of the crepe with a spatula and turn to the other side. Cook for about 30 seconds longer or until the center is firm and the edges are slightly browned. Proceed with the remaining batter, brushing the skillet lightly with oil for each new crepe. Transfer the crepes to a wire rack and cool. The crepes can be made in advance, stacked, wrapped in plastic wrap, and chilled for up to 3 days or frozen for up to a month.

Basic Pie Pastry Dough

- **2 cups all-purpose flour**
- **1 teaspoon table salt**
- **12 tablespoons (1½ sticks) unsalted butter, cut into small pieces and chilled**
- **4 to 6 tablespoons ice-cold water or more as needed**

MAKES ENOUGH FOR TWO
9-INCH TART SHELLS OR A
DOUBLE-CRUST PIE

When you make pastry dough, you have three main choices about which kind of fat to use: lard, shortening, or butter. Lard is used mainly in the South and produces wonderfully flaky dough. Shortening also produces a very tender crust, with the added benefit of helping the dough hold its shape. (My crimped edge holds its shape much better with shortening.) But butter has the flavor edge, which is why I recommend it over the others.

Three crucial things to keep in mind when you're making pastry dough: Keep all your ingredients cold, cold, cold, don't overwork the dough or it will be tough, and chill the dough in the fridge for at least 1 hour before rolling it out.

Mix the flour with the salt in a large bowl. Add the butter and use 2 knives or a pastry cutter to blend until the mixture resembles the texture of small peas. (Alternatively, combine the flour and salt in a food processor and pulse once or twice to blend. Add the butter and process until blended, about 20 seconds, then transfer to a large bowl.)

Make a well in the center of the mixture and add the water. Mix quickly with a fork to form a soft dough. Add another teaspoon of cold water if the dough appears to be too dry. Turn out onto a floured work surface and work gently into a rough ball. Wrap in plastic and refrigerate for at least 1 hour. (The pastry dough can be made up to a day in advance or kept frozen for up to a month.)

variation: For sweet pastry, reduce the salt to ¹/₂ teaspoon and add 2 tablespoons sugar to the flour and salt.

Quick Raspberry Sauce

1 pint fresh raspberries

1 tablespoon fresh lemon juice

$^1/_2$ to $^3/_4$ cup confectioners' sugar

MAKES 1 CUP

Sometimes you finish making a dessert and discover it's missing something in the way of flavor or color. Think of this delicious and easy-to-make sauce, then, as dessert helper. Faced with having to conjure up dessert for a last-minute dinner party, you can drizzle some of this sauce on a store-bought angel food cake, add some sliced fresh fruit or berries, and garnish with a sprig of mint. Everyone will think you're a genius.

This sauce keeps for a week in the fridge or for several months in the freezer. If it is not raspberry season, you can use unsweetened frozen raspberries.

Combine the raspberries, lemon juice, and $^1/_2$ cup sugar in a food processor. Taste and add additional sugar if desired. Process until well blended and strain through a fine-mesh strainer.

The Best Raspberry Sauce in the World (aka Raspberry Vinegar)

8 cups raspberries
2 cups cider vinegar
4$\frac{1}{2}$ to 6 cups sugar

MAKES 3 TO 4 PINTS

When we first started going to Massachusetts in the summer to visit my grandparents, my folks rented a cottage on the property of two nice ladies from Boston. The big house was a grand place with lots of land, a pool, a tennis court, an enormous barn complete with a deluxe kids' play house, and beautiful gardens. My sister and I used to sneak into the kitchen, where Irene Fortune, the cook, could often be found whipping up a big batch of cookies.

Every so often the two nice ladies would honor us with an invitation to dinner. I remember putting on my party dress for the occasion, but the details of the meals themselves, which must have been elaborate, are lost in the mists of time. I was a plump little kid with a sweet tooth. It is the cookies that were memorable.

Irene taught this recipe to my grandmother, who passed it on to my aunt Jean. Every summer Jean raids the big patch of raspberries out back at our family farm and makes up many bottles of raspberry vinegar. Occasionally there's still some around at Christmas, but more often it's long gone by then. It's just too delicious to use sparingly. So which is it—a vinegar or a sauce? Although it is made with vinegar, its sweetness absolutely qualifies it as a dessert sauce.

Pick over 4 cups of the berries and rinse well. Place in a medium bowl and use a fork or potato masher to crush. Pour in the vinegar. Cover with plastic wrap and place in a warm spot for 24 hours. Strain through a strainer and press on the solids to extract as much liquid as possible. Discard the seeds.

Pick over and rinse the remaining berries. Crush and add to the strained raspberry juice. Cover and keep in a warm spot for 12 hours. Strain through a strainer and press the solids to extract as much liquid as possible. Measure the liquid and add half as much water as there is liquid. Measure this new liquid, and for every 1 cup stir in $1^1/_2$ cups sugar. Pour into a large nonreactive saucepan. Bring to a boil over medium-high heat, stirring just until the sugar dissolves. Skim off any foam that rises to the top. Strain through a strainer lined with a double layer of rinsed cheesecloth. Pour into sterilized pint jars and process according to the jar manufacturer's instructions.

Vanilla Sauce

This is the base of many other sauces and desserts, including ice cream. The French call it *crème anglaise*. Feel free to add whatever flavorings you like: freshly grated citrus zest, melted chocolate, liqueurs, extracts, you name it. The sauce can be used with cakes, fruit, soufflés, puddings, or just about any other dessert.

2 cups whole milk

1 vanilla bean,* halved lengthwise

5 large egg yolks

$1/3$ cup sugar

$1/8$ teaspoon table salt

*Available at specialty food shops or see Mail Order Sources.

MAKES 2 CUPS

Combine the milk and vanilla bean in a small saucepan. Heat over medium-high heat until small bubbles form around the edge. Remove from the heat, cover, and infuse the milk for 10 minutes. Scrape the seeds of the bean into the milk. Rinse and dry the bean and save for another use (such as putting it in your bag of sugar, which will turn it into vanilla sugar).

Whisk the egg yolks with the sugar and salt in a large heatproof bowl until thick and light, 3 to 4 minutes. Stir in the hot milk. Return the custard to the pan and stir over low heat until slightly thickened or until a finger drawn across a wooden spoon dipped in the sauce leaves a mark (about 160°F). Do not boil, or the sauce will curdle. Strain into a large bowl and cool to room temperature. Cover with plastic wrap and refrigerate until well chilled, at least 2 hours.

Simple Sugar Syrup

1 cup sugar

¹/₂ cup cold water

MAKES ABOUT ³/₄ CUP

Simple syrup is nothing more than sugar and water, heated to dissolve the sugar and then cooled. Pastry chefs always have some on hand to brush on cakes and as a base for sauces and sorbets. Fine restaurants have started putting little pitchers of it on their tables in the summertime, because simple syrup sweetens iced tea or coffee instantly—unlike granulated sugar, which never fully dissolves in a cold liquid. Simple syrup is easy to make and adds a wonderful touch to summer entertaining.

Combine the sugar and water in a small saucepan. Cook over medium-low heat, stirring gently, just until the sugar dissolves. Cool completely, then store in a clean glass container. Keeps, refrigerated, for up to 2 weeks.

Marshmallows

Once I decided I was going to put a recipe for really great hot chocolate into this book (page 334), I knew I also had to come up with one for marshmallows worthy of that hot chocolate. Why bother? Because homemade marshmallows are so much more tender than those bouncy guys for sale at the supermarket. The only difficulty presented by this recipe is that you will have to buy a candy thermometer if you don't already own one. (Of course, then you can also use it for all the deep frying you will be doing with my encouragement.)

If you are concerned about salmonella, I've got just the product for you. Called Just Whites, it is pasteurized dried egg whites. All you do is add water according to the formula on the back. Not only does this product eliminate the possibility of salmonella, but it is also ecological; now you are not throwing out egg yolks because all you needed was the whites.

About 1 cup confectioners' sugar for dusting

2 envelopes (2 tablespoons) unflavored gelatin

1 cup granulated sugar

$^1/_4$ cup light corn syrup

$^1/_4$ teaspoon table salt

2 large egg whites, or 4 teaspoons Just Whites mixed with $^1/_4$ cup water

1 teaspoon vanilla extract

MAKES 36 PIECES

Oil the bottom and sides of a 9-inch square nonstick baking pan and dust with some of the confectioners' sugar. Tap out the excess.

Pour $^1/_2$ cup cold water into the bowl of an electric stand mixer. Sprinkle on the gelatin and set aside to dissolve for 5 minutes.

Combine the granulated sugar, corn syrup, and salt in a large saucepan. Pour in $^1/_4$ cup hot water (115°F) and heat over low heat. Stir just until the sugar has dissolved. Increase the heat to high and bring to a boil without stirring. Boil until a candy thermometer reads 240°F. Start beating the gelatin mixture, and with the beater in motion, carefully pour in the hot sugar mixture. Beat until thick and very white, 5 to 7 minutes.

Beat the egg whites with the vanilla in a separate bowl until stiff but not dry. Add to the sugar mixture and beat until just combined. Pour into the prepared pan and sprinkle about 2 tablespoons of the confectioners' sugar evenly over the top. Chill, uncovered, until firm, at least 3 hours and preferably overnight.

Run a knife around the edges of the pan and invert onto a cutting surface. Trim the edges with a sharp knife and cut into 1-inch pieces. Transfer to a large bowl and toss with additional confectioners' sugar. Keep in an airtight container for up to 1 week.

Pairing Wine with Food

a commonsense guide to the pairing of wine and food
by Michael Green

Wine is one of civilization's oldest and most enduring pleasures, and the pairing of wine and food is a thrilling and never-ending exploration. Oddly, however, this happiest of subjects is often written about in the most offputting way, offering up hard-and-fast rules combined with loads of pretense. Although the subject can indeed appear to be infinitely complex, the basic rules of wine and food combining are eminently simple and commonsensical: Your personal taste and preferences are the ultimate guide.

Still, the subject is immense. Wine is produced from a variety of grapes, hails from many different lands, and is crafted by winemakers to create many different styles. Walk into a wine shop and the huge variety of bottles—thousands of them, stacked up side by side and floor to ceiling—may set your head spinning. "How do I know what a wine will taste like before I buy it?" you wonder. Even more confusing is the vast difference between different styles of wine made from the very same grape: If you like Chardonnay because of the oaky richness that defines the Chardonnays of California's Napa Valley, you may be surprised, and perhaps even disappointed, by the unoaked Chardonnays of Chablis, France. Add food to the equation, and it is not surprising that the gastronomic pursuit of successful wine and food pairing can seem daunting.

Fear not! There's a simple way to learn about wine and wine and food pairing that dispenses with the study of grapes and regions. The focus is rather on the taste of the wine and its relationship to the food you are serving. Ultimately you are looking for a combination that achieves balance and delivers pleasure. Our touchstones are weight, similarity and contrast, seasonality, regionality, and occasion. Follow them and you'll soon be able to figure out for yourself why some food and wine pairings are celestial while others disappoint.

The Weight of Wine

Watercolors and oil paints are both paint but of different weights and textures. Skim milk, whole milk, and cream are all milk but have different weights or body. Likewise, a French Chablis and a Napa Valley Chardonnay are both wines (in fact even made from the same grape) but are of very different weights. Thinking about the particular weight or body of a wine allows you to begin to distinguish among the myriad types and styles of wine—and is very helpful when it comes to pairing wine and food. Lighter wines tend to be unoaked, with higher acids, lower tannins, and lower alcohol levels. Usually these will be produced in cooler growing areas. Heavier wines—fuller-bodied and more mouth-filling reds and whites—usually see some type of oak treatment and hail from warmer growing areas. In fact, if you know a little bit about geography, and the general climate of a region, you can often anticipate what the weight of many wines will be. Again, light wines are from cooler areas; fuller wines are from warmer areas.

A fun way to experience weight in wine is to give yourself a blind taste test. Select three different versions of Chardonnay: one from France, one from California, and one from Australia. Put each in a brown bag to conceal its identity. Now, can you taste the differences in weight and style? Which one is the lightest? Which one is the heaviest or fullest? And, most important, which one do you prefer?

Now, when it comes to wine with food, simply match the weight of the wine to the weight of the dish. Lighter foods work well with lighter

jot it down!

One simple way to remember which wines you like is to jot them down. Record your experiences. Keep a small pad in the kitchen and make notes of all the wines that you sample. For example: "2/5/2002—John Jones Chardonnay. Full-bodied and oaky. Served with salmon and lentils. Liked very much." Also, the next time you enjoy a wine at your favorite restaurant, ask your server to write down the name of the wine on a piece of paper. As you would with your favorite recipes, keep this information close at hand—in either a notepad or a file.

wines. Richer foods pair well with richer and fuller wines. A crisp light white wine like Pinot Grigio is a wonderful match with a nice light poached fillet of flounder. A hearty California Cabernet Sauvignon would pair up beautifully with Seared Hanger Steak with Mustard Basil Butter (page 112). Matching weight in wine and food is an easy and successful pairing strategy.

Contrast and Similarity

Another way to achieve a harmonious pairing of food and wine is through the contrast or similarity of different flavor elements. Let's take wine out of the equation for a moment. Certain foods in combination strike us as classic. Think of baked potatoes and sour cream, salmon and lemon, lobster and butter, peanut butter and jelly. These combinations make sense to your taste buds, the kind of sense that shouts pleasure. With baked potatoes and sour cream, it's all about *contrast*—the contrast between the hot potato and the cold sour cream, between the blandness of the potato and the sharpness of the sour cream, and between the dryness of the potato and the moistness of the sour cream. Similarly, the crisp acidity of lemon contrasts beautifully with the rich oiliness of salmon, while sweet, moist jelly provides welcome contrast to dry, salty peanut butter.

On the other hand, it's not the pleasure of contrast but of *similarity* that tells your mouth to get happy when you magnify the richness of lobster by dunking it in butter.

Now let's restore wine to the equation. Caviar served with a crisp white wine or Champagne is a classic combination. Why? Because the oiliness and saltiness of the caviar contrast beautifully with the lightness and acidity of those wines.

tannin

Found mostly in red wines, tannin is a compound that derives from the skins, seeds, and stems of grapes. It acts as a preservative that contributes to a wine's ability to age. On the mouth, an excess of tannin strikes us as bitter or astringent.

Another classic is a light white wine or sparkling wine served alongside a garden salad with warm goat cheese in a vinaigrette dressing. Why? Because the acidity in the salad, the goat cheese, and the vinaigrette is very similar to the acidity in the wines. With both of these scenarios, the same style of wine can offer a pleasurable combination, depending on whether you are striving for contrast or similarity. To further explore this idea, let's turn to the tongue.

Wine-Friendly, Wine-Hostile, and the Territories of the Tongue
The tongue is an organ capable of distinguishing an infinite number of gradations in five basic categories of taste: salt, sour, sweet, bitter, and *umami*. All dishes comprise a combination of these sensations. If they are in balance, the dish is wine-friendly. If any one sensation predominates, there can be trouble.

1. Salt: Using salt judiciously in a dish is fine; there will be no negative interactions when that dish is paired with most wines. However, a very salty dish will often reinforce the bitterness and astringency of a wine, especially a red wine. If you like Red Sea amounts of salt on your food, your wine may even taste metallic. For recipes where salt is a dominant flavor, seek out wines that are high in acidity and/or wines that have a touch of fruitiness. Acid and sweet elements in wine pair beautifully with salty foods.

2. Sour: Acidity is a crucial element in cooking, sharpening or brightening a sauce with a squeeze of lemon or wine used in deglazing a pan. Often acids in food are balanced by other elements such as sweetness. But food that is too acidic will make many wines taste flat or dull in contrast. Dishes that are high in acidity pair well with wines high in acidity. Another direction is to select a wine with a touch of sweetness—sweet and sour are delicious contrasting flavor elements.

3. Sweet: In a well-balanced recipe, the sweet is often offset by the sour. But stay away from pairings of dry wines with sweet dishes. It will make the wine seem even drier, more astringent, and even sour. With desserts, a sweet food/sweet wine pairing is a match that works.

4. Bitter: Bitter foods like endive, arugula, radicchio, and walnuts are often combined with ingredients that will balance and offset the bitterness, such as sweet or acid. However, if you enjoy bitter elements in food, then you can select a wine that has elements of bitterness as well, such as one with tannins present like a full-bodied red wine. If you want to offset the bitterness, choose a wine that will add another dimension of flavor, one with a touch of sweetness or high acidity.

5. Umami: This taste sensation, relatively new to the West, was isolated and identified about a century ago in Japan. Literally translated as "savory taste," the flavor is described as somewhat mushroomy. Foods high in MSG contain loads of this sensation, as do cured meats, braised dishes, and dried tomatoes. A dish high in *umami* will make bitter wines taste even more bitter, including white wines with loads of oakiness. With foods high in *umami*, look to wines that have low tannins and high acidity.

Season

Our tastes change with the season. We crave crisp salads and lighter foods in the summer, hearty stews and richer fare during the winter. The same is true of our taste for wine. When it's cold, we tend to favor bold, full wines. When it's warm, we reach for lighter wines. I once attended a wine and food festival in Phoenix, Arizona, where many stellar full-bodied wines were poured. And yet in the 113-degree heat—yes, I know, it's a *dry* heat!—the wines that pleased me the most were the lightest and crispest of the bunch. I would have preferred to savor some of the more serious and fuller-bodied wines during cooler months.

Regionality

Doesn't it seem like common sense that the wines of a given place would pair nicely with the food of the same region? Also, there is something psychologically fulfilling about pairing regional wines with regional foods. In residence for a week at a cooking school in a village near the Tuscan coast, I tasted local and lesser-known Tuscan wines that partnered fabulously well with the whole gamut of Tuscan foods. Likewise, on a road trip to the wine region of Long Island, my *Gourmet* colleagues and I savored the local Long Island wines paired with dishes made with the local produce. Wines as varied as dry rosé, Merlot, and Chardonnay all worked beautifully with roast Long Island duck and fresh corn. The next time you prepare a dish where certain ingredients or preparations are linked to a specific region, consider a wine choice from the same region.

Occasion

Wine and food often thrill us when they match the occasion and the moment. Think of Champagne and caviar on New Year's Eve or opening up an older, distinguished wine for a special occasion. Any wine that for any reason holds a particular significance can elevate a meal. For example, I often serve a wine from the Alsace region of France when I want to make an occasion truly festive, simply because my personal passion for wine was kindled in that part of the world.

Now with a grasp of these basic concepts—weight, similarity and contrast, seasonality, regionality, and occasion—you can begin to put wine and food together in a way that will achieve balance and make you smile! Pairings can often be done before you have even tasted a dish if a recipe is well balanced. Really! If you can isolate and dissect the dominant elements and flavors in a recipe and keep in mind the other touch-stones that we addressed, you are on the road to creating a pairing that will be pleasurable and memorable. Let's look at several of Sara's recipes and put our wine and food pairing fundamentals into action.

A Romantic Dinner for Two

Smoked Salmon and Salmon Roe on Crispy Potato Pancakes with Horseradish Cream and Pickled Onions (page 24)

Rosemary-Scallion-Crusted Rack of Lamb (page 105)

Mashed Potato Cakes (page 249)

Creamed Spinach with Crispy Shallots (page 234)

Almond-Stuffed Pears in Pastry (page 272)

Half-bottles of each selection will be plenty for the two lovebirds in question and work wonderfully well here, giving you the opportunity to sample several varied offerings. Here we have an elegant and romantic first course. The smoked salmon—rich, smooth, and salty—becomes even more luxurious with the addition of the briny caviar. While the horseradish cream beautifully balances the salmon and caviar, I would pair this dish with a wine that cleans the mouth of salt and fish oils and leaves it ready for the next bite. (In effect, the wine will function like a squeeze of lemon.) What is the weight of the wine we're dreaming of? It is light. Broadly, I'm thinking of light whites and sparkling wines with bright and shining acidity. If we consider occasion as well as weight—in this case a romantic dinner—it's easy to settle on Champagne.

on wine, taste, and price

There is often no correlation between taste and price. Paying a lot for wine does not guarantee great taste. In fact, many of the most delicious, ready-to-drink wines are the most modestly priced. Today there is a world of wine available from well-known as well as unknown and undervalued regions, so the name of the game is to explore, sample, and enjoy the journey.

Our main course, Rosemary-Scallion-Crusted Rack of Lamb, is rich and succulent. The lamb partners well with many fuller styles of wine, but—ever attuned to regionality—I'm tilted in the direction of the Mediterranean by the rosemary in the crust. Accordingly, my first thought is of the medium- to full-bodied wines of sun-kissed Rioja, Spain. While a fuller-bodied Merlot or Cabernet Sauvignon would also partner well with this dish, I'd be more inclined to stick with a big wine from the Rhône Valley's Côte Rôtie, another star hailing from a Mediterranean climate.

Almond-Stuffed Pears in Pastry is a lovely presentation and a lovely way to end the meal. Playing on the technique of similarity, I'd be inclined to amp up the sweetness in our dessert by pairing it with a sweet dessert wine. Specifically, I'm thinking of either a lighter late-harvest Riesling from Washington State or from Germany or—if the goal is sweetness coupled with power—a ruby port.

A Winter Meal for Six

Three-Mushroom Tart (page 216)

Roast Tenderloin of Beef with Cornichon Tarragon Sauce (page 121)

Roasted Lemon Potatoes (page 252)

Magda's Cauliflower (page 245)

Giant Chocolate Turnovers with Orange Custard Sauce (page 296)

We begin with the hearty, flavorful tart, a great start to a cold-weather meal. If contrast is your method, you might pair the tart with a relatively light wine, Sauvignon Blanc or Beaujolais, for example. In colder weather, though, I'd probably be looking for similarity and choose a full-bodied red, perhaps a Pinot Noir from the Burgundy region of France. (For additional contrast, consider serving this bottle slightly chilled. This will increase the wine's acidity and make it even more refreshing.) If you'd prefer to start with a white wine, try a full-bodied, warm-climate Chardonnay such as one from California or Australia.

The Roast Tenderloin of Beef with Cornichon Tarragon Sauce is a substantial and dramatic main course. The sauce is savory and aromatic, with the cornichons adding potent snap and tang. But these miniature pickles present a problem to the wine pairer—wines that are low in acidity may taste flat in comparison to the cornichons. Accordingly, I would select a light- to medium-bodied style of wine with good acidity. Consider two unsung grapes from the Piedmont region of Italy—Barbera and Dolcetto. Both combine loads of flavor with bright fresh berry acids. Alternatively, a full-bodied, fresh, and spicy Zinfandel might be just the ticket.

On to dessert. Chocolate desserts are often so rich that they can overwhelm a wine, making it seem thin and astringent. The orange liqueur in this dish, however, makes it more wine-friendly. A full-bodied fortified dessert wine like port or sherry—endowed with the flavors of raisin, fig, and even chocolate—is sweet and rich enough to partner well with this dessert.

There has never been a better time than now to explore the relationship, synergy, and ultimate taste of food and wine together. The joy is in the discovery. Over the years at *Gourmet*, Sara and I have had the unique opportunity to eat a lot, sip a lot, and learn a lot. Today truly great wines come from all over the world, and not all of them are expensive. Indeed, some of the most gulpable and delicious wines are priced modestly, with many great selections available for well under $15. Every day is a discovery, and with every sip and bite you can catalog a new experience and sensation. And that is the ultimate joy of the wine and food journey.

Some Classic Wines by Weight and Intensity of Flavor

Sparkling Wine:
Champagne (France), Cava (Spain), Prosecco (Italy), Sekt (Germany), and other sparkling wines from around the world

Light White Wine:
Pinot Grigio (Italy), Pinot Blanc (Italy), Galestro (Italy), Muscadet (France), Soave (Italy), Chablis (France), Aligoté (France), unoaked Chardonnay (for example, versions from the Loire Valley, France), Riesling (Germany, New York, and Washington State), vinho verde (Portugal)

Medium-Bodied White Wine:
Sauvignon Blanc (California), Semillon (California, Washington State, and Australia), Vouvray (France), Albariño (Spain), Pinot Gris (France), Mâcon-Villages (France), Pouilly-Fuissé (France), Sancerre (France), Pouilly-Fumé (France), and village white Burgundy (France)

Full-Bodied White Wine:
Chardonnay from California and Australia, Viognier (France and California), premier and grand cru white Burgundy (France)

Light Red Wine:
Beaujolais (France), Chinon (France), Bourgueil (France), Bardolino (Italy), Grignolino (Italy), Chianti (Italy), Dolcetto (Italy), Barbera (Italy)

Medium-Bodied Red Wine:
Côtes-du-Rhône (France), simple Bordeaux (France), Pinot Noir (California and Oregon), Pinotage (South Africa), village Burgundy (France), Chianti Classico (Italy), Rioja (Spain)

Full-Bodied Red Wine:
Bordeaux, (France), Cabernet Sauvignon (California and Australia), Zinfandel (California), Hermitage (France), Amarone (Italy), Brunello di Montalcino (Italy), Côte Rôtie (France), Châteauneuf-du-Pape (France), Nebbiolo (Italy), Barbera (Italy), Barbaresco (Italy), Barolo (Italy), Merlot (California), Syrah (California and France), premier and grand cru red Burgundy (France)

Sweet Wine:
Sauternes (France), late harvest Riesling (Germany, California, Washington State, Australia), Muscat (Italy, France, and California), Hungarian Tokay (Hungary), port (Portugal), sweet sherry (Spain), Madeira (Portugal)

mail order sources

Adriana's Caravan
321 Grand Central Terminal
New York, NY 10017
http://adrianascaravan.com
(800) 316-0820
Saffron, herbes de Provence, crystallized ginger, green peppercorns, Spanish chorizo, sherry vinegar, tahini, dried porcini, Turkish bay leaves, truffle oil

Asian Connections
537 Newport Center Drive
Newport Beach, CA 92660
http://asiakitchen.com
Asian chile sauce, rice vinegar, cellophane noodles, dried wasabi powder, panko bread crumbs

Bridge Kitchenware
214 East 52nd Street
New York, NY 10022
http://www.bridgekitchenware.com
(212) 688-4220
Spaetzle maker, microplane

Broadway Panhandler
477 Broome Street
New York, NY 10013
http://www.broadwaypanhandler.com
866-cookware
Spaetzle maker, microplane, flexible cutting board

Brown Trading Company
Merrill's Wharf
260 Commercial Street
Portland, ME 04101
http://www.browne-trading.com
(800) 944-7848
Finnan haddie, smoked salmon

Chukar Cherries
320 Wine Country Road
Prosser, WA 99350
http://www.chukar.com
(800) 624-9544
Dried cherries

D'Artagnan
280 Wilson Avenue
Newark, NJ 07105
http://www.dartagnan.com
(800) 327-8246
Organic poultry, poussin, truffle oil

Dean and DeLuca
Customer Assistance
25266 36th Street
Wichita, KS 67219
http://www.deananddeluca.com
(877) 826-9246
Aged balsamic vinegar, truffle oil

Ethnic Grocer
162 West Hubbard Street
Chicago, IL 60610
http://www.ethnicgrocer.com
Asian (toasted) sesame oil, cellophane noodles, corn husks, Thai chile paste, masa flour, porcini, polenta, tahini, panko bread crumbs

Gaucho Gourmet
25011 Granite Path
San Antonio, TX 78258
http://www.gauchogourmet.com
(877) 837-0521
Dulce de leche

Indian Harvest
1012 Paul Bunyan Drive Southeast
Bemidji, MN 56601
http://www.indianharvest.com
(800) 346-7032
Lentilles du Puy

Jamison Farms
171 Jamison Lane
Latrobe, PA 15650
http://www.jamisonfarm.com
(800) 237-5262
Natural lamb

Kenyon's Cornmeal Company
Usquepaugh
West Kingston, RI 02892
http://www.kenyonsgristmill.com
(401) 783-4054
Johnnycake meal

The Kitchen Market
218 Eighth Avenue
New York, NY 10011
http://kitchenmarket.com
(888) 468-4433
Panko bread crumbs, sesame oil, Thai curry paste, coconut milk, corn husks, masa flour, lentilles du Puy

Mexgrocer
P.O. Box 2888
La Jolla, CA 92038
http://www.mexigrocer.com
(877) 463-9476
Maseca flour (the best masa flour), corn husks, chipotles in adobo sauce

Morse Farms
1168 County Road
Montpelier, VT 05602
http://www.morsefarm.com
(800) 242-2740
Grade B maple syrup

Niman Ranch
1025 East 12th Street
Oakland, CA 94606
http://www.nimanranch.com
(510) 808-0340
Natural beef, pork, and lamb

Pacific Farms
88420 Highway 101 North
Florence, OR 97430
http://www.freshwasabi.com
(800) 927-2248
Fresh wasabi

Pacific Rim Gourmet
11251 Coloma Road
Gold River, CA 95670
http://www.pacificrim-gourmet.com
(800) 618-7575
Thai curry paste, coconut milk

Pasta and Co.
501 Eighth Avenue
Seattle, WA 98109
http://www.pastaco.com
(800) 943-6362
Walnut oil

Penzey's Spices
P.O. Box 924
Brookfield, WI 53008
http://www.penzeys.com
(800) 741-7787
Vanilla beans, paprika, herbes de Provence,
Turkish bay leaves

The Smithfield Collection
P.O. Box 487
Smithfield, VA 23431
http://www.smithfieldcollection.com/1
(800) 628-2242
Country ham

A Southern Season
1800 East Franklin Street
Chapel Hill, NC 27514
http://www.southernseason.com
(800) 253-3663
Grits, country ham

The Spice House
1941 Central Street
Evanston, IL 60201
http://www.thespicehouse.com
(847) 328-3711
Turkish bay leaves, paprika (sweet, hot,
smoked), saffron, tahini, vanilla beans,
chipotles in adobo sauce, wasabi powder,
green peppercorns

Sun Empire Foods
1220 South Madera Avenue
Kerman, CA 93630
http://www.sunempirefoods.com
(800) 252-4786
California apricots

Tienda.com
4514 John Tyler Highway
Williamsburg, VA 23188
www.tienda.com
(888) 472-1022
Sherry wine vinegar, Serrano ham,
chorizo, saffron, smoked paprika

Sources for Publishing a Family Cookbook

Cookbooks by Morris Press
3212 East Highway 30
Kearney, NE 68847
(800) 445-6621
http://www.morriscookbooks.com

The Cookbook Company
2523 El Portal Drive
San Pablo, CA 94806
(510) 234-9700
http://www.cookbookco.com

Walters Publishing Co.
1050 8th St., N.E.
Wasem, MN 56093
(800) 447-3274
http://www.custom-cookbooks.com

To produce your own cookbook at a copy shop or electronically, go to *http://www.kinkos.com* or call (800) 2-KINKOS for locations, rates, options and a downloadable free file prep tool.

index